# GETTING TO NOW

## 67 YEARS OF TECHNOLOGY EVOLUTION

## ART DICKERSON

Order this book online at www.trafford.com
or email orders@trafford.com

Most Trafford titles are also available at major online book retailers.

Print information available on the last page.

ISBN: 978-1-4907-6158-9 (sc)
ISBN: 978-1-4907-6159-6 (hc)
ISBN: 978-1-4907-6160-2 (e)

Library of Congress Control Number: 2015910071

*Trafford rev. 06/20/2015*

 www.trafford.com
North America & international
toll-free: 1 888 232 4444 (USA & Canada)
fax: 812 355 4082

# Contents

To Shari and Chris

And in memory to Collie

# GETTING TO NOW

It was Sunday, December 7, 1941, just a little after 11:00 am in the small Texas town of Seguin. Four young men rode in a brand new black 1941 Chevrolet sedan, loaned from the father of two of them, the local Chevrolet dealer. The men were each a year apart in age. William Lovett 18, Dick Ryan 17, Thomas Lovett 16 and myself, Art Dickerson 15. I was in the front passenger seat admiring the new car radio which had a novel short-wave band in addition to the AM band which was tuned to WOAI in San Antonio. The sounds of "Chattanooga Choochoo came over the radio We were tapping our feet. Abruptly the music stopped and a voice announced, "There has been an attack by Japanese aircraft on U.S. Navy ships at Pearl Harbor, Hawaii. This is real, it is not a test."

We sat stunned and silent. I recall thinking, *this changes everything for all of us*. The future proved the accuracy of that thought and the difference a year of age could make. All four of us would become officers in the coming World War II. Not evident was the tremendous technical progress that World War II would engender and how this would change a nation's lives far into the future.

Willy Lovett, 18 a student in engineering at Texas A&M, would join the Army Air Corps and become a P-51 pilot. Flying in China in 1944, his plane was shot up by the Japanese.

1

Wounded he attempted to land at Kunming airfield. He crashed a 1/4 mile from the end of the runway. Kunming was being evacuated ahead of Japanese occupation. He and his plane were simply left in place. Willy was an accomplished cello soloist and the most co-ordinated football linebacker with whom I had ever teamed. His abandonment was to me unforgivable, evacuation notwithstanding.

Dick Ryan, 17 a student at the University of Texas Seminary in Austin would become a Navy deck officer. He participated in the 1944-5 island-hopping campaign in the Pacific. At one point his Destroyer was ordered to test the accuracy of Japanese artillery on an island in advance of its' invasion. They drove at flank speed directly toward the island to test the distance at which firing would begin. When it did, they wheeled about and steamed away, testing accuracy. They survived, the Japanese did not. Dick was very bright and an excellent basketball player. He would survive the war and become a minister as was his original intention. He served happily at a church in Fredericksburg, Texas.

Thomas Lovett, 16 also became a Navy deck officer. He was late for the Pacific Island campaign, but in 1945 suffered through the Great Pacific Typhoon, which just before the bombs were dropped on Japan, caused the loss of two destroyers capsizing in the winds up to 150 miles per hour. He also survived and became a minister as he longed to be. He proudly served a church in Seguin, Texas.

I, Art Dickerson 15, a student in Seguin High School would graduate in 1943. Classed as 4F because of 3 amputated fingers, I would not be drafted. The amputation was the result of a science experiment in 1939. In class we saw a match struck and while blazing put into a test tube. It consumed the oxygen and extinguished. At home I tried the same experiment with a small copper tube I found at a construction site. It was a dynamite detonator.

I did not face the draft, but received an interesting offer from a Navy recruiter. If I would enlist, he would approve me for either the V-5 or V-12 officer training programs. This was too good to pass up. I considered both programs. The V-5 led to a commission in the Naval Flying Service. The V-12 led to a commission as a Naval Deck-Engineering officer. My father, bless him, did not lean on me about the choice. V-5 had the glamour of being a combat pilot. V-12 led to an electrical engineering degree which the family could not otherwise afford. At that time the Navy considered the war would not end until late 1947. My class would be scheduled for the invasion of Honshu, the main island of Japan in 1946 when I would have just turned 19. I opted for V-12 and engineering There would be plenty of war left then for me to serve my country.

In 1945 the atomic bombs on Hiroshima and Nagasaki ended that plan. As Secretary of the Navy, Louis Johnson began the dismantling of the worlds most powerful fleet. This was so thorough that in early 1946 there were no navy black shoes size 9 1/2, the most common one. No new orders had been placed. My class graduated with a BSEE and a Deck-Engineering officer commission. We were promptly transfered to the USNR with blank orders for active duty if required. This initiated a feeling of shame that the Navy had furnished my rations, quarters and training for 2 1/2 years and I could not repay America that debt.

* * *

The major progress in various technologies during the war was not generally envisioned at the start and in any event was highly classified at the time. The present-day analysis of massive arrays of data to discover hidden patterns owes its' beginning to "Operations Research" which began in 1942 as a tactic against the German U-boats which torpedoed inbound ships of food and came close to starving England in 1941-2. All known reports of sightings at sea, spy messages on land or aircraft radar contacts were put into a common data base which early computation searched to determine the number of submarines entering and exiting the Bay of Biscay off of France. When the total was high, massive aircraft attacks were launched at night in the bay to detect the subs on the surface charging their batteries. When the number was low, routine maintenance of aircraft and crew relief was in order. In 1943 this tactic destroyed so many U-boats that they ceased to be a threat to England's supply lines.

I have a friend who was the Engineering Officer on a German sub at that time. He stated that they would surface at night and with no indication on their radar signal detectors they felt confident they were safe. Then in the sky, searchlights would come on and an aircraft would drop depth charges. They concluded that the threat was new infra- red detection equipment on the aircraft. In truth it was Operations Research plus aged German radar detectors that did not sense a change of the Allies radars to new higher frequencies. The Ops Research doctrine was that whenever the kill-rate of subs sunk as a percent of subs in the bay dropped, the radars would shift to a new higher frequency. In 1943 the U-Boat fleet came close to destruction. In 1944-5 hunger began to appear in Germany as land forces reduced German farming.

Radar itself changed hugely during the war. At the start the antenna towers in England were up to 160 feet long. By the end of the war antennas of only 4 foot long were in use on aircraft.

At the start, anti-aircraft shells were fired with no kill unless they hit the aircraft. By the end, they carried small Doppler radars which caused them to explode at the closest approach to the aircraft. Kill rates jumped hugely. These antennas were only inches long.

Thus, in WWII technical progress accelerated exponentially leading to the total change in life we see today in the mid 2010's. This book is an interior insight of portions of that progess as viewed from the memoirs of an electronics engineer participating in the developments of that age

# TWAS BRILLIG

My father once said that the fascinating thing about history is that it's baked fresh daily and so shows the amazing variety of human experience. This is particularly true in times of rapid change.

The year 1946 brought great change in the United States. A military force of 14 million men and women was reduced to 3 million.. The returning 11 million found housing in short supply and many foodstuffs still rationed. The manufacture of military supplies stopped abruptly and the changeover to industrial and residential goods began to fill the shortages generated by four years of exclusive focus on military needs. I was one of the 11 million, a newly commissioned naval officer, no longer needed and so transferred to inactive reserve. However, with the orders came my freedom to get married. The Navy had wanted no active duty married ensigns and I had given them my word. So there I was, newly married to Collie Dickerson, twenty years old, a graduate engineer with a specialty in what would later become "electronics".

This situation attracted an offer from General Electric to be a "test engineer" on probation for one year at a pay of $1.00 per hour. The good news was a raise to $1.18 per hour for reasons I never learned, but probably indicating a poor response to the $1.00 scale. I also had an offer from Aramco at

$1.60 per hour, but that was in Arabia with the status of wives unclear at that post. So, Schenectady and GE was the objective as Collie and I packed our entire belongings in the trunk of a 1937 Plymouth coupe, a gift to us from my Dad.

The GE test program was well conceived as training for new engineers. They spent at least one year in three month assignments at various GE manufacturing locations, testing the products of each plant. This allowed the management to get a perspective on the individual and the new prospective hire got a "hands on" education in the company's products. At the end of a year, the "test-man" could negotiate a position with any location where he had served. If none of them were interested, it was back to the street. For 90% of the applicants, it was a success for both parties.

I presented at the main gate of the GE Schenectady works with my offer letter in hand. That earned me a temporary pass and directions to the test office. The big guard in the blue uniform pointed and said, "About half a mile down the main road here. It'll be on your left. Has big columns out front. Don't look like no other building in the plant. You can't miss it."

I started down the main road, surprised to see buildings on both sides stretching for close to a mile. Most of them were dirty red brick with a uniform style dating back before the change of the century. Passing the open door of one building I saw a vertical lathe turning with a steel work piece that had a diameter of at least 15 feet. The machinist was actually inside the work and rode it around past the lathe tool which turned off a spiral of steel which immediately oxidized to a brilliant blue color. Clearly this plant did things on a massive scale.

The guard was correct, the test office resembled a bank or city office in contrast to the old red brick buildings. Inside, I sat for an interview with the test scheduler, who was interested

7

to learn that I was a Navy communications officer. He pointed out that GE had a contract to develop and produce the "Mark-56 fire control" for shipboard guns of 5"-38 caliber. He thought that would be a good match as the main effort was on the computer that controlled the tracking and pointing of the guns. So I walked back almost to the main gate and presented my orders to the supervising engineer at the Aeronautics and Ordnance Department. His desk was located on the ground floor of a comparatively modern three story building. The second floor had been removed to permit the installation of a 5"-38 naval gun turret, which at that moment was pointing almost straight up, extending well through the space where the second floor had been.. The heating ducts along one wall extended from the ground up to the third floor and showed extensive damage. Noting my fascination with this, my guide observed. "Yeah, the control has some stability problems. It got loose last week and the gun barrel cleared away some of the heating ducts." He though for a moment then said, "I'm sending you up to D.D. Scott. He's in charge of the potentiometer production. They've been having some problems."

\* \* \*

While I was settling down inside GE, Collie was out looking for a place for us to live. In that place and time this was nearly impossible. She eventually located a 10x12bedroom over *Wah Lee's Laundry* and next door to *Hogan's Bar and Grill*. We came to know Wah quite well as there was no way to do laundry in the bedroom except for socks and underwear. Wah did not put your name inside a shirt, he put his name, WAH. He sent the shirts out to be washed and ironed. With his experience he remembered the customer as soon as he saw the shirt. I was puzzled, but delighted that he never lost one of my shirts.

The 10x12 bedroom rented for $35. per month and the pay of $1.18 per hour put severe restrictions on our eating style. Collie had a hot plate that served to prepare hot dogs and canned beans. Lunch was cheese sandwiches and breakfast was corn flakes. Hamburger at that time was $.38 per pound and Velveeta was $.79 for a two-pound loaf. We found that if we were careful, we could afford a movie once every two weeks.

With gasoline at $.19 per gallon, travel worked out to about a penny a mile and furnished low-cost entertainment. Upstate New York was truly beautiful and our weekend activities soon included car trips with friends to the wonders of Lake George and Thatcher Park.

* * *

Back at the Aeronautics and Ordnance Department, I settled in with D.D. Scott to learn of the problems with potentiometers. Scott had been a Signal Corps officer in Germany. He produced several boxes of instruments shipped as his personal reparations program before leaving Germany. These he had assembled as a test fixture to give a precision reading of the resistance of the potentiometers, which were like the volume control on a radio. That had been done before I arrived, but the test readings varied over time and were simply not trust worthy. Scott's order was simple – "fix it."

I sat with the test fixture and the marvelous collection of German instruments for the better part of a day, watching the drift in the resistance reading. I arranged a 150 watt lamp so that I could examine the setup in good light. When it was turned on the reading began a speedy shift and settled to a new value. I puzzled over this with no results and decided to call it a day. When I turned the light off, the reading began a movement back to its' initial value. It was several minutes before my brain came through with a possible explanation --- the error was the result of temperature changes in the test fixture. Memory searched back to physics lectures and found the term *Peltier Effect*. It occurs when two different metals touch each other. A small voltage is generated and the value of the voltage changes with temperature. The lamp was changing the temperature of the wire contacts and hence the voltage in the circuit. This voltage was the source of the resistance reading. Hence the drift in reading was caused by a change in temperature of the wires.

The next day I located a heat gun and used it to repeat the result I had seen with the lamp. The drift was there alright, multiplied by the greater temperature generated by the gun. I found Scott and demonstrated the effect to him suggesting that we have the wireman take the entire fixture apart and redo it being sure that only one metal, copper, was used throughout. He was skeptical, but had no other way to go, so he ordered it.

Now, doubt assailed me. This was my first assignment. What if I had caused this extra expense and Peltier Effect wasn't the problem? Would they fire me outright or just ship me off to some hopeless assignment testing technology that had not changed in 50 years.

Two days later the job was finished and an unhappy wireman was giving me a doubting look, but carefully not saying any thing. I recorded the reading and then turned on the heat gun, directing it straight into the test fixture. I assumed my most confident expression, but a trickle of sweat came on at the hairline. The reading held rock-solid. I continued with the gun for five minutes, there was no change in reading. The wireman breathed a soft, "Son of a bitch." He smiled, nodded his head and left the room.

Scott showed up just as I was writing up the experiment. I repeated it for him. His smile went from ear to ear and I received a good slap on the back. He returned with Dr. Harold Chestnut, who was the contract leader. The experiment with the heat gun was repeated and reference showed that the reading had not changed through three repetitions of the heat gun cycle. Chestnut smiled and said, "Very nicely done. That's one less problem."

None of us knew it at the time, but Hal Chestnut was one of a group of General Electric engineers who would be leaders in the development of electronics as a vital industry and source of change throughout the world. He would become the recognized father of "Control Theory" and the President on the Institute of Electrical and Electronic Engineers. The IEEE became the world's largest professional society. Other GE alumni included Simon Ramo who formed Ramo-Woolridge and George Haller who formed Haller, Raymond & Brown which bought Singer Sewing Machine to form HRB Singer.

I would later receive a job offer from Ramo to join Hughes Aircraft at a significant increase in salary. But, that was a few years in the future and it would be a further twenty two years before I would join Hughes.

# THE SLYTHY TOVES DID GYRE AND GIMBEL

Three months later with my assignment at Aeronautics and Ordnance finished, I reported to the Test Engineer office with an excellent rating for my work. Proud of that first appraisal, I looked forward to some glorious next assignment. A mild shock came when I saw my next job would be in Magnetic Controls. Here I was, one of the first engineers educated in the new field of electronics and with practical experience too. Instead of an electronics assignment I was being sent to a fifty-year-old technology that was virtually dead except for use in submarines.

Being only four months out of the navy, I said nothing except "Thank you" and started my walk to Magnetic Controls. I was only 50 yards down the street when there was a sound of shoes running on the cobble stones and a voice said, "Are you Dickerson?" Conforming this I saw a young clerk who then said, "Please come back to the Test Office, I think they want to change your assignment." I complied and wondered what they could find that would be worse than old-time Magnetics.

Back at the office, I faced the manager who said with a big smile, "Just after you left we had a call for a new spot on the test program. One of the departments just received a big foreign order." He handed me a new assignment sheet. I glanced at the typing to see I was going to Electronic Controls. Now the big smile was on my face. GE was a leader in this field and I was on the way to see the products supporting that lead.

The department was located in a large open factory building with a small area for engineering offices in the front. My first job was testing welding sequence timers. A sophisticated control that allowed a factory worker to automatically make a repeated a sequence of spot welds of different current and time duration, all programmable from the front panel. The unit was a nice design, but after the first dozen units, testing it became tedious. I shared the test cubicle with Jim Olin who would in time become the general manager of GE's fractional horsepower motor department. However, that day he was, like me, just out of the service. He had been an Army Signal Corps officer and was wearing khakis. I was wearing my Navy greys, both of us dressed for dirty work and wearing out our former fatigue uniforms on the assumption we had no further use for them.

We both found the tests boring. Jim suggested we race to see who could complete the greatest number of units. This put spirit back in the day as we started our competition. Two hours later we had filled the test cubicle with finished control units and ran out of space to move. Each unit weighed about 50 pounds and was the size of a large microwave oven. I yelled for a truce so we could clean up the place and start again. Jim called for a porter, saying that the union had a strong grip on this plant and we should not move anything out of the cubicle or there would be the threat of a strike. We waited until a thin white-haired man arrived with his cart to take away the finished product. Our strong union worker looked at the stacks of control units and at Jim and I and said, "Hey, them things is heavy. You guys want to put 'em on the cart for me?" Jim and

I looked at each other and I said, "I'll race ya!" When we had finished the loading, the slithy tove did gyre and gimbel away with his pushcart.

* * *

In retrospect, I'm amazed at how little attention was paid to safety at that time. I am not blaming GE, it was the same everywhere. Perhaps the casualties of the war had pushed industrial accidents into a distant second place. The chief safety problem at Electronic Controls Department arose because the equipment had to withstand high potential. The tests, called Hi-Potting, ranged from 2500 to 7500 volts. The test engineer used a wooden probe with hand guards to push a high voltage wire onto the test point. Shortly after arriving, I witnessed a test man ruin his right arm by reaching over the hand guard to get a more accurate position for the voltage probe. That shift left his hand touching a lightly insulated conductor with 7500 volts. He moved to get a better placement of the probe and his elbow contacted the frame of the test cubicle. The result was a loud crack and a badly burned blackened arm. At first his face turned white and then later the red typical of electrocution accidents. He did not lose the arm, but its functional ability was greatly reduced. He learned to become left-handed.

My safety problem came while working on a steel mill rolling control that operated on 480 volts. I knew that most 480 volt accidents were fatal as that supply had the full force of the utility generators behind it and the voltage level was enough to break down the skin and penetrate to the inner muscles fibrilating the heart.

Collie had bought me for a Christmas gift an identification bracelet. It was heavy silver links and a solid plate with my name on it. It seems strange today that men would wear bracelets, but it was popular at the time and may have been a civilian reaction to freedom from wearing dog-tags. My problem was a lack of imagination. I was working the steel mill control with the voltage on. The control was about the size of a large refrigerator. The high-voltage power connections were held in place by sturdy bolts and nuts. I reached deep into the control to make some adjustment. When I withdrew my hand the bracelet caught on a bolt inside the cabinet. A quick glance confirmed that it was one side of the 480 volt supply. If any part of me touched the frame of the equipment or the test cubicle, that was it. I immediately had a rush of ice-cold sweat from toes to hairline and froze rigidly in place. It would not do to yell for help. All anyone could do was turn off the power. That would create a surge well over the 480 volts. In fact, as I thought about it I hoped no-one would try that. I had to get out of this without help.

My dad's advice in hunting had once been, "If you're hung up with a loaded gun on a barb-wire fence, just stop and take ten slow breaths." That seemed like a good idea. While I breathed, I thought. The way out became clear, but frightening. I would have to insert my hand further into the equipment then raise it so that the bracelet would clear the bolt. then I could withdraw it slowly past the voltage fittings. I took one more breath and started the process very carefully. I slowly moved forward and got the bracelet clear of the bolt. There was a great urge to jerk my hand out. That urge was suppressed to the accompaniment of another rush of sweat. Then came the slow movement out of the equipment. I cleared the enclosure and stood still, and repeating the Lord's prayer with emphasis on "Thy will be done." Slowly I removed all jewelry, class ring, wedding ring, bracelet and watch. Ever after that I worked "hot" only with gloves and no bling.

* * *

The "big foreign order" that prompted my reassignment proved to be interesting, educational and in a way historic. The order was from Russia and it was for 2 of everything in the catalog, one to operate and one to disassemble and reverse engineer. It included stuff that was hopelessly obsolete but also the newest and the best. We were just beginning to learn about our former ally. The Berlin airlift was 5 years in the future. A larger slithy tove did gyre and gimbel on the wabe.

For the Russian order I got to test mark-register controls that permit a newspaper printing press to register the three separate inks that make up a color printing. Also going through two at a time, like Noahs animals were cigar cutters, welders, and motor speed controls. One of the senior control engineers told the test men that he was angry with them. His beef was that in 20 years he had not seen all the GE products and here was a bunch of "kids" that got to see the whole catalog in one three-month pass.

* * *

Collie, with diligent searching managed to find an apartment for us. It was in the old Italian neighborhood on Summit avenue. We moved away from Wah Lee's laundry and started washing our own clothes. The apartment was the rear half of the second floor of a flat. The living room was so small that we could pass a pack of cigarettes from one to another without getting up from two chairs in opposite corners. But, it set us back only $50. per month plus $5. to park in a lot across the street. That proved absolutely necessary as the snow plows used the whole street width, so there was no street parking in the winter. Collie also found the City Library, which was well stocked and provided our typical evening entertainment as TV was not yet on the market (see the next chapter). The kitchen stove was a kerosene unit which also served as the heater for the apartment.

Life began to settle into the long-night style of an upstate New York winter.

# ALL MIMSY WERE THE BOROGOVES

Our 1937 Plymouth coupe had no heater. It was a southern auto. As winter set in this became an evident limitation, but with no spare cash, nothing could be done about it. A necessity, apart from the heater, was a pair of snow boots to make the trip from the GE parking lot to the workplace. A surplus pair of Air Corps flying boots proved both cheap and serviceable. At least my feet were warm.

Snow began early that year and before the spring arrived the cumulative fall would reach eight feet. Snow-plows did not remove snow they simply piled it on the sidewalks which soon were under banks rising to twelve feet. Tunnels were dug from front door to street so that folks could catch a bus. The road looked like a white canyon with periodic caves in its walls.

As the snow piled up I noticed that some people tied little colored ribbons to the radio antennas of their cars. I naively deplored this as a vain display. Then one night as I left work, I found and dug out a coupe only to find that it was not mine. The ribbons took on a new meaning.

The assignment at Electronic Control Department ended with a good rating and I reported to the Test Office to see what was in store for the next three months. I delightedly learned that survival of two assignments allowed me a voice in my next job. The Electronic Tube Department was just what I wanted and fortunately they had an opening.

I reported to Ray Knight, who ran the Application Engineering section. He was impressed with my practical and academic experience in electronics, but started me off on a typical "new boy" assignment. GE made tubes, such as the type 1620, that were designed to serve in the microphone amplifiers of radio stations. The rapid growth of FM radio, with its excellent sound reproduction created a strong requirement for noise-free amplifiers. That was fine, but someone had to test the tubes individually to determine they were "noise free". The worst offense in these tubes was a "noise burst".

Subsequent research showed these noise bursts were caused by a charge buildup on the insulators inside the vacuum tube. When the peak was reached this charge broke down the insulation and rushed to the amplifier producing a load CRASH. at least several hundred times as loud as the normal noise level. When the mechanism was finally discovered, the effect would be overcome by design. But, these were early days and the solution was for the "new boy" to listen for five minutes to the quiet ambient noise using head phones so as to avoid disturbing others. If there was a CRASH sound, the tube was rejected. If not it passed to provide quality, classical music broadcasts to American homes.

The problem with this test was the long five-minute wait with the uncertainty of an ear-splitting CRASH. The tension grew through the day. By nightfall I was as tired as if I had dug ditches all day.

Fortunately after a few days another Test Engineer appeared and became the "new-boy-on-the-street". I graduated to designing and building what would later be known as a "Hi-Fi

Amplifier". I designed a similar unit during my Navy training so this was a technical snap.

One of the older engineers gave me an engineering model of a high-fidelity loudspeaker and I appropriated the chassis of a GE FM radio that completed its tests. Collie and I now had the wherewithal to enjoy quality classical music. To fully use the ability of that Hi-Fi speaker, we needed a baffle to exclude the sound from the rear of the unit so that it would not cancel or interfere with the pure sound from the front. This was solved using the access panel to the attic of our apartment. We bought a piece of plywood the size of the panel and made a cutout for the speaker. This was installed to replace the original panel which was carefully saved for the day we would move.

The night came when we tried this arrangement – it worked beautifully. It is hard to describe today the grand improvement in sound quality that FM brought to the radio listener. We take that quality for granted now, but in 1947 it was a welcome revelation.

* * *

As winter furthered its clamp on life we discovered that our street was correctly named Summit Avenue. The back of our apartment faced the entire Mohawk River valley. In summer this was a grand view, but in winter it faced directly into the prevailing west wind and the soot from the smoke stacks in the GE plant. Although the windows fit well into their frames, there were no storm window covers and so the soot built up on the inside sills and with winter came the cold breeze. The apartment was heated from the kitchen stove downwind of the leaky windows. Finally, enough was enough.

The outside temperature was 10 degrees F. Saturday was the day. I filled a bucket with water at the sink and walked onto the back porch. With a great heave, I splashed the water over the outside back wall. It slowly ran down the wall and then, as I had hoped, it began to freeze. Another bucket provided a second layer. Leaving a full bucket outside to cool close to freezing helped and after fifteen buckets there was a layer of ice at least a quarter inch thick on the entire wall. We retreated inside and found no breeze in the bedroom and no soot seeping onto the sills. We southerners were learning how to live in an upstate New York winter. We crawled into a warm bed and listened to Swan Lake on the FM station.

* * *

I had never experienced blizzard conditions and my first exposure came early one morning in the huge GE parking lot. The sun was not up and the temperature was around 15 degrees. The wind blew at 20 to 30 knots and a heavy snow was falling. When I turned off the headlights and stepped out of the car, visibility dropped nearly to zero. At that level it compared numerically to the wind-chill factor. I was not frightened, but rather concerned. The plant was surrounded by an eight foot steel fence topped with barbed wire. The huge parking lot was on the outside. There was only one gate and the fence was over a mile long. I took a reference on the angle of my car and started in the direction where the fence should be. When I had walked further than I thought necessary to reach the fence, concern changed to worry. I stopped to see if I could hear anything to use as a guide. The sounds of the plant were completely masked by the wind. However, I could hear garbage cans being blown around by the wind. Great! If there were garbage cans outside the fence, that meant they were close to a gate, nobody would put them where they would require a long walk. I aimed for the sound of the cans and soon ran into the fence. The cans were on the inside. So much for a reasoned approach! At least I'd found the fence, all I had to do was follow it to the gate.

Then I recalled the fence was over a mile long. Which way to go, right or left? If I went right and the gate was behind me, I'd wind up almost a mile away from the gate in a deserted area behind the plant. I tried to think how long a person was supposed to last at a wind chill below zero. All I recalled was the verbal training to keep moving and don't go to sleep. If I went left, the worst that would happen would be a half mile walk to the main entrance of the plant. That was a long way from where I worked, but they had a stove. The decision was a no-brainer. I walked left with one hand on the fence. Within fifty yards a light appeared alongside the guard shed at the main entrance. I was only a little late to work

\* \* \*

An additional discovery for us southerners was the short daylight hours of winter in the far northern latitudes. In December and January the sun did not rise until after one arrived at work and it set before departure. So if you ate lunch inside at work, you simply didn't see the sun except on weekends. This had different effects on different people. By late January, Collie developed "Cabin Fever", an old settlers name for a depression brought on by too much time indoors. Going to a movie was obviously no cure for this. We tried drives with the car on weekends. This was a help, but snow was a problem once we arrived where we were going. We simply had to live with it.

Then one weekend, the sun shone and the temperature was all the way up to 32 degrees. I recall standing outside in pants with just a skivvy shirt on top and feeling quite comfortable. The realization that my blood had "thickened" was a surprise. One southerner had physically converted.

# Beware The Jabberwock, My Boy

Returning to the Test Office in early April, I learned more about the way the system operated. The Electron Tube department had decided they wanted me permanently. However, the Test Office insisted that I complete the full year of assignments. Tube Department then said, "why not send him to General Engineering Lab. Both he and the Lab would benefit from that." So I was on my way to the Lab. This was very promising as the GE Lab was just one cut below GE's Research Lab which at that time ranked with Bell Labs and MIT's Radiation Lab in the electronics field.

I reported at the Lab to a section managed by E.D. MacArthur and would later learn that in GEs grapevine his initials were said to stand for "Egotistical Devil". I began to realize the basis of that nom de guerre. Quietly working at a test bench, I turned to see E.D. enter the room with a VIP visitor. He proudly proclaimed, pointing to a photo of a power supply, "That's the power supply that made the atom bomb possible." I knew that supply and regarded it as precise and reliable, but so were several competing products. Also, it was perhaps only 0.1% of the equipment involved in development of the bomb. The chief support of the claim was that E.D. himself had designed this unit. I chuckled inwardly and thought to myself,

"How fortunate his name wasn't E.D. von Schnaubert. We'd all now be learning to speak German."

As a first assignment I began the testing of a German tape recorder made by Telefunken and returned as part of the booty from the occupation of Germany. The U.S. had only wire recorders at that time and the Telefunken drive mechanism appeared an impressive design that could go from full forward to full reverse seamlessly without breaking the tape. The tape was a marvel itself, being plasticized paper with an iron-oxide coating.. The Germans had tested it with recordings of both Roosevelt and Churchill speeches taken from short-wave broadcasts. It was novel to hear FDR doing a fireside chat through the noise and fading typical of short wave reception.

I carefully examined the interior of the recorder and found the workmanship and design impressive. However, the German engineers made one huge mistake in the design of the tape carrier. Later U.S. tape reels would have a plastic circle on both sides of the wound tape. However, the Telefunken unit had a support only on one side. This made dismounting and moving the tape a ticklish business. The dismounted half-reel looked like a dinner plate with the tape roll served as an entrée. I learned to lift the plate carefully with a pencil inserted through the center and my thumb pressing against the outside of the roll so as to hold it fast against the pencil. This worked fine until one day when a co-worker asked where I had left a certain tool. I did what came naturally and pointed with the hand holding the reel, "It's right over there." To my horror that movement slipped the tape off the reel and it lay on the floor like a 200 foot snake coiling and uncoiling. What had I done to this one-of-a-kind specimen? Red crept from my collar to my hairline.

Fortunately the workroom was on the sixth floor of the lab overlooking an enclosed courtyard. I conceived a plan and with some trepidation threw the head of the tape out the window. Slowly the snake on the floor unwound to follow its head out into the courtyard 60 feet below. When the tape end was in sight, I stopped the movement and rewound it on the reel. Sure enough, the six-story drop furnished enough distance for the coiled tape to straighten itself out and after 15 minutes of red-faced labor, it was all back on the one-sided reel ready for replay.

* * *

GE had a contract with the Army to develop a novel locator of artillery fire to fix the coordinates of enemy guns and direct the counter-battery fire. The scheme used a surveyed line of four microphones to triangulate the muzzle blast of the enemy artillery piece. I learned that the blast of a 105 mm cannon was very nearly a perfect half sine wave of 30 cycle frequency. That simplified the design of the microphone amplifiers. However, one problem remained. The sound level of the muzzle blast varied greatly, being a function of distance to the muzzle and the angle with respect to the microphone line. I was tasked with designing a compression circuit to reduce the amplitude of loud sounds and raise the amplitude of weak sounds. The circuit would use a new GE component called a Thyrite Resistor. (no relation to the later thyristor). This was a component with properties not previously available and known to only a few. With curiosity I studied the research reports and determined that a design using two amplifier stages in series would be necessary to meet the requirements.

This design was presented to the assembled group of E.D.s engineers. When I finished, the senior engineer criticized me severely for using two stages, "when one stage would do the job and be simpler." He had not used the new component and misinterpreted its properties. I verbally explained its properties and the need to use two stages. This was my first mistake. No one argues with E.D.s senior engineer. He replied heatedly. Then I made my second and major mistake. I wrote out the mathematics to prove my case and cited the research report of the inventor. That did it. He fumed and left the room. Nobody throws mathematics at the senior engineer in front of his subordinates. My mathematics had been better than my politics. However, the two stage amplifier when built did its job very well.

When the rating was made for that assignment, my gross error was demonstrated by the low score that I read with shame and angst. That same day I received a phone call from the test program director in the Tube Department where I hoped for permanent hire. His voice was clear, "get down here in 30 minutes or you'll be off the payroll." It was a half mile to his office and Collie had the car. I started a pace of 100 yards walking fast then 100 yards double time repeated over and over. I was at the Tube Department in about 15 minutes. He smiled, "I just wanted to see how fast you could move."

"Then it doesn't have anything to do with my rating?"

"Don't worry about it. The labs ratings don't mean a damn thing."

"Here's your employment agreement. You'll be assigned to Application Engineering as soon as you sign." I made a fast signature and forgave him for his little joke that prompted a new speed record between General Engineering Lab and the Tube Department.

\* \* \*

Back on Summit Avenue, our ice wall melted with the arrival of spring so we resorted to a careful taping of the windows on the windward wall to reduce the soot. With the snow off the roads, we could venture out and discovered the beautiful scenery of the Mohawk Valley. Of particular attraction was Washout Road on the opposite side of the River from Schenectady and a few miles up stream. We sat in the luxurious green grass and dreamed that someday we might be able to build a home on a gentle tree-covered hillside a few miles back from the river. Our dream could not imagine all that would happen over the next 13 years before we would return to Schenectady.

Friends were found among GEs young engineering men and their wives. These included one classmate and wife that we had known in Texas. They were driving a Hupmobile which trumped our Plymouth for "Aging Car of the Year". The owner claimed it had a multi-cycle engine that ran first on gasoline until it heated enough for the water leaks to let it run on steam, then the oil leaks let it run on diesel.

A small raise that went with permanent assignment helped our finances, but we were still selling the war bonds that we had dutifully piled up during the war.

* * *

Our landlord, an aging Italian, Giuseppe with his daughter Angela, ran a small grocery store across the street, next to our $5/month parking lot. Giuseppe, a trusting sole never mastered American money. Normally Angela made change in the store. In Angela's absence Giuseppe would hold out a hand full of coins and trust you to take the correct amount and leave him with the rest. However, in other matters he proved craftier. One day he showed up at the apartment with a gift bottle of homemade red wine in a paper sack.. The sneaky part emerged from a second paper sack which contained a broken food grinder of the hand-driven, clamp-it-to-the-table type. His simple explanation said it all. "You are engineer. Maybe you can fix?" I thanked him warmly for the wine.

Fortunately, the repair presented no problems and the next day I returned the unit to a delighted Giuseppe. The wine we found to be potent, but cut with ginger ale, it made a fair aperitif. We were starting to learn about international barter.

# AND THE MOME RATHS OUTGRABE

The job at Tube Department proved fascinating and challenging. As a first step I received a briefing on a long-standing problem for which no one had provided a solution. A machine was required to replace a skilled human operator in measuring the distortion produced by a tube audio amplifier. The soaring popularity of FM radio and what would later become HI-FI records increased the demand for low distortion amplifiers. The Tube Department published optimum operating conditions for its products. The problem was that determining these conditions took a considerable effort by a skilled technician. The measurement required a special setup, multiple adjustments and some math calculations to do the job. In short, it cost money.

I spent some time understanding the need, a procedure known as "inducting the problem". Like the preceding engineers, I saw no clear solution and decided to play a game, saying to myself very sternly, "On August 14th I want a solution to this problem!" Thus, excused of immediate responsibility, my concentration shifted to the more visible routine problems.

Two months later August 14 arrived. At 9:00 am I received a jolt similar to a hit on the back of the neck. My sub-conscious that had been working the problem for eight weeks demanded a debriefing. Grabbing a clean tablet of ruled paper, I started to write and sketch. Information literally poured onto the tablet, including both text and sketches. Sometimes I asked this weird inner voice, "how can I do that?" This produced reasonable answers for everything except one mathematical calculation. With the session completed, the tablet contained 6 pages of sketches and notes. The clock showed 11:00 am. The session consumed 3 hours. Emotionally worn out, I solemnly promised not to ever play that game again.

I first addressed the math function that had no visible means of implementation. It involved summing the squares of several functions then taking the square root of that value. With programmable digital computers today, that would be a cakewalk. However, in the time of analog computers, that was a major task. Serious thought produced a way to approximate the function. When tried, it worked, but with some small inaccuracy.

I consulted Ray Knight, the section head as to how much inaccuracy we could tolerate. His answer astounded me, "To hell with the root-mean square, just take the average." That was truly a cakewalk in analog computers – I was in.

The implementation of the idea into a working machine involved real work. After all, automating the efforts of a skilled technician at a time when even the word automation was not yet in use passed beyond the everyday job. However, by December a prototype machine was working and doing its job well. We decided to ship it to Owensboro, Kentucky where it could be used at GE's receiving tube plant. I would take the same train as the machine and demonstrate it for the engineers in Kentucky.

All went well until unpacking in Kentucky. I had not paid attention to the mechanical design beyond that required for laboratory use. Five years later I would learn, while working for the Air Force, that the most damaging environment for electronic equipment was shipment by train, but then naivety was mine. As we unpacked, I became both horrified and embarrassed to see broken mounting bolts and the heavier components lying loose inside the case.

The Kentucky engineers were both understanding and helpful. In a few days the repaired machine did its job well and I swelled with pride to see my first design applauded by my peers. For the next 60 years I would be addicted to electronic design.

* * *

Not all of Electron Tube Engineering was work. There were a few pranksters in the outfit, such as Ken, who delighted in spoofing those not as quick as himself. I saw something afoot when his head appeared over the cubicle wall in the test lab. There Lloyd was performing a power measurement on a microwave tube. Crude microwave instruments, in those days measured power by noting the increase in temperature of a water load that absorbed the microwave energy. The operator adjusted the volume of water-flow while watching the water through a glass window and recording the readings of inflow and outflow thermometers. The water reservoir up on top of the cubicle wall supplied the water flow. That's where Ken's head appeared unnoticed by Lloyd.

I puzzled over this stunt until I saw Ken's hand holding a chunk of Potassium Permanganate over the reservoir. This chemical dissolved readily in water and turned the fluid a lovely red-purple color. Ken's timing was perfect. Lloyd flipped the switch to turn on the microwave power. Immediately he saw the water change to wine. He was a good Christian boy and the vision wrote a shock on his face. He had performed a miracle!

The shock held until Ken's laugh let him in on the prank. Lloyd had the good grace to smile.

\* \* \*

On Summit Avenue winter returned, but not as severely as the first year. We iced the windward wall and settled in for the dark period. Collie bought a sketchbook and pencils and began to draw scenes as medicine against cabin fever. It worked somewhat, but the upstate New York winter was always a trial. This year we had television – an old GE set that completed its tests at the plant. It had a greatly simplified design and many problems, but pointed the way that TV would go in the future. Schenectady had its own TV station, WRGB, the initials of WRG Baker, VP of Electronics. The station proudly originated its own programs. They were noticeably light on commercials and really quite interesting. We had the TV in the bedroom as the living room was really too small. That particular model had a peculiar problem. After it was turned off, a dim white ball of light appeared on the screen and stayed there for several minutes. We concluded that it watched us and always behaved ourselves until it blinked out and disappeared.

We were learning to live through a New York winter.

# And Hast Thou Slain The Jabberwock?

Ray Knight, my boss at Tube Department, handed me the 1948 tech manual for the RCA 630-TS television receiver with simple and clear instructions. "I want you to study this set until you know the engineering value of every component in it and why the designers selected that value. When you do, come back and we'll discuss what comes next."

Ray's challenges always seemed like compliments that you were the only person that could carry out this task. The 630-TS, a marvel of complexity at the time, set the gold standard for TV design. The task of inverse design proved tedious as there were 30 tubes in the set. It had been designed carefully by engineers dedicated to excellence with little thought of economy. All told the unit comprised over a hundred components. The reverse design seemed nearly impossible at the start, but became reasonable when the individual functions of the receiver were viewed one at a time. In three days I returned to Rays desk to learn what came next.

"Alright, Art, you say you know why the 630-TS is what it is. Now, I want you to try something out." He reached into a desk drawer and produced a high-voltage transformer about the size of a pint carton of whipping cream. "This is something our people in Syracuse have produced to replace that unit with the iron core in the 630-TS. Instead of iron it uses a magnetic ceramic. They say it requires much less power to generate the high voltage and it moves the spot across the screen more smoothly than the iron core. Find out if that's true and what kind of tube we need to drive it."

If the claim were true, this would be a boon to TV designers. That part of the set used the most power and thus produced the most heat. I talked to the people in Syracuse that had invented this thing and got their picture of it. They particularly stressed its linearity. The TV picture was drawn one horizontal line at a time. This unit drew the horizontal line so perfectly so that a circle seen by the TV camera appeared as a circle on the screen, not an oval.

I substituted the new unit in the RCA chassis and found that it did produce more horizontal line width than needed. That meant the power could be reduced, I incorporated a safety component to prevent tube burnout. That worked. Now a simpler, cheaper tube could be defined to do the job. The Kentucky engineers started that new design which in time became the industry standard.

Ray wanted a little credit for what we had done to make TV pictures that showed circles as circles. He scheduled a demonstration for a GE vice president. The night before, I checked the picture using the TV station test pattern featuring a large circle with a picture of an Indian. Everything looked great. The circle was a circle. The Indian looked happy.

The next morning when the set was turned on, there was the same test pattern, but instead of a circle it was egg shaped, fat at left side and skinny on the right. The Indian looked fierce, facing a demonstration that would be a calamity. I went to work and adjusted the circuit to produce a reasonable circle.on the screen. Then the vice president walked through the door. As if on cue the technician at the TV station discovered that the test pattern card was crooked in its holder. He straightened it. Now we had an oval that was skinny on the left and fat on the right. The Indian looked livid. Ray went to work explaining things. I'm not sure the VP ever believed that he was not being conned.

The exercise had thoroughly educated me in the design of horizontal deflection circuits. This would prove useful two years later when I would become the field engineer for GE Tube Department in New York and the boroughs

* * *

The 1948 presidential election was preceded by a campaign of sound and fury. The Republicans featured Thomas E. Dewey, governor of New York and viewed as a competent administrator. The Democrats put forward President Harry Truman, who at the time appeared as a second-rate, albeit decisive president. The electorate backed him on the decision to end the JapaneseWar with two atomic bombs. His promotion of the Marshall plan to rebuild Europe was seen as fitting for the worlds newest and greatest power which also provided a home for the new United Nations. The problem was that Roosevelt cast such a huge shadow following his death in 1945 that it was difficult for a mere human to shine out.

On election night the *Chicago Tribune* had it all figured out and put forward an issue trumpeting a Republican sweep of the Congress and topping it off with a front page headline declaring "DEWEY DEFEATS TRUMAN". The election was close, but by the following morning it was clear that Truman had won and the Democrats had taken both houses of Congress. The Tribune had distributed 150,000 copies of the paper before it corrected both the headline and the congressional appraisal. As a Democrat, I had a good laugh at the red-faced Republicans.

\* \* \*

FM and HI-FI continued to grow. Ray set me the task of defining and measuring all the sources of 60 cycle hum in audio amplifier circuits that came from the utilities AC power sources. This proved to be a interesting task. One facet involved the mystery that a particular RCA tube design was lower in hum than GE's model of the same type. Conventional measurements showed the difference, however the hum was the same when the tubes heaters were energized by Direct Current instead of the conventional alternating current. Clearly something was different about the heaters in the two designs. I didn't want to destroy the RCA tube by opening it, so decided to try X-ray to see any internal difference. A sort of VAT scan of the heaters.

We had a very good X-Ray technician. I posed the problem, telling her I wanted to see the heaters in the two tubes to determine any difference. She asked what was the structure of the metal tubes. I had to admit that the heaters were inside three concentric metal cylinders. She took my estimates of thickness and made some calculations on a pad. "OK, let me have them. We'll see what we get." She set up the X-Ray and stepping behind her safety screen hit the switch.

Taking the film, she said, "hang in there a minute we'll see what we got." and disappeared into the darkroom. It was only a few minutes later when she reappeared and handed me the film. I put it the illuminated viewing screen. The lady's skill showed clearly, through six layers of steel she had brought out the heaters as if they were a portrait. The solution was immediately evident. The clever RCA guys had used a heater of two strands twisted on itself like a rope, while GE's was laid out in a number of straight lines. The twisted turns canceled their magnetic field from the heater and removed that source of hum. The design solution was clear. We started twisting heaters.

The work on hum sources resulted in a paper which I presented at a leading technical conference in Chicago. It was well received. The paper had been passed by Don Fink in GE, recognizing his status as a technical author. His review was, "everybody knows those things." I was crushed to have spent a month learning what "everyone knew". Nevertheless, the RCA Radiatron Designers Handbook cited the paper in its editions for the next twelve years. Apparently not everyone was at Finks exalted level.

* * *

Our secretary, Dottie Kells served a bull pen of ten engineers who dictated their reports and correspondence on wax Dictaphone cylinders that were stacked on Kells' desk for transcription. She was a remarkable person that was not only ambidextrous, but could simultaneously write forward with one hand and backward with the other. When she transcribed my first cylinder, she did me a great service. Turning to the office she shouted, "Hey guys, Art has set a new record – 37 "duhs" on one cylinder!" I had developed the habit of inserting a "duh" whenever my tongue had outrun my brain. My face reached a new red as a roar of laughter filled the room. Kells succeeded in wiping the sound, "duh" permanently from my vocabulary. I became careful to insure that my brain was well ahead of my tongue at all times.

* * *

It is exciting to be part of the inventing side when a technology is in a booming expansion. However, this can't always be the case, sometimes competition takes the lead and engineering gets down to the nitty-gritty. This was the case when Ray called me to his office. "RCA has a neat new wrinkle on the horizontal deflection circuits. They are recovering part of the energy expended on moving the spot and this has reduced the power consumed and made the circuit cheaper. There's no doubt it's a winner."

"OK, what do we do to catch up?"

"I thought you'd never ask. What we need is a life test rack for the additional new tube this scheme requires." He shoved a schematic in front of me and explained, "You see this new tube gets a thousand volt pulse between two of its electrodes where normally there might be 10 to 20 volts. This implies a heroic design change and we need to be able to test the life of the first trial designs."

"I suppose we could build ten positions of the complete circuit."

"That's not a good idea, Art. A life test rack must be far more reliable than the tube it's testing. Failure of other components in the test could produce surges that would prejudice the results and we wouldn't know what we had. We need a solid professional source for the thousand volt pulses."

"Do we have any old radar pulse modulators left over from the war?"

"I don't think so, but hey, we do have an old pulse generator in storage. As I remember. it was built like a battleship. If it's still working it would be ideal. Go to storage, get it out and make a test setup. If it works we can have the techs make a ten unit rack and be in business."

That pulse generator predated my joining the department by at least three years, but I found it, dusted it off and had it moved to my test bench. It was about the size of a restaurant refrigerator and had front panel adjustments that would produce just what we needed. I clobbered together a test circuit for the tube and fired up the jury-rigged arrangement with appropriate instruments attached. It worked! Right off the bat it worked! I stood back and marveled for about two minutes. Then there was an explosive arc inside the generator. I hit the off switch and carefully opened the case of the unit. There was a lot of dust inside, but no damage was visible.

I decided to try again. The result was the same. After two minutes there was the same explosive arc. Again, there was no evidence of damage, I decided to do an inside examination and removed all the panels from the case of the unit, defeating the safety interlocks so I could watch this mystery develop. Decked out in safety glasses and gloves, I started up the test. The problem was immediately apparent, but so fascinating that I couldn't stop watching the process. Mice had invaded the unit in storage and their fecal droppings littered the plate under the high voltage transformer. In operation the transformer had a high DC voltage on one terminal. This charged the little droppings and they climbed one on top of another like acrobats forming a pyramid. Finally the top acrobat reached the terminal. There was a blinding flash and a cloud of mouse dropping dust floated in the air. When it settled there was no evidence of damage, but a sufficient supply of old droppings to repeat the process.

I borrowed a vacuum cleaner from the janitor and thoroughly cleaned the rugged old instrument. When it was then fired up everything worked and we had the basis for our life test rack.

\* \* \*

With the boom in housing construction, rental units became available. Collie found a third floor flat on Crane Street across the ravine from our place on Summit Avenue. In the new Polish neighborhood we were welcomed with relief that we had escaped the terrible Italian side of town. We moved in and began a make over of the space. This included sanding and varnishing the wood floors, new carpets, new indirect lighting, refinishing the kitchen counters and repainting the place from one end to the other. Our landlady, Mrs. Kosinski thought we were the greatest. Actually all we wanted was a good looking place to live. When our overhaul was complete we invited the fellow people from application engineering over to admire the place.

Finally we had arrived socially.

# THE JAWS THAT BITE, THE CLAWS THAT CATCH

The year 1948 proved to be loaded with change, both internationally and locally. Not only was the State of Israel created, but the World Health Organization was established. Russia elected to close access to Berlin on the ground, prompting the Berlin Airlift in which the USAF flew round the clock transports into Templehof Airdrome loaded with food, medical supplies and coal. The same government which two years before ordered two of everything in the GE controls catalog now discovered that it could not shut down the jointly held capital of Germany by denying access to roads through the Russian Zone of Occupation.

In the GE Tube Department change flourished. My esteemed boss Ray Knight left GE to become chief engineer for ARINC, the engineering consortium for the airline industry. ARINC aimed to increase the reliability of aircraft electronic equipment. They put in place an office in every major airport of the U.S. to gather data and conduct tests. I had the good fortune to do some work for ARINC before Ray left. This concerned the effect of redundancy on reliability. The results were counter-intuitive and opened my eyes to the power of statistical analysis in the reliability field.

The big boss, Black Pete, insisted that I attend the short course of the Sales Analysis Institute. GE considered the SAI course an absolute requirement for anyone having continued contact with customers. Basically it stressed the necessity of observing carefully peoples' verbal and body language and carefully building up a picture of their motivations: Money, Fear, Fame, Prestige, Love. The course stressed a non-judgemental approach. What you saw in another person was neither good nor bad, it simply was what it was and not your job to change it. You should frame a proposition that would appeal to the person's needs and protect against their fears. This course was aimed at business, but proved valuable in the social sphere as well. I completed the course and was ordained to contact GE customers.

\* \* \*

Simultaneous with Rays' departure, the application engineering force received total re-organization. In effect the Schenectady branch was dissolved and the people re-assigned to field engineering posts in Chicago, Los Angeles and New York. I received the territory of New York City and the Boroughs. This was known as a tough "10% territory". The back-office description was "90% of the customers and 10% of the billing." However, it was not the quantity of customers that created the difficulty, it was the brutal competition among the small fast-growing TV manufacturers. Some names, such as Emerson, exist today. However, Teleking and Teletone, significant at the time have passed away.

Ken, he of the water-to-wine joke on Lloyd, introduced me to the New York customers before he left for Chicago. One company president when I was introduced said to Ken,

"Whatcha want me to do? Get him laid?" I discovered later that his organization was well equipped to perform that service which I really didn't need.

My style was quite different from Kens'. He put effort into taking the management to lunch and dinner. I went directly to work with the engineers, particularly assisting in design of the newer more efficient horizontal deflection circuits. Word got around among the engineers who readily talked to each other independent of the competition at the management level. Soon I received requests to review the designs of horizontal deflection circuits.

Inevitably the question arose, "What's so-and-so doing about this circuit?" That was a path I dare not step onto – my standard reply was, "I won't tell you that any more than I'd tell him what you're doing." The message got through. I knew I'd gained trust the day that I was asked by a customer t evaluate a GE competitor's solution to his design problem. Privacy didn't work for competition.

Things were sweet with the TV engineers, but not yet with the management. I received a phone demand to come immediately to the plant of a TV manufacturer who will remain nameless. His plant was on the West Side dock area of lower Manhattan. These docks loaded coffee and chocolate. The aroma was marvelous. I walked through the TV assembly floor and saw rejected sets piling up so high that in 4 hours there would be no room for workers. I walked into the managers office and received a glare and in a loud voice, "You stupid son-of-a-bitch. Anyone who works for GE is a stupid son-of-a-bitch." He didn't know my IQ or my parents so I could look upon this as pure conjecture. However, the tirade continued non-stop. After 20 minutes I had passed through surprise to anger to cold logic. He took a deep breath and continued, "Your lousy tubes are costing me real money. They don't work. How can you stay in business with such a worthless product?" The rant continued. I conceived a plan. At about 30 minutes into the harangue he paused and I injected. "I want to thank you for that flattery. When I walked through your plant I guessed this was costing you about $20,000. an hour. Here you have spent a half hour -- $10,000. just to enjoy my company. I couldn't ask more of you. Suppose I go out now and get to work on solving your problem." A massive silence was followed by "Get out there." I did and in less than an hour his problem was solved and the foreman set up a line to repair rejects with the circuit change I'd suggested and which had proved itself on the main assembly line. For the sake of both of us, I couldn't speak to the boss. I asked a thankful foreman to give him my regards. I failed to state what kind.

The word of this affair got around with astounding speed. Apparently standing up with cool to a ranting boss was the mark of a "mensch". The management attitude changed to gracious and smiling. This was reflected at the end of a year when I left New York for Chicago. Needing a new car for the Chicago job, I was handed by a customer, a purchase order with fleet discount for a Ford sedan delivered to a Chicago dealer. I had to pay the price, but the fleet discount was a handsome gift and a reminder of the way business progressed in New York.

\* \* \*

Our first daughter, Sheryl Melody was born in Niskayuna, a suburb of Schenectady May 5, 1949. It was a Thursday supposed to be the doctors day off, but Shari would only become strict on schedules later in life. She was a strong and happy baby. I designed and built a special chair for her. It sat on the floor with a tilted back and cushioned headboard. Her rump was supported in a sort of sling with two holes for her legs, which allowed her feet to touch the floor. In front of her was a small board to hold toys. This contraption sat on the kitchen floor where she could watch Collie fix dinner and bang on the board with whatever came to hand. This prompted great cries of delight from Shari and murmurs of pleasure from Collie. I felt like a successful father.

# Flossie Trumps A Floozie

I should introduce Flossie Bucklin whose name appears in this chapter heading, but she will not appear in action until later. Flossie was a top heat transfer engineer in GE's Schenectady engineer establishment. She was gracious, pleasant and above all one outstanding engineer. Aside from her industrial labors, Flossie's interest was to produce a mathematical explanation of a baking Apple Turnover. I'm told that hers were excellent, but she despaired of a solid math explanation for the turnover phenomena. At that time Flossie was about 60 years young and could pass in any grocery store as a dumpy housewife. Before we see how this leads to problems, I need to set the tone and schedule of living in Schenectady while assigned to work in New York City.

In the new organization, three of us were assigned as field engineers respectively to New York, New Jersey and Pennsylvania and allowed to live in Schenectady. This speaks mainly of the "family" style of corporate organization at the time. That would soon change and people would live where they were assigned.

The style was to catch the New York Central coach on Sunday evening to New York and return on Friday afternoon. This consumed a lot of coach tickets from Schenectady to NYC. Wendell, the sneaky one of the group had his own approach.

Out of Albany, the conductor would use his personally coded punch to put a hole in the ticket and stick the punched stub in the back of the seat ahead. Each punch had a unique die which identified that conductor. The punched shapes ranged from five-pointed stars to imaginary figures and designs. The punches were all very sharp and well maintained.

Wendell would smile and hand his ticket to the conductor who would punch it, hand it back and pass on to the next car. Wendell would then lick his index finger and retrieve the small punch from the floor, fitting it back into the hole in the ticket. The precision punches insured a keen fit and with a little rubbing, a "new" ticket emerged. Wendell would then put an old punched ticket in the seat back ahead and he was good-to-go to New York City. The "new" ticket would be re-used four or five times before its "holey" nature was too risky to use.

Wendell carried his ticket business one step further when New York Central raised the rates to NYC. He bought a number of tickets and when the new rates went into effect started selling them to his fellow travelers at a small discount. This proved beneficial to all until one day it was discovered that he was selling reconstructed tickets as new ones. This put Wendell on the outs with his fellows, but not with management which put him in charge of the new sales office in Clifton, NJ.

* * *

One of my largest customers was Garod TV, in Brooklyn, just across the bridge from NYC. I took the subway over and got off to walk the final few blocks to the Garod plant. The first unusual thing was two cops at the cross street. Going on, I found another two at the next cross street. Obviously something big was on in Brooklyn. Halfway between streets a van pulled to the curb in front of me. The back doors opened displaying two racks of men's clothes. A husky voice said, "Hey, Mac, wanna buy a suit?" I sensibly concluded they didn't have my size. The doors closed and the van moved on. Business in New York was done in unusual ways.

Garod TV was a mixed blessing as a customer. GE had 95% of their tube business. Regardless of my performance, sales could only go down or stay the same. To avoid any negative report, I spent a major effort on design of the horizontal deflection circuit in their new model. This worked out very well and Garod was happy. I was happy and my boss "Black Pete" was happy.

Black Pete, E.F. Peterson, was distinguished from "Red Pete" by the color of their hair. Black Pete was the big boss. Being on his good side was clearly desirable. Red Pete handled the department's finances and was thus less visible in day-to-day matters. However, I found him in the waiting room at a customers' plant when I arrived for a routine visit. His face matched his hair color and I was surprised to hear him address the receptionist, "I'm the head of credit and collections for GE. Your boss has kept me waiting out here for 30 minutes. Tell him that in 15 minutes if I'm not in his office, I'm leaving and taking with me the full GE credit extension to his company." The lovely young lady looked horrified and rushed off to deliver the message.

I watched Pete cool for a minute and then said, "That was a little sharp? What's he done?"

"Our stupid salesman told me that Louie Pokrass stood behind the credit we extended to this company."

"Well, Pete, as I understand it Pokrass is worth well over 20 million. He's good for it."

"Oh he's got the money alright, but he's not standing behind the company. He's not an officer of the company, he's just a stock holder. That idiot in there." He motioned toward the closed door. "He waves Pokrass' name in the air and is holding up payment of his bill. Our salesman swallowed a bad story." I knew that the salesman was much too keen to be taken in by that story, but was not about to enter a fight that wasn't mine.

At exactly 14 minutes after Pete's 15 minute threat, the door opened and a smiling face appeared to welcome him to the inner sanctum. It wouldn't be kosher to appear too anxious. Five minutes later Pete returned, stuffing a check into his pocket. His face had returned to its' normal color. You just have to know how to do business in New York.

* * *

My routine settled into a different style. As a new father I wanted to be with the family as much as I could. Instead of going to New York on Sunday night, I had a standing order with the cab company to puck me up at 0530 each Monday morning. I would be dressed in a suit and topcoat over my pajamas, carrying my suitcase packed for a week of hotel living. The cab delivered me to the Schenectady station where I boarded the train and promptly went back to sleep. When the train stopped in Harmon and changed to electric propulsion for New York City, I walked to the bathroom, shaved, dressed and at 0830 was ready to step off the train at Grand Central Station. A cab took me to the Lexington Hotel on 48th street and from there it was a short walk to GE headquarters at 53rd street. I arrived promptly at 0900 bright eyed and ready for work.

The reverse routine occurred on Friday afternoon. With luck I could catch a train that would put me in Schenectady in time for dinner and the chance to spend three nights with my family. This train was popular with other GE men who were on the same schedule. I put my suitcase on the overhead rack in the coach and walked back to the club car. I really didn't want a drink, just a chance to read the papers and enjoy the view on the route up the Hudson River. When I walked into the club car I received a dazzling smile from a young lady who was strategically seated just inside the door. I smiled back and continued on to the mid point of the car, taking a seat where I could watch the view of the Hudson and incidentally the young lady by the door. The next entrant, a dumpy housewife, smiled graciously to the young lady and me, took a seat further into the car, appropriately ordering an "old fashioned" from the waiter.

Once again the car door banged open and a handsome man of perhaps 30 entered receiving the dazzling smile from the young lady. He paused and then looking further in the car his face lit up and he walked over to the dumpy housewife, announcing in a loud voice "Hello Flossie! Great to see you." He ordered an extra dry Martini and they settled into an animated conversation.

This routine repeated twice, each time with a joyous cry of "Hi Flossie!" and total neglect of the dazzling smile that only wanted a couple of free drinks on the way to Albany. To make matters worse each time the conversation descended to indecipherable technical discussions. When it happened one more time, the dazzler looked daggers at Flossie and with a snort of disgust stomped out of the car. One of Flossie's companions asked, "What was that about?" Flossie, who missed very little said, "I think she's just worried about her apple turnovers. I would be.".

# Chicago Is A Different World

Black Pete described it in a very promising way. He said, "Art, you've done well in New York. I have good reports and you've learned one way of doing business. I want you to move to Chicago so you can see a different business world." It sounded good to me, so Collie and I packed up the Crane Street flat and put our furniture into storage. She and Sherry went to Texas to live with her parents until I could find us a place in Chicago. We were sufficiently well off by that time to consider buying a house. Finding one would take a little time.

* * *

The Chicago job was the same work as New York, but centered on out of town customers in Minneapolis, Minnesota, Fort Wayne and Indianapolis, Indiana as well as Cedar Rapids, Iowa. The 1937 Plymouth coupe with no heater served us well as a local car in Schenectady, but clearly wasn't up to the long distances and the Midwest winter. I sold it and was ready to pick up a new Ford sedan in Chicago at a fleet discount price courtesy of my New York customers. Collie and Shari took the train for Texas and I was off for Chicago. It was the end of 1949 and changes were still coming at an exciting rate. Russia exploded an atom bomb, setting up the race with the U.S. on nuclear armament. China became a communist country and Taiwan seceded from China to assume its' independent status. The 45 rpm record was introduced, replacing the large 78 rpms and the first Polaroid camera was sold. RCA demonstrated color television. The economy was glowing and ladies hemlines dropped below mid-calf, a decidedly unflattering level. Other than hemlines, America's prospects looked great. I was greatly pleased.

* * *

In Chicago I picked up the new Ford sedan. Wow! What luxury, an actual working heater! Finding a hotel room at a weekly rate on the North Side, I drove out of town during the week and looked for houses during the week ends. For the first time I knew true loneliness. My new boss, was cold and remote and seemed to resent my being there. The first week he angrily confronted me, "You're only 23. What are you doing in this job?" I reminded him, that I'd been working for GE as an engineer for three years. He backed up a little saying, "Well, Black Pete says you're OK. We'll see."

I learned two years later that he thought of me as a threat to his job. If Black Pete thought I was Ok, maybe I was there to replace him. Nothing could be further from the truth. I looked at Chicago as a learning experience and was aiming at something quite different from his job. My dream was shaping up. I wanted to serve in every job of both marketing and engineering and then step into general management with a first hand understanding of the key jobs that reported to me. I began to see a career.

* * *

The house hunting began with the decision on which railroad to take into Chicago. There were three choices, one from the North side, one from the west and one from the southeast. After visiting all the regions, I settled on the west route using the Aurora & Elgin Railway. This was a short-haul line, but it went directly into the loop where the GE office was located in the Merchandise Mart, the worlds largest office building. Further searching narrowed the field to the town of Lombard which announced itself as the Lilac Capital. The next step narrowed to houses within walking distance of the Aurora & Elgin train stop. With this selection, I found a well constructed two-bedroom house on Chase Street. and mailed a floor plan to Collie We discussed it by phone. According to her it would fly. .We made an offer, telling the broker that this was absolutely the top we could go. He did his best and soon we owned a house and a mortgage. I got the furniture out of storage and moved in..

Collie and Sherry were still in Texas when I came home one night to find the living room floor 6 inches deep in snow with a long trail leading to the front door and up the wall to the switch for the front porch light. The coal furnace had gone out during the day and the fierce Chicago wind drove snow through the outside light fixture to the switch plate and onto the living room floor. After a trip to the hardware store, I had the wind path sealed, the snow shoveled .and the coal fire restarted. Something had to be done about that furnace. Refitting it to fuel oil went to the top of the "to do" list, as soon as we had the money.

I stocked the house with groceries and went in the new car to pick up Collie and Sherry from the train station. Everything was ready including Sherry's chair on the kitchen floor. Everything went well, the car was admired, the snow held off and the house proved just what Collie wanted. At last we had a home of our own. I was a proud and happy father.

* * *

My most fascinating new customer was Motorola. It was a complex company making an excellent TV set, advanced military equipment, and a top-of-the-line mobile communications radio for police and taxis. Their TV design skill was a cut above any in New York. They had two TV engineering groups. When one group completed a design, they followed it into the factory and became the manufacturing engineers. When their model passed out of production they reverted to be the new design engineer group.

This arrangement insured that the lessons learned on the factory floor were plowed back into the design process. The employees all shared in the profits of the company. I was surprised one day in the factory to hear one woman berate another who had spilled something on the floor, "Pick that up, do you want somebody to get hurt and sue the company?" Black Pete was right, business was done differently in Chicago.

Delco Radio in Kokomo, Indiana was another novel case. They made the radios for General Motors automobiles. The model year began for them in late August and production ran like a freight train through to the following July. The designs were frozen in early summer and the suppliers for the upcoming year were approved in July. To be a supplier of the entire kit of tubes was a significant piece of business. Each kit was worth about $4. and GM made around 6 million sets each model year. The $24 million pie was split about half for the lead supplier and a quarter for each of two others. Thus the gold ring was worth $12 million and second place only $6. The award was based on

% of rejects in the preceding year and the amount of help given in development and design during the engineering phase.

The kindly Swedish gentleman in charge of Delco engineering assured me. "I hev a proyeckt to redoose reyeckts." I took that as my mantra and concentrated on insuring that GE's internal testing matched and insured performance to the GM specifications.. On one occasion I loaded the GE test set into my car in Kentucky and drove it to Kokomo to insure that correlation of performance specs was maintained. Surprisingly, this was a new step as the competition simply stood fast, maintaining that their test sets were right. We got the preferred supplier spot that year and the next. It felt good to win!

\* \* \*

Thanks mainly to the efforts of my former boss Ray Knight, I was placed on the "go team" for design review when reliability problems arose in AIRINC airline equipment and also the "go team" for U.S.Navy missile equipment. The team comprised one engineer from each of the four leading tube companies, RCA, Sylvania, Raytheon and GE. This work was fascinating. Speed was of the essence and the team was typically picked up and flown to the manufacturer's site in Charley Bank's Beechcraft Bonanza. Charley was an AIRINC employee and a former Navy pilot, thoroughly knowledgeable about aircraft..

I once kidded Charley, saying during a Chicago winter it would be good to have an Eastern Airlines emergency so we could fly to their headquarters in Florida. One day the phone rang and Charley reminded me, saying "Hey, I got that Eastern Airlines problem for ya." I thanked him. It was 10 above that day in Chicago. "Problem is the Eastern plane is in St. Paul, Minnesota."

"I didn't know St. Paul had an airport."

"You'll see when we get there why you didn't know about it."

With this mystery in mind and dressed in my heaviest overcoat, I waited for Charley at Midway airport. He arrived and I discovered that I was the complete "go team". You're lucky, it's a GE tube that only you folks make and it's in a piece of Collins Radio equipment, type 51-R2."

"What's the problem?"

"That's the main communication set for the airlines. The communication is just fine until the plane approaches the airport about at the outer marker. The pilot is talking to the tower getting his landing instructions then the reception breaks up. He can't understand the wind velocity, which runway is his, nothing. It's all chopped up. You can understand why they're upset." I grunted an agreement. If I were a pilot, that would be a white-knuckle experience. "Course they got a second radio, but by the time they get it on line they've lost the line up and have to go around. That's an insult to the pilots skill and he doesn't take it kindly."

I thought about that for a few minutes. "Charley, what's a typical distance to the outer marker where this happens?"

"Oh, maybe eight or ten miles."

'I assume your AIRINC people have a complete receiver on the bench for test."

"Yep. If there's anything you need ask for it now and it will be yours."

"Ask them to be sure to have a VHF signal generator and a cable to fit the antenna input., a tech manual and a good voltmeter."

As we lined up for the final approach at St. Paul, it was evident why I didn't know it had an airport. The runway was bordered by the Missouri River at one end and terminated by a 200 foot vertical cliff at the other. It was no problem for Charleys' Bonanza, but must be a sweaty experience for some of the commercial airliners that came in for repair. The risky runway had reduced it from a passenger terminal to a maintenance depot.

Charley was as good as his word and called the St. Paul AIRINC agent. When we walked into the hanger there was the receiver set up with the signal generator and the voltmeter waiting on the bench. Introductions were made all around. I sat down, and using the tech manual found the spot I was looking for in the Collins receiver.

I had made a guess that the breakup had nothing to do with any equipment at the outer marker -- that was just a description of distance to the airfields' transmitter. The mystery breakup was related to the signal strength received from the airfield. That was a guess and it was all I had at the moment. Putting on the headphones, I tuned the receiver to receive the output of the signal generator then slowly increased the strength of the signal. Suddenly the sound in the phones simulated a hoarse chicken clucking. I backed off on the signal strength and the chicken slept quietly. The sound was distinctive. It was the so called squelch signal turning on and off. A quick use of the voltmeter proved this to be the case. I asked one of the Eastern pilots to confirm that this was the problem. He tried the phones and confirmed loudly, "That's the son-of-bitch." The squelch signal is designed to relieve the pilot's ears of hissing noise at low signal levels. It turns on his audio only when there's enough signal to be useful. This squelch signal was doing the reverse of its ordinary function. When the signal level got large it cut off the audio.

Now we knew what was happening, the question was twofold; 1 what causes it and ; 2 What do we do about it? Using an oscilloscope we made traces of the waveforms for all electrodes of the squelch amplifier. There was no question, the little devil was oscillating all on its own whenever the signal strength reached a high level. An oscillating amplifier is not a simple proposition, but for this one I made a second guess and soldered in a resistor from one electrode to ground. It was my night for guesses. The oscillation stopped and the amplifier worked properly.

I turned to the Collins Radio man and said, "I don't recommend this as a circuit change at this point, although you might have the Cedar Rapids guys consider it. I think this is a tube problem that occurs with aging. Has this been happening on new tubes?"

"No, it's only on sets that are in service for 18 months or so."

"OK, I want the tube from this set and any other failures you have. I've got to take them back for tests that are more complex than I can make here. I can promise you that if it is a tube problem, we will fix it. We have a commitment to airline reliability and we'll carry it out." That was a brave statement, but it was company policy and at that time field engineers had a surprising amount of authority in making customer promises. Ironically, three years later that authority would be substantially withdrawn back to headquarters and I would be the one tasked with carrying out the withdrawal. But that was in the future.

The tests were carried out and my old Hungarian compatriot Dr. Lou Hamvas explained the results while puffing on his Hungarian cigarette. "We have a case of *Insul-bildung*. My German was limited, but it sounded to me like "island building". Lou conformed that saying that as the tube aged, little islands of electrically conducting metal were deposited on the insulators that separated the electrodes.. At low voltages this had no effect, but high voltages broke down the spaces between the islands and allowed a short circuit to develop.

In the present squelch amplifier, the voltage was low until the receiver had a large signal from the airfield. Then the higher voltage caused a breakdown and shut off the audio. Instability caused it to oscillate back and forth cutting the audio on and off. Lou had a simple suggestion of how to fix this with additional parts to shield the insulators from the metal deposits. We put together some samples and sent them out to Collins, starting our own accelerated life tests at the same time. The change was put into production and completely cured the chopped audio problem. It was a prime example of how the expanding use of vacuum tubes in new applications created new problems requiring new solutions if progress was to continue at this accelerating rate. It was an exciting time, even if hemlines were dropping. I felt proud again that I had solved a very complex problem and Lou had provided the cure. GE was a good place to work.

# Expansion Of Both Viewpoint And Family

The year 1950 continued the course of technical and political expansion at an accelerating rate. President Truman authorized production of the Hydrogen Bomb. In June, the North Koreans invaded South Korea and Truman ordered the US Army and Navy into the conflict. It was strangely not a declaration of war, but conflict was conflict and death was death. The week following the North Korean invasion, my father died of a heart attack. There is little doubt that he feared the start of WW III. He had long worried over the rise of China and saw conflict with the US as only an accident away.

Collie, Sherry and I flew to Texas for the funeral. His death struck me deeply as we had been very close. The sorrow was partly relieved to see the response of so many people to his passing. He had been a Bell Telephone Pioneer, working for the company for 45 years. In that time he touched many lives. The news spread through the company and telegrams arrived from distant states as well as remote locations in Texas. It was my task to clear up his desk at home. There I found many letters over the years expressing thanks for assistance and advice. He was loved by many whose lives he touched.

When we returned to Chicago, my boss advised that Naval Intelligence had called on him. When I asked what that was about, he smiled, saying, "They're just checking up on you." Anything that made me uncomfortable made him happy. About a month later I received notification from the Navy that my reserve status was moved up from "inactive" to "ready", bypassing the grade of "active". This looked like a recall, so we talked with my mother and found that she would be delighted to have Collie and Sherry living with her in a house that seemed lonely with Dad gone. We waited for the notification of duty station to come. Six months passed and then the letter from the Navy appeared announcing that I had been moved again all the way back to "inactive". I never learned what that was about, but did find later that my fellow classmates had the same experience. Probably one of the seizures the Navy was experiencing in a rapidly changing world. I felt relieved.

* * *

As a member of the "go team" for Navy missile design, I had a chance to work on the *Regulus* and *Talos* missiles and in a later and different capacity on the *Tartor* and planning for the submarine launched *Poseidon* missiles. This was a new experience for the Navy and surely a new one for me. The operating conditions on board the missiles differed greatly from anything experienced before in addition to the new equipment functions. The US military was building up rapidly and unfortunately the quality of engineering was less than in the profitable TV field. This would be corrected by the mid fifties, but at the start of the decade it was a sad fact.

I was called out for a Navy "go team" on the Regulus missile at Chance Voight Aircraft in Fort Worth, Texas. The problem involved a small gas-filled tube used as a pulse generator in the missiles radar. I had little experience with gas-filled tubes and so got a quick briefing from an old buddy in Schenectady whose experience encompassed that rare animal. When I arrived at Chance Voight I found that the responsible engineer for the pulse generator was a young fellow much less experienced than I with gas tubes. For my good fortune, the problem was one that the Schenectady buddy had cautioned me about. I seemed well prepared and the suggested changes did indeed cure the problem.

The pleased Chance Voight people gave me a tour of their facility which proved interesting. The last F4U Navy fighter aircraft was on the assembly floor. It was a very advanced gull-winged aircraft from WW II that proved deadly against the Japanese in the final year of the war. It was now in use in Korea and had changed markedly from its' forebearer. The presence of massed ground fire had prompted the complete lining of the underside of the pilot compartment with steel armor plate The beautifully tooled air-scoops in the wing-roots that supplied the oil coolers were now blocked off with a sheet of aluminum, but the graceful scoop was still in place. The oil coolers had moved elsewhere.

Out on the airstrip I witnessed an exciting piece of aerobatics by a Marine Corps pilot testing a new F4U. He came down-wind over the strip at perhaps 250 knots. At the end he pulled up vertically to around 1500 feet and just before stalling, did a wing over and dived back at the runway approach lights. He pulled out sharply and landed exactly on the numbers, leaving me with an Adam's apple high in my throat and wondering how many times he would pull that stunt before something went wrong and he strewed plane and pilot all over the strip.

That did indeed happen on the Regulus, which was in competition with the Army's Matador missile. Both were sub-sonic, air-breathing cruise missiles with nuclear payloads. The Department of Defense, DOD asked whether the Navy could use the Matador in place of the Regulus. Pride in its mission caused the Navy to say NO and back this up with a plan to use the vacant nuclear payload compartment to house a landing gear and remotely controlled autopilot so the missile could be recovered and flown again during it's extensive test phase. This plan worked, at least enough to convince DOD.

Engineers tend to shingle beyond the ridge pole and in this instance they exceeded the pole substantially. There were seven flights with successful recoveries before a slight wind gust during landing flipped the missile upside down and scattered 10,000 pounds of parts down the runway. Investigation showed that the roll rate of the missile with its' stubby little wings was faster than the brain to hand reaction time of the earthbound pilot. There was simply no way to correct a landing error. It was 1951, the cold war accelerated and in the pentagon inter-service rivalry flared. I was puzzled.

\* \* \*

The Chicago office served as field engineers for the Cathode Ray Tube and the Transmitting Tube Departments as well as the home teams' Receiving Tube Department. I knew many of the engineers in those departments from the Schenectady days, so it was natural that I was asked to fill in for them when a local problem arose. The first of these involved a psychological warfare equipment that used a transmitting tube to furnish 3000 watts of audio for dissing the enemy in Korea at long distance. The application was straight-forward and presented no problems. The customers' engineers decided that all work and no play was a poor life. They mounted the portable unit in the underbrush at a remote railroad crossing and loaded it with the recording of a steam locomotive approaching, passing and then disappearing in the distance. They waited in the bushes until a farmer approached in his truck. He could hear the train and knew enough to stop even though there were no signals at this remote crossing. While he was sitting there, the sound of the train approached, rumbled past at 3000 audio watts, complete with the Doppler frequency shift as it passed and then gradually quieted into the distance. All of this happened with nothing visible on the track. He got out of the truck, looked fearfully down the track in one direction, then the other, jumped in the truck and sped off on his way home. The engineers chalked it up as a successful field test. I've often wondered if the farmer had the courage to tell anyone of <u>his</u> experience.

\* \* \*

The cathode ray tube department introduced a large 24 inch metal tube which was to be used in a GE TV set. The Underwriters Lab in Chicago would conduct the test to determine the effect on anyone in the room if the 24 inch tube exploded. I was tasked to witness the test for GE. The setup was impressive. The TV set stood on a platform ablaze with high power lights and covered by two high-speed movie cameras. A technician with face mask, gloves and heavy overalls stood alongside the TV set with a sledge hammer, ready to drive a plunger through the cabinet and against the metal shell of the tube. In this first test, the safety glass had been removed from in front of the tube. The 24 inch screen looked huge and without the safety glass, thoroughly threatening.

A dry run was made to check timing and then the real test started when the hammer began it's descent.. There was a huge explosion, the cameras whirred and glass flew spectacularly to a distance at least 30 feet in front of the set. A careful review was even more frightening. It showed that the entire front screen of the tube collapsed backward into the conical metal shell and then owing to the shape was concentrated and reflected forward out the front in a stream of small fragments. The electron gun assembly from inside the tube came flying out last as a saw-like mass of metal and glass to spear anything that the stream of glass fragments had not destroyed.

With a new tube installed, the test began again with a safety screen in place. Happily the entire catastrophe was contained inside the cabinet. That was the purpose of the test and the Underwriters were pleased to put their stamp on the product. I trembled inwardly from the results of that first unshielded test.

Within a month I went to Motorola to authorize return of some 24 inch tubes that they claimed were the wrong screen color. We went to their stockroom and I opened a cardboard box to inspect the front face of the tube. As I was looking at it and pondering the terrible explosion at the UL test, I saw a crack start at the edge of the metal cone. The huge 24 inch screen started to crack. For the second time in my life I experienced the cold breakout of sweat over my whole body as I jumped backward onto the floor. I lay there breathlessly as the screen quietly completed its single crack without an explosion of glass fragments. The customer was knowledgeable of CRT explosions, so I received a hand up and no wisecracks about my backward jumping. I authorized return of the shipment without the courage to examine each of the other tubes.

\* \* \*

Our home on Chase Avenue proved to be well constructed and a joy to live in once we had the furnace converted to fuel oil. The previous owner left a huge pile of clay where the driveway was dug out. I moved this by wheel barrow to the back of the lot and buried it under good black Illinois topsoil that I stripped off the surface. This gave us a vegetable garden raised about a foot above the surrounding ground level and resting on a bed of clay. That turned out to be a marvelous planting area. We enjoyed corn, beans, okra and broccoli that literally leaped from the ground. I built a fence around the inner part of the back yard to give some running room for Sherry and built a stone patio off the back of the house and even a large sandbox for Sherry to play in. The cat decided the box was for its private use so we had to clean it weekly. Life settled down to be good.

# THE KOREAN CONFLICT RAGES

In Korea, the year 1950 had closed with the battle of Chosin Reservoir in which US forces, both Marines and army, were thrown back in North Korea by Chinese troops that arrived in astounding number. In early 1951 Douglas Mc Arthur advocated using nuclear weapons on the Chinese. It looked like Dad's fear was about to materialize. Truman fired him proving that in the US, the military was under the command of elected civilians. The US was able to recapture Seoul and ground forces settled into a static position. The air war continued violently with the new US F-86 aircraft holding well against the Russian MIG-15s in some cases flown by Russian pilots. Two of my high-school classmates, F-86 pilots were killed in Korea that year. One died back at his airbase, the other was seen to be captured alive and walking, but was never reported by the Koreans as a prisoner. Ethel and Julius Rosenberg were convicted of spying for Russia in the transfer of nuclear weapon secrets and were sentenced to death. The United Nations building opened in New York and Remington Rand delivered their first UNIVAC computer.

In 1948 I had co-authored a paper with Al Haas which introduced a high gain ultra low-noise tube for the Hi-Fi market. Al designed the tube and I designed the Hi-FI amplifier which demonstrated its' capabilities. The circuit used a trick which went back to the ITT correspondence course that my Dad had ordered for me while I was in high school. It was common in radio frequency circuits, but this was the first usage in audio. The paper caught up with me in Chicago in 1950 when I answered a call from Lear Development An engineer stated that Bill Lear was planning to use that tube in a new autopilot they were designing. I had conflicting emotions. It was nice to have my earlier work recognized, but the idea of that tube subjected to the vibration and operating conditions of aircraft flight with human safety in its' care was a jolt.

I visited Lear with samples of the new tube that resulted from the chopped audio event in the Collins receiver. It was something of a sell, as the price on the new tube was at least three times that of the audio product. However, the emphasis on long life and mechanical ruggedness won out, particularly with the units performance tied to Lears' own name. I breathed a sigh of relief a month later when they called to say that they would use the military version of the tube in the new F-5 autopilot. It was the first autopilot to be used in jets and won Bill Lear a Collier trophy from President Truman.

* * *

As summer advanced, Collies' pregnancy became a load in the hot weather of the mid-west Finally in late July, Crystal was born in Elmhurst, Illinois. It was indeed a dark and stormy night. Lightning struck the hospital, but the Dickerson family was delighted. Collie thoughtfully bought a doll for Sherry so that she too could have a "baby". Sherry wasn't sure this was a good idea as the attention shifted from her to Chris who had severe digestive troubles. After many changes of formula and some two months she began to sleep through the night. The poor kid was exhausted and so were her parents. I recall getting up at 0430 to drive to my customers in

Fort Wayne, Indiana and then driving back that same night so as to relieve Collie on the care and feeding duty.

We found a partial solution with an old floor-type vacuum cleaner set under Chris' crib. The noise of its' running seemed to quiet her and in no time she would sleep. As an adult, she told me that the sound of a vacuum cleaner motor was quieting to her as a result of the childhood experience.

Soon Chris began to put on weight although not as much as we or she would like. In stead of crawling, she learned to move by digging her heels into the carpet and pulling herself forward in an upright position. It looked strange, but she moved with surprising speed. A characteristic that became her signature in later life, moving quickly with head upright and eyes forward.

\* \* \*

I became part of a three-man "go team" for a problem on the Navy's Talos missile. The nature of the problem escapes my memory, but it was simple. I did learn a useful technique from the Sylvania engineer on the team. Confronted with the problem, he took out a jewelers folding magnifying glass and carefully examined the sample tube in detail. I subsequently asked him, "what did you expect to see? That was obviously not a visible problem."

"I didn't expect to see anything. The magnifying glass is a gimmick. It allows me time to get my thoughts together on how to tell them they've screwed up in their design."

I learned a valuable point from him. I seldom used a glass, but did learn to be diplomatic in the face of poor design practice. Mainly, I recall the incident as a prelude to a much later situation on the Tartar missile, a descendant of Talos.

\* \* \*

The year 1951 stretched on into 1952 with no progress in the Korean War situation. My personal status had been resolved to "inactive reserve", which I welcomed as the head of a growing family. Underneath, I felt that I owed something to the Navy and America for that first-class engineering education. Then the opportunity arose for a small payback of my debt. GE and the Air Force were going to try something new. A contract was signed for GE to supply three engineers to work at Wright Field in Dayton, reporting to the civilian head of Electronic Device Development, but still on the GE payroll.

The team would be headed by Walt Kirk, former Manager of Engineering at the Owensboro, KY department. I knew Walt well, having done circuit analysis for him while I was in Schenectady. All I needed was approval of my Chicago superiors to apply for the job. My boss was delighted. That would be a neat way to get rid of me with no skin off his nose. With a little back stairs selling on my part (Black Pete was told that this was a chance for me to see how business was done from inside the government), I got the OK and Walt Kirk welcomed me to his three-man team.

So, in 1952 we put our Lombard house on the market and I went to Dayton to start work and look for a house. We discovered to our delight that there was a good market for houses in Lombard and in fact it was possible to make money by owning a home. In fact, the minimal down payment and low interest on the GI loan made the return very nice. We bought a new house in Dayton with an unfinished upstairs where my childhood carpenter skills could be put to use. We sodded the unfinished back yard and soon had a neat looking place with a view of the Ohio farmland south of Dayton.. We were experienced home owners.

# Wright Field From The Inside

The first task for our three-man team was to write a book teaching the application of statistics to the design of electronic equipment. The concept was a brilliant stroke and I think Kirk was the originator. He saw clearly that the greatly expanded usage of vacuum tubes in military equipment meant new functions for the tubes and new quality control needs. The old measurements, what might be called the "vital signs" of tubes now must be correlated to performance parameters in new military circuits.

There was a problem here. Statistics as taught to engineers in the US was simply the math of sampling and quality control. The field of parameter correlation was left to the egg-heads in the math department. As a result, we could find no textbooks of US origin that could teach the math that would relate "vital signs" of tubes to the field performance of circuits. Today, this sounds ridiculous, but in 1952 we were faced with writing the book from scratch. We even had to coin new words such as "variables" for useful characteristics and "detriments" for those that limited performance. Finally a text began to emerge.

We knew we had something when IBM, seeing an early draft, asked the Air Force for permission to publish their own issue ahead of the official Government Printing Office edition. The three of us, joint authors, swelled with pride. The GPO version continued through several editions, well into the era when semiconductors replaced tubes. The design principles were the same and translated easily from tubes to transistors.

* * *

Not all of the Dayton tasks were writing. One day a tired looking Air Force Major was introduced by the branch commander and began to tell his story. As it emerged, one could see that he had been ridiculed through the upper echelons of Wright Field and was loathe to tell his story one more time. He was the commander of a B-29 squadron based in Korea. His men were convinced they were haunted by a dead Korean Papa-San and morale had reached an all-time low.

The story was simple. "We take off and everything checks out great. We fly for 2 hours maybe a little more and then we pass over this old Korean Monastery with a graveyard. As soon as we get there the bomb-nav radar goes berserk. There are blips all over the place. it's useless. The men say that an old dead priest is upset about our disturbing his sleep and wants us to go away. I argue with them, but they've got it in their heads and nothing I do seems to help."

This sounded a little like the chopped audio problem in St. Paul. Always happens at the same place, must be a fault of the place. Just as in St. Paul, I took a guess, "What's the mission profile?"

"We cruise at 30,000 and lower to 5000 for the bomb run. The chief is a stickler for accuracy."

"OK, what are you doing when you pass over the monastery?"

"We're in the transition, maybe 6000, 7000 feet."

"So you're taking an ice-cold airplane from 30,000 feet down into the humidity. Do you have fog form inside during the descent?"

"Do we ever? You can't believe that humidity."

"OK, I've got an idea." The thought that someone might believe him changed the poor guys view on life. "That bomb-nav is an APR-23 isn't it?"

"Yeah, a pretty good set if you can keep the mechanics out of it." I had not personally worked on the APR-23, but heard the confirmed stories of repeated failures after the top lid was removed for maintenance. This exposed the internal precision gear trains to dropped screws or wire clips with dramatic results. That wasn't the problem here. What I recalled was that the unit was not pressure sealed and thus embraced whatever air stream was presented to it. If there was fog in the aircraft, there was fog inside the bomb-nav radar. That meant condensed water droplets and that meant electrical breakdown – "blips all over the place."

We talked casually about his experience in Korea while I searched through the library for a tech manual on the APR-23. Thumbing through its pages, I found exactly what I was looking for and didn't expect to find. The designers were so naïve, they had included a photograph of their design error! There it was – an oscilloscope photo of a 1000 volt pulse on the base of a miniature tube. The absolute maximum was supposed to be 750 volts under warm dry conditions. This pulse initiated the main bang of the radar. If it broke down whenever it wanted to, there would be "blips all over the place."

"There's your problem, Major." I pointed an accusing finger at the photo and in my head aimed it at the inexperienced and unthinking designers who photographed and printed their own mistakes.

"What do I do about it?"

"What you need is a big tube of silicon grease." The blank look on his face made me change the approach. "Come on down to the lab, I'll get a tube for you. This is good clean stuff. Have your techs squeeze out a glob about the size of an English pea on the top and base of this socket." I wrote down the pin numbers and the tube number. "It'll stick tight through high and low temperature and it absolutely protects against electrical breakdown." I carefully avoided saying that it should have been done by the manufacturer before the squadron ever received the equipment.

A month later the branch chief received a letter of thanks from the Major with the notation that the Papa-San had gone to sleep. I was happy with the winning of engineering thought over engineering incompetence, but wished it had never happened.

\* \* \*

I was tasked with examining the mechanical conditions of vibration and impact shock on the serviceability of tubes in aircraft. The first job was to examine the "Wright-Pat Report". This was a study of vibration in aircraft that was initiated in WWII. It had been incredibly thorough. If you wanted to know the vibration of a B-25 at frame 25 with landing gear down and all guns firing, you could find it in the "Wright Report". It had been reviewed by government employees on three successive occasions and no one could agree what should be done about it. It was a mistory of massive beaurocratic inability to take action.

I pointed out to the branch chief that none of the aircraft types involved in the study were still operational except the P-51 and it was a remarkably clean aircraft from the vibration standpoint. There was nothing there except for the sine wave frequencies related to the engine rotation. My view was that we should simply put the Wright Report on the library shelf and start a new examination of the vibration induced by jet engines, their thunderous exhaust and near sonic speed. The idea was that we no longer had single frequency vibration, but rather a cacophonous mixture of frequencies as a result of the jet exhaust and the aircrafts high-speed buffeting. The branch chief was intrigued. I had no idea what I was getting into.

One of the first assignments was to go to Boeing in Seattle to review their experiences in developing a huge bomber. Entirely by coincidence I was at Boeing on April 15, 1952 for the first flight of the XB-52. This was a watershed in aircraft development. That plane is still serving the USAF 58 years later. However, I remember it as a sudden recalibration of my view on aircraft size.

The entire Boeing workforce lined the tarmac to witness the flight. Out on the strip was this big thing with droopy wings and four jet engines that seemed to me to be too close to the ground for comfort. The aircraft started its roll and when it had used up half the runway I was horrified – it was only doing 50 or 60 knots. In my view it would need at least 100 knots to lift off and it couldn't pick that up in the runway that remained. In my minds eye there was a horrible crash coming. Then the chase planes appeared over the starting end of the strip. They were F-86s assigned to follow and photograph the flight. I knew the F-86 aircraft and they were doing maybe 120 – 130 knots. They should be overrunning the big monster whose droopy wings had now lifted to a normal angle. But instead the gap was closing slowly and then holding constant as the monster lifted clear and started its climb.

I suddenly realized how mis-calibrated I was. This plane was so huge that I could not correlate its apparent movement with its actual speed. I had been raised close to a major Army Air Corps training base and had watched planes from the age of 6 onward, comparing their speed to their apparent movement. This was a new world of aircraft size.

Boeings' experience with the XB-52 bore out my thesis on vibration. The sound level in the cockpit during taxiing was so great that it damaged the pilots' mastoids. They had to wear heavy lead-lined helmets until the sound level could be reduced. There were also cases in XB-52 taxiing where electrical fuses in wiring boxes of the wings had failed from having their contained sand blast away the fuse wire when the sand was excited by that high noise level.

Despite this evidence that aircraft vibration had entered a new phase, the high ground on theory was held by mechanical engineers who continued to think exclusively in terms of the rotation rate of the engine shafts. For them there was no vibration except at the shaft rate. I wrote an extensive report on the subject suggesting noise driven vibration testing. The report was shredded by the Mechanical Engineer establishment and I was branded as a wild-eyed Electronics Engineer who knew nothing of vibration. My only support came, oddly, from the Signal Corps. Fort Monmouth devised the "Tethered Jeep Test" for electronic equipment. The sample was mounted on the back seat of a jeep which was tethered to circle around a post on a concrete track that was crossed with numerous wooden 4X4 beams. The jeeps bouncing up and then down at each crossing produced a punishing vibration which at least had the merit of reflecting reality.

* * *

The year 1952 proved to be a fascinating continuance of the earlier '50s. The Korean War continued. In England Elizabeth became the Queen, known in Canada as QEII. Churchill announced that England had nuclear weapons. Werner von Braun published a series of articles promoting mans' exploration of space via a trip to the moon. East Germany formed its own army and the U.S. laid the keel for the first nuclear submarine and exploded the first hydrogen bomb. UFOs repeatedly buzzed Washington, D.C. with visual and radar sightings much to the chagrin of the Air Force which maintained they didn't exist.

Wright Field was the home of "Project Bluebook" the aim of which was to prove the non-existence of UFOs. Despite that two aim, two F-94s were maintained on ready status at Patterson AFB on a runway exactly aligned with the hilltop building where I worked at Wright Field. On at least three occasions I recall putting my head on the desk with my mouth open and fingers in my ears when the F-94s did an afterburner scramble which placed them climbing the hill directly over our building. Of course that had nothing to do with UFOs.

Wright field was also the home of research on aerial photography. This produced surprising exposures. One evening, Collie and I put the kids to sleep and then stretched out on lawn chairs in the back yard to chat and view the night sky. We were far enough from downtown Dayton so that no nightglow disturbed this view. There we were, eyes upturned and dilated when a brilliant explosion occurred in the sky. I recall losing my vision for the better part of a minute while thrashing about in the lawn chair. I learned the following day that tests were made using a large phosphorous bomb for illumination of night photography.

A similar event occurred one evening as I left our hilltop workplace. A B-25 at about 100 foot altitude was climbing up the hill with a brilliant fire in the port engine nacelle streaming smoke behind it. I hit the irrigation ditch alongside the road face down with hands over my head. The next day I learned this was a test of a new technique for precision ground photography in which the shutter was simply a thin slit past which the film was moved at the ground speed of the aircraft. A phosphorous flare provided the intense light for the thin slit. Somewhere the USAF has a high precision photo of the correct "duck and cover" procedure used in a roadside ditch.

We were becoming accustomed to things that go bump in the night.

# Doing Business Inside
# The Government

The year 1953 formed a pivot for the world as well as the Dickerson family. General Dwight Eisenhower replaced Harry Truman as president of the U.S. Joseph Stalin died and was replaced by Kruschev. The war in Korea ended with an armistice. Captured POWs were returned, but not my high school classmate who disappeared under the care of the North Koreans. Some prisoners were found to have been psychologically treated -- the term "brain-washed" entered the language. On the technical scene, Watson and Crick discovered the structure of DNA, starting a renaissance in biological research. The Univac 1103 became the first to use random memory, moving computing into a new stage. The first color television sets went on sale and the term "electronics" entered the language.

\* \* \*

At this time the Air Force grew exponentially. The B-36 entered the operational inventory of aircraft. In my opinion it was the worst bomber design ever put in production. The air Force steadily maintained that it was invisible to radar at its operational altitude. A statement so ridiculous that most knowledgeable people simply refused to discuss it fearing that some inscrutable scheme was afoot and that pooh-poohing it would bring instant firing or worse. As a gross ergonomic mistake, the flexural frequency of the airframe closely matched the resonant frequency of the male body cavity. Takeoff with crosswind virtually insured a vomiting pilot as the whole airframe twisted and rolled in synch with the human innards.

* * *

A debate began in the technical arm of the military as to whether short-term burn-in of electron tubes would increase their subsequent operational reliability. The thesis was that early life failures due to poor workmanship would be removed by simply operating all tubes for 100 hours in burn-in racks. Then the survivors could be installed in operational aircraft with assurance of long life. That was the thesis and if there were early-life failures, that would eliminate them – no argument with the theory. The problem was the total absence of data showing early life failures. Lack of data did not halt the theorists and so a large study was demanded to "prove" the thesis. I was tasked to design the study. It didn't matter that I didn't buy the thesis for one minute. They wanted someone to lay out the working plan and I was sitting there.

The design of an experiment is more complex than might be thought. First is the accuracy desired – one significant figure, i.e., 10% accuracy? Two significant figures, 1% or, perish the thought 3 significant figures? Fortunately the USAF would go for 1%. Next is the question of how many groups of data would be involved. This is so that you can afford to discard any data that becomes contaminated and still meet the 1%. The USAF wanted the work to go on at 17 Air Force Bases. Then there is the procedure to insure that the data does not become contaminated and finally the in-process tests to spot any contamination that does occur.. What's this data contamination stuff? Hang in there, we'll get to that.

I sat down and did the organization plan of the work – the experimental groups, the control groups, the blinds which insure that the people performing tests don't know which group they are testing, etc. Then began the writing of the mathematic procedures of analysis and the in-process tests to see if the randomization and the "blinds" were really working. Lastly were the decision points at which we would declare a string of data suspect and the level at which it must be declared contaminated. All told, about a week of work. At the end there was a design review and the test plan was declared valid. The process was started.

I was assigned three newly minted 2nd lieutenants to do the leg work and detail in-process analyses. All I really needed was one, but the USAF does things big and I think they considered this a form of training for the young engineers. All were 1952 Cornell graduates with BSEEs in electronics.

About the third day of operations all three came to present me with a problem. I believe they thought there was strength in numbers or maybe they felt I would blame them for what was happening. The story was simple, the tests for equality among the experimental and the control groups before any processing began showed the randomization at the start of the experiment was not working at one AFB. All other 16 AFBs showed the jagged back and forth quality that accompanies true random grouping, but Kelly AFB in San Antonio, Texas was developing real significance between four test groups right from the start, before anything had been done to them.

I complemented the Lieutenants and took the data to the branch chiefs' office. "Amos, we have a problem with the burn-in experiment. One of the AFBs is showing significant differences between the control and the test groups before anything is done to the tubes."

"Sit down, Art." I did. "What's the chance that this is just a statistical fluke that will go away?"

"That's always possible, but we set this first trip point at one chance in a hundred. It got there in just three days. I think we will have to send someone down there to find out what's going on. I wanted to warn you for budgetary and travel request purposes before it gets worse."

"Who should we send? Do you want to go?"

"That's home territory for me, but I think we should make it look as routine as possible. A young 2nd Lieutenant will do just right. How routine can you get?"

"How about David? I think he has more street smarts than the others and he looks deceptively routine?"

"Sounds fine."

Two days later I had to tell the chief we had reached the point of labeling the data contaminated, but that if we had to throw it out we still would have enough for his 1% accuracy. David went to San Antonio and in two days was back. The branch chief asked me to sit in on his debriefing.

"So, David, what did you find?"

"A lot, sir To begin with the supervisor decided to ignore the instructions to identify the lots only by their serial numbers and to assemble them by random choice each day. In his mind that was stupid. He labeled them A,B,C,D and started testing lot A the following morning and went on to B,C,D in sequence."

"Why would that matter? I admit I thought it odd myself when I read the instructions."

"Well, sir. Next morning the test ladies started taking readings on Lot A just like they'd been told and the supervision was always late – say about 45 minutes. The net result was that lot As were always tested with no supervisors present and the other lots always tested with supervisors present. The ladies seemed to feel that if their supervisors were present, they had to be extra diligent. So, there were always fewer rejects in the lot As and more in the other lots. There was a built-in bias to the data even before the experiment began.."

"What did you do about it?"

"Nothing, Sir – I was sent to find out, not to correct."

The branch chief thought at length then raised his head and asked again if we could get by without the Kelly AFB data. I assured him we could.

"OK. Kelly is an Air Material Command base and that's a different command than the one we are in. The least common denominator has at least three stars. So, Art. You discard the data from the experiment but don't either of you say anything about terminating the test at Kelly. OK?"

My selling point to Black Pete when I wanted to be transferred to Wright Field was that I'd learn how business was done inside the government. I was learning.

* * *

In the military, the rapid growth of electronics caused the formation of the Joint Engineering Development Electronics Committee, JEDEC. I became the Air Force representative on the standards subcommittee. Pondering this, I concluded that the Air Force regarded our GE group as more worldly than their newly minted second lieutenants or civil service employees. They had several former German scientists, but their appearance on a JEDEC committee would be suspect, so the task fell to me.

This assignment led me to fly often on the Military Air Transport Service or MATS between Dayton and Washington. This revealed a new side of the Air Force. At the end of WWII there were hundreds of squadron and wing commanders who had distinguished themselves valiantly in Europe and over Japan. The Air Force felt a great obligation to them, but recognized by the early 50s that many of them would never make it to General Officer rank. The result was that they were kept on at desk jobs on Patterson AFB and their flight pay status maintained by assigning them occasionally to fly C-47s on MATS flights. This virtually guaranteed that the left hand seat on MATS coming into Dayton would be occupied by a bird colonel of monumental flying experience.

That experience became evident one night landing on the long runway at Patterson. When the plane flared out a foot over the runway, the engines were not cut, but the plane was rolled slightly until the right wheel came within inches of the runway. It was held there for a few seconds, enough for the wheel to start rotating from ground-effect airflow. This was then repeated with the left wheel and then the nose was raised to a perfect "three-point" attitude with all wheels just inches off the concrete. The throttles were slowly closed and a landing was made without the usual "eerp – eerp" sound that left rubber on the runway. There was an immediate enthusiastic applause from a dozen bird colonels who were passengers that night. It's nice to see a thing done "just right".

A JEDEC meeting in Washington educated me in the British calm and patient deportment. The committee was headed by an officious Signal Corps officer. He made a decision which I had opposed in conference. On the way out I said to the

British representative that I thought it was a dumb mistake. His commented, "It's not what you or I should do, but he is the chair, and after all old boy, there you are." I was learning what Black Pete wanted, to see the way the government did business with friends and enemies.

* * *

### DAYTON – THE BEGINNING OF THE END

One MATS flight. from Dayton to Bergstrom AFB in Austin, Texas stands out in my memory. The aircraft was the ubiquitous C-47 and the weather was awful. I had my favorite bad-weather seat in the last row opposite the exit door. An air force master-sergeant occupied the seat next to me. I liked the C-47. It had very light wing loading which made it safer. It could fly fine on one engine. However, in bad weather this blessing was a curse. Wind buffeting caused the plane to rise and fall abruptly for what seemed like huge distances. This night the curse was in full operation. The pilot had tried seven landing approaches, each with a series of upward thrusts and downward falls terminated by a full throttle gunning of the engines and a pull up to get on top of the cloud deck. By that time the aircraft stank of vomit as most of the passengers used the regulation "barf bags" supplied at each seat.

The sergeant and I were blissfully ignorant and discussing the problem. We concluded that there was a problem with the fields' Instrument Landing System or ILS. Maybe the pilot couldn't find agreement between his compass and the track given to him by the non-human ILS system. As things drug on we decided that they had gone over to GCA or ground-controlled-approach, using radar for location of the aircraft and verbally instructing the pilot how to fly the plane. I described being on a Airinc Beechcraft Bonanza testing the newly installed GCA at Louisville during a day with perfect visibility and seeing that we were being directed to fly straight into a large steel mill alongside the airport. That's what test flights were for.

We had exhausted the GCA possibility when the pilot did his seventh pull-up. I had gone to school in Austin and knew the layout of the city, explaining to the sergeant that the field was out by the river and the land past the runway was going uphill to the location of the town.

This time, the pilot didn't try another approach. Instead he turned and flew south until he found a hole in the cloud deck, then went down to find the river. He then turned and followed the river back to the airfield. On landing under the low-hanging cloud cover, I could see that there was no ILS antenna array. There went that theory..

The sergeant and I were first off the aircraft. I asked a duty sergeant at the gate, "Where's the GCA radar antenna?"

"Well, sir there ain't no GCA on this field." I thought in horror, 'could that pilot have made seven blind approaches to this field?'. Just then the pilot walked off the plane. His light blue Air Force shirt was stained with sweat all the way to his waist. That was my answer. I gained a new respect for senior pilot dedication to the mission.

\* \* \*

My recollections of Dayton always include the winter of health problems. All four Dickersons were down with flu at the same time. It was a severe flu and we had no relatives or care givers nearby. We made it by simply taking turns to tend the kids and each other. It was a bleak week, but the furnace worked and we stayed warm. Between the canned goods and a well-stocked refrigerator we ate consistently.

Shari showed some vision problems which prompted a visit to the eye doctor. He reported severe visual problems and prepared glasses to correct them. I remember with tears the day they were fitted to her. We walked out of the doctors' office into the hallway which was tiled with little black and white squares. Shari, three at the time, bent down to feel the floor. She had never seen a floor in detail. It was the same way with the sidewalk and the rug at home. What a dismal world she had been trapped in before we finally noticed the problem. I felt for her and kicked myself for not being sharper in observation of her.

\* \* \*

Kirk was a delightful boss, intelligent, very strict but fair and straight arrow in all respects. He continued to live in Kentucky while heading the mission to Dayton. He would travel up each week and so Collie and I had him over to dinner several times. He was always welcome and brought a bottle of Isle St. George sauterne from Ohio. Collie became accustomed to entertaining and so when Crosley announced a contest to "Design Your Kitchen With Crosley Appliances", she was right on to of it. Her theme was to design for entertaining and her artwork did a great presentation of the anticipated results. At that time Crosley made everything one could imagine to go into a kitchen – she had an open choice. To her great surprise, Collie won the contest. A man named G.E. Smith came to see her, present kitchen and announce her prize. We had to tell him that we were moving and there would be no chance to do the kitchen here, but we would be happy to take the material with us and design a new kitchen where we planned to build a house. He was very kind about the whole thing and agreed with our approach. I learned later that Crosley had decided to go out of the appliance business and so this was no great loss to them. In any event we then had a kitchen-in-a-box. However, I'm a little ahead of the story. Let me tell you of the events that led up to our leaving Dayton.

* * *

The work of the GE team at Wright field was appreciated by the Branch Chiefs. Mutual respect had developed and this led to entrusting us with the drafting of a new purchase specification for vacuum tubes. I went to the field one morning to find an irate Walt Kirk and our third member, Karl. Kirk said that he had just resigned from GE and Karl echoed that thought. They urged me to do the same. I finally got a explanation. Kirk had been approached by his boss and told to slant the specification so that it favored purchase of the GE product. He did not say so, but I got the impression that he was threatened with firing if he didn't. Kirk was a straight arrow of the old school. You didn't order him to commit a crime and you surely didn't threaten him. His response was to resign from GE. Karl was devoted to Kirk and his response was the same. I had been on a trip and missed the whole show until now.

My response was "No, I'm not going to resign. I wasn't involved in this. I'm going to Schenectady and find out what is going on. You can be sure that I will have no part of slanting a specification." I phoned Kirks' boss, Gene, and arranged to visit him in two days.

In Schenectady I found Kirk's boss chagrined. Apparently Black Pete, noting Kirks resignation had questioned Gene and gotten to the bottom of the matter. I gather that Black Pete chewed him heavily and spit the smaller pieces in the waste basket. Anyway, with a multitude of smiles he asked, "would you assume charge of the GE contract with the Air Force?"

"Under no circumstances will I slant a specification and if that is part of the job, you can count me out."

"No, that's not part of the job. You can run the show the way you want."

"Alright, if GE continues the contract I'll take charge of it, but I suggest that would be a mistake. As long as there are GE people at Dayton it will be a reminder of this incident. I have the trust of the Branch Chief and I can retain it, but my very presence will be a recall of the attempt to skew the purchase specification. I suggest that GE and USAF mutually agree to end the contract."

He lowered his head thought for a moment. "Hang in here just a minute."

He returned with Black Pete in tow. I smiled and shook hands with Pete.

"I commend you Art on your recommendation. I think you are right. We'll end the contract. There's just one problem, what will we do with you?"

# A New Hometown An Old Occupation

Pete's question went right to the point. What did I want to do and what was possible? I heard a rumor that Bob, the manager of application engineering for the whole division was about to retire. I had held the spot of supervisor for an application engineering sub-section four years before. The answer seemed natural. When I voiced it, Black Pete said, "I heard the same rumor. When I checked it I found it's not true. He has every intention of staying on and he won't retire for another 8 years."

My face turned deep red, "Pete, I've made a terrible mistake. He is a good manager. If he's staying on, excellent – we should consider other possibilities. Please accept my apology for this mistake,"

"You needn't apologize. It was a rumor with the sound of truth. I think I know how it started, but that's another story. Let me suggest something to you. He has an open position under him as supervisor of application engineering for entertainment products. If you would take that, I think you'd find yourself in the manager spot in a very few years. You'd have to trust me on that."

In my six years in the division I had noticed the remarkable way that events played out on the lines that Black Pete desired.

Could I trust him? The odds beat anything I could think of. I stuck out my hand, "OK Pete, you've got a deal."

* * *

On the plane back to Dayton, I couldn't help wondering, "What have I gotten myself into?" First I had to explain it all to Collie. She didn't like Dayton, so leaving would be no loss, but she wouldn't get to build the new kitchen she had won in the design contest (one negative). We would be moving to Owensboro, Kentucky – a dyed in the wool southern girl like Collie would be right at home (one positive). Her East-Texas accent would sound strange to the natives at first, but it surely wasn't Yankee talk. She'd fit right in. When we sold the house in Dayton, we could build a new one in Owensboro with her kitchen just the way she'd designed it (another positive). I shouldn't have worried, Collie was a trooper. If the job was in Owensboro, she'd make it work out right.

* * *

I should explain at this point what application engineering involves so we can follow the way that Petes' Plan played out over the next few years. There are three activities involved, First, and the most fun, is the analysis and design of circuits for new products such as color television. Second, and the least fun, is the resolution of customer complaints that our product was defective and did not perform as it should. Sometimes that would be true. Although the fault was in the factory, the application engineer was the one with the red face who had to tell the customer that we had screwed up and would ship him a new lot of product. At other times the customers' use of the product was faulty. Here was fun – a chance to do the circuit design properly and be seen by the customer as some sort of hero. Third is the published data and technical papers describing new products. This work has a high tedium content.

* * *

On assuming the supervisor spot, I found that most of my engineers had morale problems from serving a continuous stream of customer complaints. They saw only the bad side of the work and soon believed that GE was a sloppy outfit. My first move was to establish a schedule in which each engineer served 6 months on complaints and then 3 months to research a new application of his choice and produce a paper describing the correct way to use the product. It took a few months for the first people to finish their research and then the morale problem faded. GE had become a leader in the quality area as far as its' application engineers were concerned.

* * *

A second innovation was taken directly from the publication we worked out for the Air Force on the use of statistics in the design of electronic circuits. The goal here was to construct our internal quality control specifications so they correlated with the needs of the customer in the most frequently used circuits. The first need was a working knowledge of statistics. A night course was arranged for the application engineers, taught by one of our accountants who minored in statistics during his college years.

The proof of this new scheme came one week when our internal specifications were shown to be much too loose on one specific product. There had never been complaints, but the factory had always run well above the internal limit. When the product slipped down to the limit, I had a long talk with the factory manager which ended with my walking out on a limb to say, "Right now we are shipping product that won't work and it's only a matter of a few weeks before we get hit with complaints like we've never seen before. You won't agree to our proposed tighter specs, so please get the product back up where it used to be."

"Art, you're talking into the wind. I don't hear any complaints and nobody's rejecting our product. We'll continue as we are."

Within 10 days we were hit with a massive series of complaints. The factory manager found himself taking back product and with $1 million of defective product in his warehouse. He asked me over to his office to say that the statistical approach had been proven and he would support our recommendations on spec changes.

* * *

In Owensboro Collie found a rental house on 21st street to occupy while the Dayton house was on the market. The house had a full basement, which was rarity in northern Kentucky, but which furnished ideal storage for Collies' "kitchen in a box". We sat down to design the house that we would build in this charming southern town. Included in our plans were a bedroom for each of the girls and a small studio for Collie behind the 2-car garage.

* * *

My fondest memory of 1953 was at Easter when Collie dressed the two girls in pink dresses to go to church. We both sang in the choir and the girls spent the time in child care. We went home to a fine Easter dinner.

## THE NEW HOUSE, THE NEW JOB

The new house plans occupied our spare moments. We produced a full set of drawings that showed all construction details and boasted a front dominated by a limestone chimney and lined flower bed in the shape of a vertical letter L. The basic house was in pastel rust-colored Roman brick with limestone ledges for the windows. We established a good relationship with Howard, the contractor who would build the house. He owned the land for this new development. Our house would be the first built. He liked the modern look of the place and so we got a good deal for the land and construction. When our Dayton house finally sold, we signed the contract for the Owensboro house.

Howard had a fine dry sense of humor and when he found an error in my drawings, he made the best of it. One day with great seriousness, he showed me the main floor plan which showed a door on the second bathroom labeled B on the door schedule table. In all seriousness he said, "We are a little backward here in Kentucky, but even for progressives like yourself it would be far out to have a clear glass Galousie door on the bathroom." We both got a laugh out of that and I changed it to a wood-core door and initialed the alteration.

Howard also insisted on a sump pump for the basement. Basements were unheard of in Owensboro and the Ohio River was "right down there on second street". My citation of a 70 foot elevation above the river didn't count, "You just can't trust that river." So we had a sump pump, which never ran in the 7 years we lived there.

\* \* \*

The advent of color television had the tube business up to its' ears in development of new products to perform the functions of this promising entertainment device. RCA marketed its' first color TV, a 12" unit selling for $1000. A behind-the-scenes conflict that went unrecognized by the general public was that two standards for color TV coding were under consideration by the FCC. In addition to the scheme in use for the past 55 years, CBS had proposed a simpler, mechanically-oriented arrangement in which a large wheel rotated in front of the picture tube, alternately presenting red, green and blue (RGB) filters. The cathode ray tube (CRT) presented as white screens, the sequence of the RGB frames and the wheel rotation fooled the eye into seeing a "color" picture. The RCA proposal performed all of the color magic by electronic coding, avoiding the huge rotating wheel and providing a base for future development into "digital" TV. The industry engineers thought the CBS proposal was "insane", but the FCC gave it consideration. When the final decision went to RCA, there was a huge sigh of relief. Color TV would be able to grow with electronic capability and not be limited to the size of mechanical wheel that consumers would allow in their living rooms.

The focus of many engineers on a common problem showed again the opportunity for "simultaneous invention". A problem of the period was the cost and complexity of the "shadow mask" picture tube. It used a metal mask with over a million tiny holes to separate the RGB phosphorescent dots on the screen and maintain their registry with the electron beam that turned on each dot. The mask used in manufacture was locked in place and became a part of the CRT for life. The color picture was good, but the cost was high. Sylvania, a real competitor in the field conceived of a tube in which the color image registry was obtained by using vertical stripes instead of dots and identifying them by applying a coating to one color which returned electrons when the electron beam struck it.

This scheme promised to greatly reduce cost. Sylvania did not want to lose its' inventor's rights, but needed another tube manufacturer to develop the implementing products so that its' customers would have the safety of a "second source". They picked GE and insisted on the tightest secrecy. As a result only three people in GE knew about the Sylvania invention, even though we were developing tubes to implement it. I was one of the three and sworn to absolute secrecy.

My top engineer went on his honeymoon to Miami. When he returned, I congratulated him duly and indicated we might talk for a while. To my surprise he had little to say about the honeymoon. "Art, I've got a problem. I have a great idea for a color CRT, but I don't know what to do about it."

"Well, John tell me about it. I'll keep it secret and maybe we can get someone interested."

"I was in a bar in Miami and there were two guys at the next table. One of them said – 'vertical RGB stripes and one has a secondary emitter coating' All of a sudden this idea came to me ---"

John then described exactly the Sylvania invention down to the secondary details and the possible reduction in cost. Now I was in the soup. My stomach muscles tightened and my voice went up at least two whole tones. John was very bright and an honest, straight error guy. I concluded that the best approach was to swear him to secrecy and let him in on the secret completely, depending on his sense of honor and decency to maintain the secret. So, I told him the whole story and then said, "John, I'll give you a choice. Either this can be just between you and I and you will keep the secret or we can go to the Engineering manger and I'll fill him in on your honest invention. He knows the whole secret and he can take charge of the matter."

"That's not a hard decision, Art. I don't trust him. I'll go with you and keep my mouth shut."

John did as he promised. The Sylvania plan did not come off, owing to manufacturing problems. However, a modification of the vertical stripe idea, later known as the Sony Triniton, did come off and proved to be a cost winner.

# EVENTS FORETELL THE FUTURE

The year 1954 turned out to be a pivot point leading to the problems of the next three decades. Mamie Eisenhower christened the U.S.S Nautilus, the worlds first nuclear propelled ship and the leader of Admiral Richtover's nuclear submarine fleet. In a decade, no place on earth would be beyond the reach of a nuclear missile.

The French Foreign Legion was defeated by the Viet Minh in Dien Bien Phu, Viet Nam. President Eisenhower warned against US involvement there. Secretary of State John Foster Dulles accused China of sending troops into Vietnam to train the Viet Minh. He also ended any possibility of the US assisting France in Vietnam.

Senator Joseph McCarthy began hearings on the Army being soft on communists. An associate of mine at Diamond Ordnance Fuse Labs in New Jersey was arrested and handcuffed in front of his employees on the charge of being a communist. His engineers were struck dumb. Had he sold classified secrets? Would he be replaced? Were any of their associates in on this? It turned out much later that his only crime was having the same name as someone of McCarthy's list. At year end, the Senate condemned McCarthy.

The Boeing 707 was released to production, initiating the worldwide commercial jet travel service. The Supreme Court ruled that segregated schools are illegal, initiating a decade of conflict in the US. The Boy Scouts of America desegregated. The first TV dinner is marketed.

* * *

Collie and I rediscovered music in Owensboro where we both sang church solos and participated in the Christmastime rendition of Handel's Messiah. The new house had a small studio for Collie and in the basement, a work area for the girls and a shop for Art. Life was beginning to expand.

* * *

I had observed "Black Pete's'" organizational changes work out in the past and marveled at the smoothness and naturalness with which they occurred. One day there would be an announcement and people would look at it and say, "Don't know if I'd have thought of that, but it makes sense – kinda seems the natural way to go."

My promotion to Manger of Application Engineering followed that pattern. The Quality Control Section of the Owensboro plant had a reputation for falsifying records. This very naturally led to arguments with the Manager of Application Engineering when his careful analysis of a customer complaint showed that the product was indeed defective by our own standards.

So, it was no great surprise when one day it was announced that the Manager of Application Engineering was the new Quality Control Manager. The very natural thing was for me as the senior supervisor to succeed him as Manager of Application Engineering and indeed that appeared in a separate announcement. The general response in the engineering bullpen was, "Hey, that figures." With a new man in at Quality control, the noise should calm done and the quality rise.

Inside my new office, I faced a different problem. My two supervisors asked for an audience and made it clear that they could not serve with the man I had picked to be my replacement. "Art, he has bad morals with the girls in town. We can't have any respect for him and won't cooperate with him. If you've been forced into this by higher level management, we can understand, but if you chose him that's different."

I had to admit to myself that they made their case clear. Now it was up to me to make my case clear. "Gentlemen, there are some things you should know and a few you have overlooked. I chose him myself, he was not forced on me. I chose him for two reasons, he's a competent engineer and a very good manager. He's not the top engineer in the unit, but he is the most promising manager and I need that."

I paused to let that sink in. "Now, the morals thing. I'd have to be blind and deaf to not know about that. However, please know that I made one thing clear when I offered him the job. What he does in town is his business, but if he has sex with any of the ladies at the plant, it had better be on the way to the alter, or his next assignment will be a lonely place where the temperature hovers around zero and the chances of promotion are a little below that. I will not tolerate even the appearance of sexual harassment by a supervisor." Again I paused to see if this was getting through. George, an army ex-sergeant, had eyes that showed he was picking up. Jack, an Army ex-captain didn't seem to be following. Again, I paused glancing from one to the other.

'Gentlemen, he is my choice and he will stay. I expect that you will cooperate with him and show him routine courtesy in the plant. What you do outside the plant is your business, but you must be civil. That is my expectation. I have never before fired two supervisors on the same day, but there is always a first time for anything. Good Morning."

George and Jack filed out. Jacks eyes finally showed that he had gotten the point. I could be argued with, debated, cajoled, but once my decision was made and published, It would be carried out. The session did not seem to prejudice our working relations.and in time Jack and I became an effective team in handling high-level customer complaints. I would meet at the customers location to do the first-level data gathering. Jack would stay in Owensboro and be the lead man on getting things fixed. The following incident illustrates how this worked.

\* \* \*

The DC-3 approached Albuquerque, New Mexico at night from the east and I was in my favorite "fair-weather seat" at the widow forward of the wing on the port side. The view was startling. The lights of Albuquerque caused a night glow that hovered over the intense black form of the Sandia Mountains. Aircraft with low service ceilings approaching from the East were required to follow the highway through a notch in the Sandias that led to Kirtland AFB (altitude 6000 ft) The Sandia peaks were well over 10,000 ft and the floor of the notch about 7000.

The required approach was strictly for safety, but it produced a developing scene which no movie could approach. As the notch was approached, a "V" appeared in the ultra-black form of the Sandias. This "V" slowly opened and deepened to reveal the glittering lights of Albuquerque spread over ten miles of black desert.

By morning the beauty had disappeared and I was meeting with a Navy Lieutenant in a conference room with a projector and large screen. He was part of the Navy Test Squadron housed at Kirtland. In later years I came to admire them as a premier flying group. However, that day he had just addressed me as "Mister" Dickerson with that peculiar inflection Naval officers use to emphasize that they were addressing a subordinate rank. I did not need the put down, I was here because one of our tubes had destroyed a Talos missile and ruined a live-fire test against a drone aircraft. I had seen the post-crash photos and could see that we were at fault, but not why or how to fix it. My task was to answer those questions and hopefully develop a working relationship with the Lieutenant. "Mister Dickerson, there is something I want you to see." He nodded to the projectionist and turned to the screen. The scene showed a section of desert with an old F6F approaching from the distance at what was probably its service ceiling, maybe 25,000 feet. In the foreground a missile was fired at the old drone.

When the film was finished, the Lieutenant resumed his role of teacher and asked, "What did you see?"

The best approach was to be brief, but complete. "I saw a Talos missile fired at an F6F target drone. For the first several seconds, the firing was conventional, then at an altitude of perhaps 10,000 feet the starboard elevator control surface tore loose from the missile which continued to rise, but with a major control surface missing, had no hope of intercepting the target drone."

"I commend your estimate of altitude, it was 10,500 feet. However, our concern is why did it happen?"

"The missile has an altitude sensing control that limits the angle that a control surface can present to the slipstream. This is to prevent excessive force on the surface by too great an angle at too low an altitude and yet allow wide maneuverability at high altitudes where the air is then. It would seem that circuit failed. The abruptness of onset implies hat the failure was likely in the final stage or driver for that surface. I assume that I am here because GE is the manufacturer of the driver tube in that final stage."

"Let me put before you some photographs of the assembly containing that tube which we recovered from the crashed missile and also a new assembly in pristine condition. What can you tell me about what you see?"

Recalling the advice of a friend on a "go-team" I took a jewelers loupe from my pocket and carefully examined the material in front of me. The purpose was not to discover, but to figure out how I would go about telling the Lieutenant what was in front of us. This was not an abstract electronic problem, it was simply the result of an unlikely combination of mechanical factors that had caused his crash.

"Lieutenant, you can see here on the pristine assembly how the metal ear of the tube socket reaches up and touches the glass bulb of the tube. What's not so obvious is that inside the bulb directly opposite the contact point with the ear is a flap on the anode of the tube. The flap is open, allowing a view into the interior of the tube."

"I can see that and it is a coincidence, but so what?"

"The so what is evident over here on the failed tube. See where the ear touches the bulb, the glass is chipped and worn away on the outside and on the inside there is a dark melted piece of glass just opposite the open flap."

"Oh! You're saying that the ear with some vibration broke through the glass and of course when air rushed in the tube became an effective short circuit and drove the control surface hard over, where the wind resistance tore it off."

"Exactly, Lieutenant. Let's think about what we can do to fix it. The vibration comes from the power plant and airframe. We're not going to change that." This was greeted with a grunt of agreement which might have been a burp, but they would have his stripes before he could get the propulsion changed.

"So there's the metal ear. We probably can't change that part, but you could ask your tech. to take a pair of long-nose pliers and bend it away from the tube just a little and squirt some silicone grease in there to lubricate the contact. That will at least delay the gouging and chipping. Now there's something I can do for you. That flap on the anode is necessary when the tube is being assembled, the operator looks through it to align two of the grids inside. But, once that's done, it doesn't have to stay open and let the electron beam burn through the chipped glass. In one week I'll have a dozen tubes in your hands with the flaps closed and you can try them in a vibration machine."

The smile on the Lieutenants face grew slowly. At last someone was going to fix something instead of arguing about who to blame. "OK, when we get the tubes we'll give it a simulated run with the silicone grease and compare it to the old design. – It's a deal."

Now came the reason for Jack staying behind in Owensboro to do the execution of any fix. I phoned and asked him to explain the problem to manufacturing, get a dozen tubes made with the flaps closed and airmail them to the Lieutenant.

This worked out well, the Talos was successful and had descendents in Terrier and Tartar. The missile is still used today as an air defense item aboard Navy ships although the silicone grease and flaps have long ago disappeared.

* * *

The year 1955 saw a hardening and deepening of crises in China and Eastern Europe plus a broadening of the U.S. Civil Rights movement. President Eisenhower announced a program to develop ICBMs armed with nuclear warheads, ironically almost simultaneously Einstein died in New Jersey. The US Congress authorized defense of the Chinese Koumintang in Taiwan against the Chinese Communists in mainland China. The US Seventh Fleet intervened to evacuate the Koumintang from Chinese Islands to Taiwan. West Germany became a sovereign country and joined NATO. Eight Eastern European countries joined Soviet Russia in a mutual defense pact. Claudette Colvin a 15 year-old black girl is arrested and taken off a bus in Montgomery Alabama when she refused to give up her seat to a white woman. I discovered one morning that half of Jack's Application engineers and Jack were absent. They were all National Guard and had been ordered out to Selma, Alabama to quell expected riots. The Civil Rights movement had long arms.

* * *

Shari was now six and attending Elementary School, where she encountered "Miss Sally" an inspiration, teacher and guide for he next five years. Chris was four and in the last throws of her childhood illnesses. As the illnesses passed, Chris' weight increased and our anxiety decreased. Collie and I moved further into the musical nature of Owensboro. Each year a musical Review, "The Follies" was presented complete with commercial direction and costumes. One year Collie did Spanish dances with morrocos clacking and voice singing in Spanish. it went over big. I did parts from Oklahoma (as Curly) and from South Pacific (as the Frenchman). This was great fun.

Life was beginning to take on breadth.

# A New Job And A New Skill

The year 1956 saw a great change in the organization of GE's Tube Department and an abrupt change in my career. The entire marketing organization was moved from Schenectady to Owensboro, KY. This presented a shock to the established uppercrust of this quiet southern town. They had experienced a few northerners in the past, but now there were several dozen of these "high earners" that spoke a peculiar dialect and bought expensive houses. For the local real estate people this was a gift, but for the "old money" folks it was a puzzle. A further puzzle, these Yankee folks all took courses that GE offered for them, just as if they didn't already know how to run a business. The difference was that GE knew the running of businesses was changing rapidly and old practices were proving the way to ruin.

One of the GE courses aimed to enhance a managers ability to analyze a problem, develop alternative cures and evaluate the merits and demerits of each cure. One session of this course required students to debate each other on two possible cures to a problem. In the morning session Randy Duncan and I debated the cures to a specific problem. I was pro cure A and he was pro cure B. I knew Randy from Schenectady and had great respect for him. He was now the chief financial officer. I think we both did a credible job on our tasks. After lunch the instructor, somewhat to our surprise called us back, saying, "Alright, now switch sides and repeat that debate." We did and I think we both did credibly in our reversed roles.

After the debate one of the "Old Money" Owensboro people came to me obviously upset. His face was red and he was close to tears. Angrily he said, "How could you do a thing like that? I listened to you this morning and felt you believed in cure A. Now you sound like you believe in cure B. What do you really believe?"

It suddenly I realized the purpose of the instructor's role reversals. He wanted to demolish the locals view that the debaters were the business equivalent of southern preachers. I put a hand on his shoulder and said, "It's not a matter of belief, it's a matter of clear-eyed think through of the issues. What you saw Randy and I doing was a job of selling the results of analysis. It was your job to weigh the pros and cons of our two presentations and make your own decision." This didn't convince him, but by the end of the course he began to separate those things where belief is required form those where analysis is possible.

\* \* \*

My new job was solidly in the area of analysis. I became the Product Planning Manager for the Tube Department with three engineers one responsible for each of the three product categories, military, industrial and entertainment. It was our job to formulate the development plans for new products, define their properties and set their prices. We also were charged with developing commercial intelligence on our competitors, being careful not to break the anti-trust laws of the Sherman and Robinson-Pattman Acts. Along with the job came a new boss and a significant increase in salary. Leo Bowles a respected Schenectady associate filled my vacancy as Manager of Application Engineering. This was significant as our two groups had to work closely and communicate freely.

The new boss was one of the top two that I had at GE. Reed was not technically trained, but was an outstanding manger and marketer. His initial order to me was typical of his style. "Art your new products will either be successful or they will be flops. I want you to shoot for an 80% success ration. If you hit 90% you're not taking enough risks for the big payoffs and if you hit 70% you don't know what you're doing." This struck me as the clearest instruction I could have. He continued. "An unprofitable product is not a success no matter how many we sell. Lastly, new product decisions in the past have generally been made ad hoc by the field application engineers. I want you to move that decision making into your authority. I believe you will know how to do that without too much upset. Within six months I want that authority to be recognized as yours alone. This could be done by a written order, but I think a natural evolution would be best."

This was a new kind of task, to appropriate to myself the authority that had been vested in me and my associates over the preceding decade. .After some thought there seemed to be only one workable solution. That was to set up a system which served the application engineers very well and which operated with speed and accuracy. Planning and implementing this became a major challenge, but the four of us were up to it. Specific procedures were established for product definition and the assessment of manufacturing cost. Program and timing decisions were made at a day-long meeting of the four of us once each month and modified if necessary in between meetings. Communication with the field Application Engineers in New York, Chicago and Los Angeles was given top priority After six months it was barely noticed that the old quarterly meeting of application engineers to plan products simply had not been called and would not be called again. Product development was proceeding smoothly and in an accelerated manner.

* * *

The commercial intelligence activity was challenging, but also educational. For example, whenever a new price list appeared, the four of us would sit down to mentally dissect it to see what the competitor that changed prices was trying to do. Once we received a copy of a new price list published by Raytheon. I scheduled a conference room for the whole day, although the task usually required only 3 or 4 hours to review the 300 new product prices. The key was to analyze one block of tubes at a time, with the block representing functionally competing products. If the competitor had raised the price on one of his own products, but not on competing products it meant he wanted to take that one off the market. However, his was not a simple decision as all the customers required multiple sources for a product before they would put it into their design. Maybe Raytheon wanted out on a single product because their manufacturing costs were too high. If our costs were lower, we might just let him drop out and accept an increased sales volume with him out of the game. Similar games existed for decreased prices.

Eight hours went past before we found a pattern in the new price list. I was suspicious, so I reported to my boss Reed, "We've found a pattern after 8 hours, but I'm suspicious. It's nearly impossible to change 300 prices without making some pattern. I think we just found the latent pattern in some endeavor we don't understand. I suggest we do not change any of our prices." Reed thought quietly then said, "You're probably right. Do it." The competitor waited a week then recalled his price changes going back to the previous schedule.

The whole event would have been a mystery until some years later I ran into the Raytheon man who had been my counterpart during that event. It would have been illegal for us to have spoken if we held our old positions, but in time we had moved on and were not then direct price setting competitors. I asked him about the price change. He scowled, "My stupid management said we had to raise prices. I argued against it, saying no one would follow us. They insisted, so I made a set of price changes that were the dumbest thing I could think of without being completely obvious. When no one followed us, they finally believed me. Like I said, they weren't very bright."

* * *

The year 1956 reflected the beginning of de-colonization with problems that would extend into the early 60's. The cold war continued, but in new areas. Nikita Kruschshuv. attacked the veneration of Josef Stalin as a "cult of personality". Hungary rebelled and was invaded by Russia with many casualtes. Soviet forces suppressed riots in Georgia protesting Kruschshuvs anti-Stalin doctrine . Fidel Castro and Che Guevara initiated the Cuban Revolution. Morrocco and Tunisia declared independence from France. Indonesia dissolved its' constitutional arrangement with the Netherlands. The last foreign troops left Egypt. Britain, France and Israel invaded Egypt..The closing of the Suez Canal caused gasoline rationing in Britain

* * *

Collie and I bought a brand new 1956 Plymouth sedan. It was turquoise and cream colored, the only one that color in Owensboro. It replaced the chartreuse Ford, also the only one that color in Owensboro. Collie painted a tree as a mural on the dining room wall. One of our cats verified it by running up and trying to leap onto a limb. The movement of Schenectady folks to Owensboro brought contact with old associates and friends. Generally they bought houses in the tract where we built the first house and we began to enjoy our enlarged community. Collie made a studio in the "mud room" behind the garage. The girls reached an age where she could start to paint again. With the girls in school and old friends in town, our life broadened..

# Miscellaneous Tasks And Studies

By 1957 it was evident to anyone technically trained and watching the development of electronic components that the transistor would replace the vacuum tube. From the viewpoint of the 21st century this appears obvious, but inside the tube business, it would have been heresy to voice the thought. Nevertheless, my job as manager of Product Planning was to structure new product development to achieve the best result against this threatening future. There seemed to be two avenues that could be pursued simultaneously. First, totally new products that by their nature would be immune to the transistor invasion; and second, advanced tubes that would delay the transistor takeover. Both avenues were worked actively with a modicum of success. The new products included light sensing components that used the automated forming and sealing techniques perfected by the tube business but depended on their performance on chemical compounds, not electrons in vacuum.

Typical of these was "Baby Boo's Belly Button", which though Baby Boo was a market failure, the photocell product found wide usage elsewhere and repaid its development costs handsomely. The idea was sound, a toy baby was equipped with a light sensing button where its navel would be if it were a real infant. A battery powered amplifier and speaker reproduced an infants crying wail if light struck the photocell. When the light diminished, the crying stopped. The routine was that Baby Boo was quiet as long as it was held against its' owners shoulder or chest. When it was put down in an illuminated room, the photocell sensed the light and the crying started. This could be stopped by either picking up the doll and cuddling it or by turning out the light.

The principle was excellent and those few little girls who received Baby Boo as a Christmas gift that year enjoyed quieting and soothing her outbursts. The problem was not with the design, nor with our production. We made several hundred thousand "Belly Buttons". The problem was with marketing and shipping by the doll manufacturer. The product was advertised too late and orders simply did not come in for the Christmas rush. A warehouse of Baby Boos were made and they performed well, but they missed the Christmas surge. Next year the manufacturer went bankrupt. However, we had a tiny photocell product, which we sampled widely among our historic tube customers and applications soon developed with orders to follow. "Baby Boo's Belly Button" became a profitable product free from transistor invasion.

* * *

A product in the second class was a vacuum tube, but one made of brazed ceramic layers that could withstand very high temperatures high impact shock and nuclear radiation. This was the second generation of ceramic tubes using new materials and processes which greatly improved upon the ruggedness of the WWII vintage of ceramic tubes. Obviously this product would be of interest mainly to the military where awareness of the effects of radiation on transistors was becoming a matter of deep concern. The first such ceramic tube of this new generation was about the diameter of a pencil and ½ inch in length.

To demonstrate the ruggedness of this product, I tee-ed up one and used my #3 wood driver golf club to hit it full force. After its flight and a lot of searching, it was found and passed its functional tests. Another publicity stunt was to heat the tube to an orange color and drop it into a bowl of room temperature water. The tube did not shatter owing to the near exact match of thermal expansion properties in the ceramic and the metal used in its' construction.

Armed with technical data and these startling tests, I made an appointment in the Navy departments Bureau of Aeronautics in Washington to test their interest. The appointment was at 0900 with a captain whose gold wing pin sparkled in the morning sun coming through the window of his office. He listened for about 45 minutes growing steadily more interested. Finally he interrupted and said, "Hold on, I think Captain So-and-So should hear this". The Captain was sent for while we discussed the background of the tubes development. Finally Captain So-and-So arrived and I began again. To make a long story short, this referral and continued interest happened five times. Each of the Captains stayed on to hear the subsequent discussion. At the end of the day I had talked for eight hours and was growing hoarse, but the Navy was completely engrossed in the prospect of a tube that could withstand red-hot temperatures 1000's of G's of acceleration and an unknown amount of radiation.

Shortly after the Navy visit I received a phone call, not from the Navy, but from Diamond Ordnance Fuse Labs in New Jersey. This was the home base of the Vacuum Tube Fuse, or proximity fuse that accounted for the heavy destruction of

Japanese aircraft in the later half of WWII. Clearly the Navy and DOFL had been talking and also clearly I had arrived on the scene too late for something rather significant. The man at DOFL was calling because we knew each other well and had developed mutual confidence. His proposition was simple, "Art, there's going to be a surface nuclear weapon test at Johnson Island soon. I cannot tell you when, but very soon. All the plans are set, but if you could let me have 100 of these new ceramic tubes by next Wednesday, I can assure you they will be exposed in the test and you will get data you could get no other way. The problem is that it is so late in the game that I can't pay you for them, but we will share all the data we get. You have my word on that."

"Sam, let me work this, I have your number and I'll call you back before 5 o'clock your time today." I immediately called my boss for an appointment and found that he was on a plane to New York. I called his boss and found that the two of them were on the same plane. It was hopeless to go any higher as the understanding of the situation did not extend that high. I was the SOPA or Senior Officer Present Ashore whether I liked it or not. I had signature authority over $10,000., but his was completely out of the blue. The value would be about $7500. I found that indeed we had 120 tubes in stock. I said a short prayer and authorized 100 tubes to be shipped to Sam by airmail that day as soon as test data cold be taken on them.

Taking 10 deep breaths, I called Sam back and advised that we would be on board and that he could expect the tubes the next day. He was ecstatic. I was a little tired.

When my boss returned I explained what I had done and why. He puffed his pipe, considered it and said, "I think your decision was right. We'll see what the outcome is, but in my view you did right to take the chance."

The Johnson Island experiment had a peculiar outcome. The yield of the weapon was definitely greater than planned and the box containing the tubes, which was supposed to be "tangent to the fireball" was actually inside the fireball and was blown out of the ground and required a careful search to locate it. However, the tubes were returned and found to be too hot to handle. However, Sam arranged for them to be tested in a segregated facility using manipulators. The mystery, which remains today is that the noise figure of the tubes improved significantly as a result of their radiation treatment. The good news was that none of the tubes were damaged and all were operational after being inside a atomic weapon fireball. This news traveled inside the military at a speed that we could never duplicate from the outside. The ceramic tubes became good sellers both here and in Europe and were highly profitable.

* * *

The year 1957 was also one of notable change. The Hamilton Company produced the first electric watch. The first Frisbee was produced and Colliers' Magazine folded after 69 years of publication. The USS Nautilus, the first nuclear submarine loged its' 60,000$^{th}$ mile, thus meeting the fictional Nautilus' "20,000 Leagues Under The Sea". President Eisenhower sent Federal troops to Arkansas to assure admittance of colored students to the high school where they had been denied by Governor Faubus, using the Arkansas National Guard. The first Boeing 707 flew. Russia launched Sputnik, the worlds first satellite. The U.S. attempt to launch a satellite failed when the rocket exploded on the launch pad.

* * *

I was on a trip to Michigan when the Sputnik launch was made. I sensed something that was not immediately noted in the press and canceled my trip to return to Owensboro and talk privately to my boss. The message was simple. The weight and size of Sputnik indicate that the Russians are very close to a capability of putting an atomic warhead into orbit, using the weight and size that I had seen when working with the Air Force. The capability to drop an atomic warhead anywhere on earth without firing from a ground launch totally changed the strategic goals of the U.S. We must be aware of this in dealing with the military, but must also recognize that the information might be classified. He sighed deeply and said quietly, "Oh god." I could not have expressed my feeling better.

\* \* \*

The girls were now respectively 8 and 6 and we took a vacation to Kentucky lake. I discovered the fun of sailing in a rented boat and the girls enjoyed the new prospect of a large lake. Collie took it all in and in later years it would come out as paintings of lakes and water scenes. Chris' health began to improve and she started school in the fall. Collie began to paint canvases in the tiny studio at the rear of our house. Our interests as a family were expanding.

# A Year Of Transitions

In retrospect 1958 was clearly a year of transitions in several sectors. In science Schalow & Townes published their paper on the theory of an optical laser. It would be a year or so before hardware ushered in the reality. Fidel Castor and Che Guevarro initiated their Cuban revolution which by year end had eliminated Batista as Cubas' leader. In aerospace, the word itself was invented and the United States was able to put up one satellite, largely based on the work of its recent enemy Germany. U.S. satellite attempts based on U.S. work were unsuccessful three times. President Eisenhower established NASA to clean up the U.S. effort. An economic depression in the U.S. brought unemployment in Detroit to 20%. The "Baby Boom" ended as U.S. birthrates plummeted . In the world political scene change was universal. The French colonies in Africa achieved semi-independence. The present political structure of the of the Mideast formed as splits occurred to form a separate Jordan, Iraq and Syria. A famine began in China which lasted until 1962 and caused between 20 million and 40 million deaths depending on government or independent estimates. The causes were partly weather, but mainly the policies of the Mao Tse Dong governmental takeover.

\* \* \*

In the U.S., the electron tube industry was threatened not only by obsolescence from transistors, but also by competition from Europe and Japan. GE's product planning operation gave careful study to this double threat and arrived at a unique defense that would prolong the life of the tube industry by a few years while at a the same time limiting foreign competition. The product came to be known as a "Compactron" stressing its small size and electron tube ancestry. Before the dust settled, GE would sell more than $200 million dollars of this product and I would get a job offer from Hughes Aircraft based on the planning work on this product. But, that was in the future.

\* \* \*

The idea behind the Compactron was threefold, first – combine basic TV functions into a single tube envelope so as to reduce cost, second, reduce the product size to give the TV designers greater flexibility in their mechanical layout, -- third, utilize manufacturing tools in place in the U.S, but not in Europe or Japan, forcing a re-tooling or withdrawal from the U.S. market.

The first question was how many pins or connections should the product have? This initiated a lengthy study of all possible TV and radio functional combinations and the number of pins each required. The final result indicated that 11 was the magic number yielding the greatest number of functions per unit cost of manufacture. The second goal was achieved by the brilliant idea of one of the planners that the tube should be made upside down with respect to the common structure. This permitted the nipple where the air was exhausted to be placed inside the circle of the 11 pins. Thus, the height of the nipple was subtracted from the total length as it occupied the same part of the length as the pins. The third goal was achieved by forming this product on a machine common in the U.S. but less common in Europe and Japan. This gave the U.S. a head start in capital equipment.

For the Compactron to be successful required at least two U.S. suppliers as no TV manufacturer would tie his whole design to a single source of supply. This of course reduced the market for GE, but was an absolute necessity. Fortunately, a little thought showed this was not as bad as it looked. There were just three big tube suppliers to the TV industry, GE, Sylvania and RCA. We had spent a lot of effort in learning how our competitors thought and planned. A careful examination showed a good chance that RCA was too proud to follow someone else in a major step for the TV industry. So we crafted our first product samples and supplied them to the top TV designers with the word that we knew they would need two suppliers, so we included twice as many samples as normal and would not object if they passed them on to our competition.

We waited and sure enough it was not long before Sylvania requested a three-party meeting with a mutual customer. The meeting with the customer put the exchange outside the anti-trust laws and kept everyone happy. We exchanged info with Sylvania and soon they produced their own samples. Within months we had the new TV designs sewed up and RCA was still debating what to do about it. Eventually they came on board as the market was simply too large to overlook. The foreign manufacturers after assessing the situation including eventual transistor takeover, decided against re-tooling. GE became the market leader in the new sets and of course the supplier of replacement parts for several years downstream.

* * *

Both Collie and I participated in the local "Musical Shows" in Owensboro. This was fun and we expanded our circle of friends. The previous summer spent at Kentucky Lake awakened my interest in boats and in the spring we bought an aged 23 foot cruiser that was in storage in Louisville. This involved launching it in Louisville and boating the 120 miles downstream to Owensboro. I talked a friend, Ken into going along as crew and Collie drove us to Louisville to pick up the boat. Ken later said of the trip downstream that he wouldn't have missed it for anything and wouldn't do it again for $1000.

The Ohio river is a major route of large cargo barges and their "pushers". These make a huge well defined wave from the aft end of the pusher, a situation that my Gulf of Mexico experience did not encompass. We got low on gas and stopped at a small town to get a jeep can refilled. I anchored the boat close to shore so Ken could jump off and carry the can into town. The river current held the boat steady about 8 feet off the edge of the bank. A huge barge tow came up river. I ignorantly watched the wave come in and was horrified when they washed the boat into a firm grounding on the shallow river bed.

When Ken returned we tried backing off with reverse engine. This didn't do it, but it did suck up enough mud into the cooling water to cause a seizure of one of the engines valves. It ran, but at truly reduced power. Finally we used a small tree trunk to lever under the shore-side bilge and with engine going astern, we rocked the lever until the boat broke free.

It was then a slow passage home running the bilge pump almost continuously to pump out water from a leak that appeared in the transom. We made it and tied up at the city wharf with bilge pump running and a battery charger working to supply up enough energy to keep it that way.

A later examination would show that the transom had an infestation of termites that would be cured when we overhauled the boat. But for then we were home with a new addition to our family vehicles. Life was becoming exciting.

* * *

# The World Changes Abruptly

The year 1959 saw landmark events in various fields. Both Alaska and Hawaii were admitted to the United States, changing the flag from 48 stars to 50. The UN declared Antartica to be a conflict-free zone in which only scientific endeavors would occur.Panty hose and Barbie doll were introduced to broad acceptance. Riots occurred in French Equatorial Africa and the first large-unit combat action took place in the Viet Nam War. In aerospace the pace of change accelerated. Russia's Luna I became the first man-made object to reach the moon and Luna III the first to photograph the far side of the moon. The U.S. successfully launched the first Titan ICBM missile and a vehicle to orbit the moon and take the first photo of the earth from that location.

* * *

From my perspective the world situation changed dramatically on a bright April day with the climate in Owensboro changing abruptly from winter to spring. I had on my staff a young engineer/physicist named John. He was tasked with monitoring radiation effects on electronic equipment as a result of nuclear weapons detonation. GE's position as a supplier of the radiation resistant ceramic tubes made this an essential step in the planning of products for the military and the space program.

John asked for a one-on-one meeting and when I nodded, closed the door to my office. This should have alerted me, as that door remained open nearly always as a matter of my style, but I missed the signal. However, the look of worry on his face when he sat down could not be missed. He began slowly, "Art, I'm afraid I've found something of terrible strategic importance in the Cold War." He had my complete attention, John was not one to exaggerate. "OK, maybe you should begin at the beginning."

"As you know, Art, our Cold-War defense depends on a strategy called MAD for mutually assured destruction, the threat that any launch of ICBMs by Russia would trigger a total ICBM response by the U.S. The MAD scenario depends on two techniques; first are decoys as many as a hundred in a single missile, each with the radar cross section of a warhead. The defender can't tell which one is the threat and his defense is overwhelmed by quantity and indecision. Second, is multiple independent maneuverable vehicles, or MIRVs in which a single rocket carries as many as 7 separate warheads plus decoys with each warhead."

"OK, I know that, so what?"

"What I've found is a defense that completely overwhelms both decoys and MIRVs with a single defending missile."

What followed was a long silence while I digested what John had just told me. Our basic nuclear strategy depended entirely on the force of our offensive ICBM capability. This force rested on two pillars, the difficulty of decoy discrimination and the barrage threat of MIRV missiles. Now John had told me there is a simple way to defeat both of these and render our strategy totally ineffective.

John shifted in his chair, his tall form rigid and his head held a little higher than usual. "You see, Art, there's a problem in the vacuum of space. When a nuclear weapon detonates there is a huge immediate release of radiation called "Prompt Gamma". We have not paid much attention to this because the atmosphere shields us from it and our sensors are typically well within the atmosphere."

"Alright John, where does that take us?"

"It takes us straight to a major problem. If the Prompt Gamma is undiminished in outer space, it strikes anything else that is also in outer space. The only reduction in intensity is that of distance. It's like a radio wave, it just diminishes with the square of the distance between the source and the receiver."

"OK, maybe I'm a little slow this morning, so what?"

"The Prompt Gamma of even a medium sized fission weapon is very intense. With no atmospheric attenuation, there will be a distance where it wrecks any electronics that it strikes. I've done some calculations and that distance is in the order of 500 miles. In short, we can destroy the electronics of anything in space with a near miss of 500 miles". This set me back. There was a long silence while I digested.

"Where did you get the data for this calculation? Is the source classified?"

"No, it's in a Government handbook for anyone to read."

"And your formula to calculate the effective damage?"

"It's Nuclear Physics 101."

\* \* \*

Later that night after dinner, I excused myself, telling Collie that I needed a walk. She simply nodded, accustomed to my occasional need of privacy. To insure that I walked alone, she commanded the kids to help clear the table. Wearing a light jacket, I stepped out of the lighted home and into a dark night under a clear sky. I needed to sort out priorities, catalog the assets that John and I had and put together a plan. The matter of priorities was easy. The security of our country and our families came first. Whatever was in second place was hull-down over the horizon. In our actions we were going to spend the money of our employer for wages and transportation and we would not be doing what the travel requisitions said. That was a small lie and the company would forgive it if they ever found out. To keep John's Formula secret, we couldn't tell them and must be very careful who in the armed services we told.

Both John and I held secret clearances, but if the problem was known, it would be classified well beyond that. Both of us had contacts inside the Air Force and some of these were charged with ICBM hardening against radiation. The plan seemed clear. We would schedule a trip to Washington to visit the Pentagon and discuss future plans for hardening of missile controls. That travel excuse was not untrue.

* * *

The Air Force Colonel was on the Pentagon's E-ring, second floor. After the conventional greeting, he leaned back in his chair and the sunlight from the window caused his eagles to glisten. As he swiveled in the chair the light fell on his manifold ribbons and the silver wings topped with a star indicating he had been not only a pilot, but at least a squadron leader.

Behind an engaging smile, his deep voice asked, "What can we do for you gentlemen?"

John outlined the problem in clear words and excellent detail. Our problem, he said, was to insure that the Air Force was aware of the vulnerability of missile electronics to Prompt Gamma in the vacuum of space. The colonel pursed his lips, swiveled in his chair and then said, "We have an excellent cafeteria here. Isn't it about time for lunch gentlemen?" At lunch he proved to be an excellent conversationalist, covering many topics, none of which came close to the subject we had broached. When lunch was finished he rose and extending his hand said, "I hope you gentlemen have a good visit here in Washington." With an engaging smile he turned and walked back toward the E ring. John and I looked at each other in astonishment.

After dinner we reviewed the possibilities for the colonels' non-response. I ventured that perhaps he didn't understand what we were saying and was too embarrassed to ask questions. John defeated that with the comment, "When did you last see a bird colonel embarrassed to ask questions of civilians?" We finally concluded that he could not admit that the Air Force was unaware of the problem, confirming their lack of due diligence. Nor could he admit that it was aware of the problem, confirming that the MAD strategy was flawed. Faced with this no-win choice, he simply dodged the whole issue.

\* \* \*

Our next visit was to Kirtland AFB in Albuquerque. John and I both knew a young colonel there who had a solid physics background. There would be no question of his comprehending the problem. We might even get a critique of the John's Formula. Perhaps there was a mistake in reasoning and we were chasing a non-existent problem.

We flew into Albuquerque at night through the Sandia Pass. After a half hour of blackness out the planes windows, the black sides of the pass opened up and there below were the lights of the city spread over the desert floor, each light brilliant in the clear mile-high air.

The next morning we sat in the colonel office on the base, enjoying a cup of coffee and admiring the string of dried chiles that adorned his wall like a prized painting. After the necessary small talk I indicated the purpose of our meeting. He immediately waved his hand and said, "We have a new radiation effects test facility here that I'd like for you to see. Let's walk over there."

Having gotten into the open air he said, "Let's hear what you have to say." John gave him the full picture including a back and forth discussion of the formula and the results. We did indeed stop and viewed the test facility from the outside, then started the trip back. After some thought he said, "Let me say that I fully understand what you are saying. I agree with John's numbers maybe within 25%, but in nuclear yield projections today, 25% is total agreement. We don't really argue short of 200%." I thanked him for his candor. He continued, "I can't confirm or deny Air Force knowledge of this situation. If it exists, it is well beyond your level of security clearance and maybe beyond mine as well." He let this thought rest for a few seconds then continued. "Let me suggest that you not talk with anyone in or outside the government about this. If that sounds like 'trust me', well I guess that's what it is."

John and I took the hint and changed the subject. Back in his office we discussed other subjects and then excused ourselves with best wishes all around.

* * *

It would be three years before I heard anything more of the gamma radiation outside the atmosphere. The actions would make a good spy mystery. The Albuquerque Colonel did try to convince the powers that be of the seriousness of the problem. The best he was able to obtain was an agreement to detonate a nuclear weapon outside the atmosphere during the 1960 tests at Johnson Island in the Pacific. When the test weapon was detonated the night sky turned green in Hawaii, over a thousand miles away. Now the Air Force listened. Then the Russians detonated a weapon outside the atmosphere at their test station in Nova Zemblya. Again, the sky turned green from the radiation as it struck the nitrogen in the upper atmosphere. Now the Russians knew, but we were not sure what they knew. Then in a totally unrelated conversation at a nuclear weapons limitation meeting in Switzerland, the Russian representative said, "It is not difficult to increase the prompt gamma yield of a weapon." It was a throw away comment totally unrelated to the weapon effects that John had hypothesized. Nevertheless, the US representative heard it differently. To him the Russians were developing a defensive weapon with increased prompt gamma output to incapacitate inbound U.S ICBMs. It turned out they were not, but this misinterpretation sealed the story for the Air Force which immediately instituted a program for hardening U.S. missiles against gamma radiation. The thing John and I were hoping to set in motion finally happened through a set of coincidences that would not be believed if they were put into a fiction book.

* * *

Our family life changed greatly in 1959. The old boat purchased in 1958 was overhauled in our driveway while hanging from an "A" frame. The refit included recovering all the decks and sheathing the entire hull in fiberglass with careful repair of the termite nest found in the transom. The girls helped me to mark and saw the plywood for the new decking. The three of us sat on the deck singing a Brit drinking song with the punch line, "Landlord fill the flowing bowl until it doth run over, for tonight we'll merry be, tomorrow we'll be sober.". It was a credit to the neighbors that there were no complaints about a father teaching his daughters of 8 and 10 a Brit drinking song.

When the overhaul was complete, we towed the boat a 100 miles to Kentucky Lake for launching. Thus began a series of weekends spent on the boat, fishing, and observing wildlife while the girls learned the elements of small boat handling. It was a unifying experience for the family.

# Colonialism Dies And A New Job Comes For Art

The year 1960 saw the literal rebirth of Africa from its' colonial state enforced by France, England, and Belgium into the multiple nation-states that exist today. The most violent of these was the war in Algeria which ended when France failed to put down the Algerian protesters despite extended military action. Nigeria was born when England, observing the Algerian situation, simply got up and left. The nation states created in that year were too numerous to cite here. It seemed that Africa's time had come, but the departure of the colonial governors left a power vacuum visible even today.

The U.S. Navy's nuclear submarine force surged to the front rank in military forces of the cold-war. The USS Triton made the first underwater circumnavigation of the earth, while a second US nuclear sub surfaced at the north pole. A Polaris missile fired from a submerged US sub reached orbit before being destroyed. A third leg had been added to the U.S. cold-war offensive capability.

Several Russian surface-to-air missiles downed a US U-2 reconnaissance plane over Russia. The pilot was captured and put on trial. Nikita Kruschev roundly criticized President Eisenhower for this violation of Russian airspace. A MIG-15 shot down a U.S. RB-47 over the Berents' Sea following its' reconnaissance of Russia. I began to worry that small engagements might lead to much larger warfare.

\* \* \*

In Owensboro, KY, GE received a complaint from the navy's China Lake Air Station in California. The Navy was trying to use one of GE's ceramic tubes in a Sidewinder missile to increase the sensitivity of the missiles infra-red detector. With increased sensitivity the little air-to-air missile could detect and lock onto enemy aircraft at greater distances. However, when the new seeker design was subjected to mechanical vibration it produced a significant output at around A over middle C. They blamed the GE tube as it was "all that had changed" from the conventional production unit.

This required someone to go out to China Lake to witness the tests and solve the problem. Past experience indicated that vibration output problems were not solved over the telephone, but only in the presence of the actual test equipment setup. This created something of a turf problem, because Jack, supervisor of application engineering for military products, had the organizational responsibility, but not the experience with the ceramic tubes. Jack had been one of the two supervisors that I threatened with firing when they questioned my appointment of my own replacement . Six years had passed and we learned to work with and trust each other. So to solve the turf problem we agreed that I would make the trip to China Lake, scope the problem and communicate by phone only with Jack. Then he would issue the instructions in Owensboro for anything that needed to be done.

I flew to Los Angeles and drove to China Lake, located in a semi-desert environment. The navy engineers were cordial, but eager to demonstrate the problem. The seeker head resembled a six inch slice from a loaf of French bread. It was bolted to the vibration machine which was the size of a refrigerator on its' side. Sure enough, as the shaking frequency increased, a resonance was reached where the seekers output increased significantly just as it would when it spotted a target. That frequency was about 500 Hertz or about G over middle C. At higher frequencies there was no erroneous output. I knew one thing the Navy engineers did not, the lowest pitch for a mechanical resonance in that tube was 16,000 Hertz, about six octaves over middle C. This couldn't be a resonance in the tube, but how to prove it? I suggested to the lead Navy engineer, "Suppose we turn off the heater voltage to the tube and let it cool down. Then repeat the test. The tube would not be operational, right?"

"Yeah. OK let's see what happens."

The test results were the same, a resonance at G over middle C. The Navy guy was still not convinced. "I could be something in the tube, right?"

I knew better than to argue that point and suggested we simply physically remove the tube and leave everything else in place, repeating the test. This was done and a technician opened the metal shell of the seeker package and with a knife sliced through the silicone rubber potting material that filled the inside of the case. when he reached the tube, he carefully snipped loose the connecting wires and left them in place. He could have been a surgeon. When the job ended, there was a neat hole where the tube had been and all else was back in its place.

The test now showed the same result as before, a resonance at G over middle C. The surgery on the seeker package gave me an idea on the source of the problem. The wire which carried the tubes output signal was suspended in this glob of rubber inside a metal can. Maybe the rubber and the can were resonant. I asked the engineer if it was possible to remove just the output wire from the rubber, leaving all else as it had been. The answer activated the technician who again exercised his surgeons' skill. The test then showed no resonance within the full range of the vibration machine.

This clearly showed the problem to be a wire in a resonant rubber block, not the tube. The wire was moving with respect to the metal case when the rubber resonated and this induced a small, but significant voltage which looked like a signal. One solution would be to run the wire inside of a small metal tube that would be grounded to the case. Then the induced voltage would be from the movement of the wire inside the tub. If it was tight-fitting, the signal would be much less. I phoned Jack to release him from his duty, it wasn't our problem. The navy did enclose the wire in a tight shield and repeated the test with the tube in place and operating. The seeker performed beautifully on the vibration test.

I learned later how the best laid plans of man "Aft tames gang aglee" when operational tests of the new seeker hear indeed showed increased sensitivity. Unfortunately that sensitivity caused the missile to lock onto the sunshine reflected from cloud tops making the Sidewinder a cloud chaser. The change was never used operationally. We don't win them all.

\* \* \*

The other big event for 1960 was a new job. The vice-president for electronic components decided to create a new operation, Advanced Product Planning and to locate it in Schenectady, NY. The unit would have the same management structure as a full profit center so that it could advise on problems within the operating profit centers. I was to be the Product Planning Manager, reporting to the manager of engineering. The unit was given a salary grade one step higher than a normal profit center and so offered a salary bracket jump for me. The challenge alone would have been enough, but that and the increased salary did the trick. So we put our house on the market, drove to Schenectady where we bought another house and returned to the land of severe winters

# A World Of Many Facets
# And Directions

The year 1961 showed the many sides of the cold war and the de-colonization of Africa and Asia. President Eisenhower gave his last "State of The Union" address to Congress and warned against the growth of an "Industrial-Military Complex". A peace compact was signed in Algeria and India invaded and annexed the Portugese colonees of Goa, Damao and Gui. Government changed by coup in Turkey and South Korea.

Outgoing president Eisenhower severed relations with Cuba. Newly sworn president Kennedy formed the Peace Corps while the first US nuclear submarines arrived in Holy Loch Scotland for foreign basing.. The "Bay of Pigs" invasion of Cuba by Americans with minimal US military support failed dismally. The Swedish ship Vasa was raised from Stockholm harbor where it sank 333 years earlier on its' maiden voyage. It was found to be woefully short on ballast, an early example of a military-industrial complex.

Yuri Gagarin in the Soviet capsule Vostok became the first human being to travel in space. Alan Sheppard in a Mercury capsule became the first US person to travel in space. President Kennedy announced before a special session of Congress his goal to put a man on the moon before the end of the decade.

Russia fired a space capsule which orbited Venus, but was unable to communicate back. Russia initiated a blockade of Berlin. President Kennedy announced "We will not be driven out of Berlin." The US Air Force supplied Berlin by air and eventually broke the blockade. Kennedy in Berlin, announced "Ich bin ein Berliner." Construction of the Berlin wall began, separating East and West Berlin and effectively East and West Germany. Russia exploded a 58 mega-ton hydrogen bomb over Novaya Zemblya test station. It was the largest man-made explosion to date. Catch-22, a novel by Joseph Heller is published and became a commentary on government procedure. President Kennedy sent 18,000 military "advisors" to Viet Nam.

* * *

My new work in Schenectady was to evaluate new business opportunities for GE in the electronic components field. The first of these was the prospect of a business in technical ceramics for the electronics industry. GE developed an excellent technical basis for technical ceramics as subsidiaries to its' existing business units. The question was whether these might be combined in a single profit center to serve both GE and outside customers. The study considered three quite different types of ceramics structural, magnetic and piezo-electric.

The structural ceramics mainly served as packages for delicate electronic components serving in tough environments. GE had two excellent products, Aluminum oxide ceramic and a proprietary process for brazing it to stainless steel, giving an extremely strong assembly. The second was the proprietary forsterite ceramic developed in Owensboro for the high-temperature tubes plus the process for sealing it to titanium. The combination of a ceramic plus a sealing process to a metal formed the basis for a packaging business.

The magnetic ceramics chiefly comprised ferrites for high-frequency transformers used in TV and radio, the TV market being the largest. In time these ceramics would be used in both small and large power supplies, becoming the dominant market for this class. The field included several different formulations of ceramic to suit the many applications.

The piezo-electric ceramics produced an electric voltage in response to a mechanical pressure. They embraced many different formulations used in sonar. However, in time they would also be used as igniters for the burners of surface units in kitchen ranges. My furnace now dispenses with a pilot light and instead uses a piezo-electric ceramic as an igniter.

* * *

A series of interviews with GE scientists and engineers involved in the development and production of these ceramics showed a dominant technical position in all except the magnetic ceramics. There, the understanding of basic principles existed at the research level and engineering knowledge existed at the application level, but skill in the intervening area of manufacturing was not developed. The skilled people were highly interested in the possibility of a centralized technical ceramic business. This was not surprising, as they would be the main players in such a scheme, whereas they were simply servants to a larger product in the dispersed situation that existed.

A market research determined the present nationwide sales level for these ceramics and the likely growth that could be expected in the future. Finally a sales forecast for the proposed business considered GE strengths and weaknesses and the market available inside GE and among outside customers. This showed a business in the range of 10 – 15 million dollars per year at the outset and which growth in time might bring to 20 – 25 million.

The question remained as to the profitability of such a business. Internal GE experience provided the base for this calculation in the structural and piezo-electric ceramics. Publicly available data on one major supplier of magnetic ceramics allowed an educated guess for that class. The business could be comfortably profitable and self-sustaining for its own capital and development needs..

When the presentation was made to top management, one of them said, "Gosh, doesn't that look good. You've done an excellent and thorough job. I'd really like to take over and manage a little technical business like that. Unfortunately, that's not what GE is looking for right now. We don't want a 20 million dollar business, We want a 200 million dollar business."

I stood at the podium dumb-struck, couldn't they see that the business would be contributing to GE profit and through its' technical advances contributing to the success of other GE businesses with larger sales volume? Apparently not. In three years I would see what this concentration on "the really big show" without doing adequate homework would yield. But, that was in the future. Now I was simply angry at GE management.

* * *

Collie took delight in her new house. The living room and dining room had glass from floor to the underside of the peaked roof. This glass looked out onto a forest of birch and evergreen trees from a level about 12 feet above the forest floor. Under the living room and dining room was Collies studio also with floor to ceiling glass, looking out on the same forest at ground level. The studio featured a two-sided fireplace which saw good use in the bitter winter climate of Schenectady. With a space of about 300 square feet, the studio allowed room for painting and sitting without crowding. The basement underneath the rest of the house became Arts' shop.

The cruiser moved from Kentucky to Schenectady under the liberal GE rules for personnel transfer. We joined the Schenectady Yacht Club and moored the boat in an abandoned section of the old Erie Canal and spent the summer exploring the historic Mohawk River.

The house in Owensboro sold slowly, but one day I happily announced to my fellow workers that one house and two cars was vastly superior to two houses and one car. The girls, now 10 and 12 found Schenectady very different from their Kentucky upbringing. At that age, school children can be mean. One of them teased Sherry about being from Kentucky. She quickly replied, "What do you know? I was born in Niskayuna, just 5 miles from here. Have you ever been to Kentucky yourself?". The family was growing up.

# Retreading An Old Tire In A World On The Brink Of War

In the year 1962 war broke out between India and China, Nelson Mandela was jailed in South Africa for disturbing the peace and Charles De Gaulle announced peace with Algeria while the French Foreign Legion packed up and marched home.

Telstar, the worlds' first commercial communications satellite was launched and carried the first trans-Atlantic TV program. Mariner 2 orbited Venus and transmitted the first pictures from another planet back to earth.

By far the most dramatic news involved the Cuban Missile Crisis. Russia sent nuclear missiles to Cuba. US reconnaissance satellites and aircraft photographed the missile firing sites in construction. Russian ships were photographed with missiles as deck cargo on their way to Cuba. President Kennedy received plans to both bomb and invade Cuba, but the Pentagon could not insure absolute successful prohibition of a firing. Kennedy warned Krushov that a firing from Cuba on the US would be regarded as a firing on the US from Russia and an immediate response would be triggered. He requested that the missiles be removed. In a secret negotiation, it was agreed that the US would remove its' missiles from Turkey and Russia would remove theirs from Cuba.

The US Navy steamed alongside the Russian ships with missile deck cargo and demanded they turn back. Eventually they did. The Turkey agreement was not announced, so it appeared that Russia had backed down. The world breathed again. The navy discovered that in matters of boarding at sea they had no choice between .45 pistols and 5" guns as the anti-aircraft 20 mm And 40 mm had been replaced by surface-to-air missiles. With slightly red faces, the Navy replaced the 20 mm guns.

* * *

In Schenectady my job took on a new perspective. I reported to Jim Keister the brilliant former engineering manager of GEs' semiconductor department. A Dr. Ovshinsky visited GE claiming to have a marvelous new invention that would make transistors much, much cheaper. His idea was an organic semiconductor. Jim and I were tasked with reviewing Ovshinskys' proposal, Jim from the transistor manufacturers standpoint and I from the circuit users viewpoint. Both of us admitted privately that the idea of an organic semiconductor was the final straw. We had started with vacuum tube electronics based on particle physics and then were retreaded via semiconductor physics to the new transistor world. I had also retreaded from the circuitry design for tubes to that for transistors which was totally different. Now it appeared we must go back and learn organic chemistry to fit into a new technical realm.

We swallowed our personal problems and took a closer look at Ovshinskys' idea. It had a serious flaw. The manufacture of cheap transistors required that the yield of good units be large. The prospect of making an organic material free of defects was slim, thus the yield for organic transistors would always be small. That is, there would be a lot more rejects for organic semiconductors than for the classic inorganic devices. We concluded our study with this observation and a negative recommendation. Our observation proved correct and the organic transistor disappeared into the sands of time, but not Ovshinsky. I would encounter him twice more in my career selling his far-out science, but that was still in the future. For the present Jim and I would not be organically retreaded. That didn't mean there would be no retreading, just not organic chemistry.

* * *

One of the things which GE did very well, was to train its' senior people. This was particularly well done, for those who might become engineering mangers. The word came down from GE headquarters that all engineering sub-section managers were requested to attend an intense course in the use and programming of time-shared computers. The word was that no-one was required to take the course, but new promotions to engineering manger status would require the candidate to have completed the study The course instantly became popular..

In GE an "intense course" lasted for 5 days and nights and was tough enough to permit only 5 – 6 hours a night for sleep. The student was immersed in the subject at a facility where the class did not read newspapers or go out at night, but ate all meals together in the same location where the classes were taught. This became known as "going into the submarine".

My computer course was taught at Saratoga, NY. We used Kleinschmidt teletype machines tied into a GE computer thirty miles away in Schenectady. The assistant instructor for the course was a lady of mid thirties who had formerly been "Miss Vermont" in the national Miss America contest. She had very dark brown hair, light green eyes and a cream-and-coffee complexion without a wrinkle. She was also one brilliant mathematician. Toward the end of the course we were each required to write code for a program carrying out our best wish for business analysis. Mine was to analyse the best combination of electronic parts manufacturers in different countries operating on a barter basis exchanging products, benefiting from both labor rates and currency exchange rates. When I presented that to her she read the code and said, looking straight into my eyes, "you have two matrices of data, but you are not using matrix algebra, you are simply mapping one matrix onto the other". The sense was that I was cheating because I made it too simple.

It took me some time to recover from being told by a Miss America candidate that I was simple minded. However, the code did what I wanted and I later reviewed it with GEs' International Business unit. They were horrified, saying, "but that's barter" and rejected it out of hand. It has been standard practice now for several decades and is one reason that GE pays no US income tax on over $12. million in earnings. I am now sorry to have been even a remote part of it. Shows that greed is contagious.

* * *

I received a phone call from Ray, my first boss in GE who was now the president of ARINC, the company funded by the US airlines to monitor and improve reliability of electronic equipment. for commercial aircraft. After the obligatory pleasantries, Ray said that he had a job opening for and electronic engineer and would I be interested. I replied that I was always ready to listen, but that things looked pretty good here in Schenectady. He described the job, only moderately interesting and then asked what was I making now. When I told him he said, "Oops, I'm sorry, Art. I can't come anywhere near that so we should probably just forget about the job." It was nice to know that I was well off. It was also nice to know that Ray still thought of me as a good electronics engineer.

* * *

As it turned out, my next job was right there in Schenectady. My boss, Jim and our marketing manger, Joe had become fed up with their mutual boss. They were old GE hands and so found good jobs elsewhere, leaving at essentially the same time. I was offered Jim's job. It would take me another three years to come to the end of my rope with the same boss. So, at age 36 I had made it to the coveted Engineering Manager title.

My first assignment was to use my new computer expertise along with an earlier GE training course, "Finance for Non-Financial Managers" to model the cash flow of a new business for various degrees of capital intensiveness. In general there are two types of manufacturing businesses, those that depend for profit on low labor costs, called labor intensive, and those that have higher costs for machines or inventory, called capital intensive.

It was not hard to see the root cause of this assignment. A new top management team at GE had decreed that all profit centers must obtain at least 7% profit on sales and 22% return on capital investment. This was, in my view, a very limited understanding of business management prompted by the narrow experience of the new GE president. There were GE businesses that faced tight competition and were limited in profit on sales, but which through careful management achieved very high return on investment (ROI). Conversely, there were others, common in the electronic components field that made high returns on sales, but were limited on ROI. It was naïve to require both results for a "One Fits All" set of goals that came to be known as the 7/22 club. However, under the new rules, good businesses were sold off for not meeting both criteria when they would have been considered profitable by the world outside GE..

So my charge was to use my new computer coding skill to write an analytical program that would model cash flow in growing businesses with various levels of profit to sales and return on investment. The program did prove useful both in demonstrating the effects of growth and also as an aid in evaluating companies that GE considered buying. One of these was a structural ceramics producer. I visited his facility in the Boston area and was not impressed with his product, although I took some samples just for the record. His great selling point was that he had a $1 million loss on the books. GE was profitable and so that loss could reduce their taxes by $300K. I thanked him and wrote in my report that GE had better ways to make profit than buying a losing business to reduce taxes.

* * *

Collie began using her studio every day and artwork quality improved. She had always wanted cats, which we had from 1948 on, but now the cat family bloomed to a total of 13, all outdoor cats. I built a large crate for them to sleep in during the winter. It was placed inside the garage and a 60 watt light bulb kept it warm. One night a family of raccoons came up from the forest to see what could be found in the garage. What they found was 13 screaming cats protecting their warm winter quarters. The screaming brought me to the front door to see two raccoons escaping around the corner and a third caught halfway under the door with its' head being clawed from inside the garage. I lifted the door and a relieved raccoon ran for the woods never to return.

Our boat was now on Lake George, one of the worlds most beautiful, providing a vacation spot in the summer and a wonderful view of the red and gold maples in the fall. We began to take interest in the history of the Schenectady – Lake George region which experienced several skirmishes during the French and Indian and Revolutionary wars. We were becoming true Up-State New Yorkers.

# WOMEN, VIET NAM AND KENNEDY

The year 1963 began with the publishing of Betty Friedmans' book "The Feminine Mystique" which reawakened the feminist movement in the US. The Russians caught on and Vostok 6 carried Valentina Tareshkova as the first woman to fly into space.

Russia, UK and US signed the Nuclear Test Ban Treaty. In Viet Nam the Buhdists and the Diem regimes continued their struggle. President Kennedy issued a directive that the Diem regime must go. A coup took place with Diem assassinated and Dong Van Minh taking leadership of South Viet Nam.

The first zip code was introduced and the US launched the worlds' first geo-stationary satellite, which has now become the common carrier type for telephone conversations and messages. The Arecibo facility was commissioned as the worlds largest antenna dish looking for signals from aliens in outer space.

The grievous news in November was the assassination of President Kennedy in Dallas, Texas. Lyndon Johnson, vice president and former Texas governor became president of the US and formed the Warren Commission to investigate the Kennedy assassination. The commission found that Lee Harvey Oswald acted alone to assassinate Kennedy. Meanwhile Jack Ruby assassinated Oswald, preventing a trial.

I was on a trip to Syracuse when the news of Kennedy's assassination came over the radio. I became too overcome to continue driving and pulled into a restaurant for a cup of coffee. The waitresses debated whether to call 911 for their "sick" customer. who was pale and distraught.. When I settled down, all I could do was turn around and drive home. All that promise of change was lost, the future looked bleak -- what had brought us to this?

* * *

My tasks in Schenectady expanded into the hardware area to create a small model shop where new possible products could be examined and samples made. This was exciting. I hired a technician and purchased on the GE surplus market the equipment for a small machine shop.

The first hardware effort was in the area of microwave ovens for home use. Microwaves for industrial and restaurant use were now on the market using magnetrons which originated for radar transmitters in WWII. The question was whether the new Owensboro ceramic tubes could perform the task of the magnetrons at a lower cost. Both the GE research Lab in Schenectady and the ceramic tube engineers in Owensboro were interested in this possibility and were prepared to lend support and cheer-leading. I obtained the case of a commercial microwave oven from the GE maker and prepared to outfit it with a ceramic tube generator. This is no small task. The microwave oven must perform in a narrow frequency range allotted to it by the FCC. The ceramic tube power generator would require a three-dimensional circuit called a cavity which would start it oscillating and keep it within the required frequency range. I designed the cavity including its internal feedback circuitry and my technician, Fred built it. The unit needed a power supply and this too was designed and made to order by another GE department. The day came to fit it all together, which was done with a dummy load that we called the "Iron Chicken". To my delight, the rig performed just as it was supposed to. Fred got the biggest pleasure as he had never before built anything like this and approached it with skepticism. We tried various adjustments and improvements and finally got the power up to 700 watts, the level of a low-power microwave today, but viewed in 1963 as being inadequate. It was the opinion of the Owensboro engineers and I that we would never make it to the 1000 watts desired by the appliance people, so a finesse seemed in order. If it was possible to improve the coupling of energy from the oven to the food, that would be as good as increasing the output power of the tube.

An idea for a new type of coupling antenna was conceived and a search made for material to make it. The invention had the side advantage of simplifying the rotation device that appears in the bottom of modern ovens to provide an even distribution of energy into the food. The energy in the microwave field is concentrated in lumps about the size and shape of a clenched fist. If no alteration is made, this will cook one part of the food and leave another raw. At the research lab this was demonstrated by accident when their rotor failed while a banana was in the oven. A cooked banana is black, so when the door opened there in the oven was a yellow banana with each end black. The lab photographer stuck his head in the door while we discussed this saying, "Wow, that's fantastic, don't move it while I go get my camera". If he photographed it there would be proof positive that the labs oven didn't "stir" microwave energy, a sad lapse in technology. The lab scientist quickly ate the banana and when the photographer returned asking, "Where's the banana?" He smiled saying, "What banana?" The photographer had been on this route before, he quietly closed camera and said, "OK you guys, have it your way."

A suitable material for the new radiator was found. Fred formed the antenna pattern on it. On large or medium sized loads it performed well. We made a beaker of tea for lunch each day. The classic problem in microwave was getting it to couple to small or dispersed loads. The worst example was pop corn where the initial load is a series of small grains. We finally got the antenna pattern correct to do even this. A demonstration was set for the vice-president of electronic components. We made tea for him and then threw a cup of un-popped corn on the antenna. I stood back and hit the switch. A 700 watt arc occurred between a point on the antenna and a single grain of popcorn that was in exactly the wrong place. A ball of fire spit out the front of the microwave accompanied by a whopping "bang". Fortunately, the Vice-president and I knew each other well and he laughed saying, "stick with it, Art." I breathed a sigh of relief. Fred was ready to faint.

* * *

I took the scuba diving course in Schenectady and became addicted to this fascinating sport. My lungs felt so good after a session that I gave up smoking and became un-addicted to that habit. The boat in Lake George provided an excellent diving platform which took up the week ends through the summer. The family became active boaters on that lovely lake. The girls learned to fish and Collie started painting lake scenes of upstate New York. We also acquired a Siamese cat which felt that it owned the boat and was incensed when young men began to buzz past with outboard motor boats to show off to the girls. The cat would sit up in the helmsman's seat and glower at them as they roared past. Unfortunately young men do not notice Siamese cats when young girls are present. The cat retreated to the hanging locker to nurse its' anguish. We were becoming a boat family with cat. In time the cat became a "Guy Magnet" which pleased everyone, including the cat.

# Vietnam, Civil Rights
# And The Beatles

In 1964 the Vietnam War escalated markedly with a bombing plan for the North proposed by the Pentagon to President Johnson. Students at Berkeley and other US schools staged protests of the war and the draft. The US Navy initiated patrols of the South China Sea. The "Gulf of Tonkin Incident" where two US Destroyers were allegedly fired on by Vietnamese gunboats caused the US Congress to grant President Johnson very broad war powers in Viet Nam. A coup in Viet Nam placed a US favorite in charge and prompted a constitution written in the US Embassy. China exploded a nuclear weapon in a test.

The Civil Rights Act of 1964 passed when cloture was voted after 75 hours of filibuster in the US congress. A case was brought in the Supreme Court which promptly decided the Act required hotels and other establishments renting living space to avoid all racial discrimination.

The Beatles rose to record positions in recording popularity in the US, furnishing Chris and Shari a signature music style for their generation.

\* \* \*

I served on an "off-the-org-chart" group in GE that reviewed proposals by operating departments to develop new technology, particularly for support of the military products of GE. The top management recognized that only the "technical insiders" of the company would be able to recognize essential technology early enough to permit decisive action. The costs of this group were off the published budgets and their recommendations went straight to GEs' headquarters. Membership was strictly by invitation with each person representing a sales level of $300 - $500 million annually as well as a source of new technology. The whole show was run by a savvy and incorruptable technologist from GEs' General Engineering Labs. I was honored to be asked to represent the Electronic Components Division. The meetings were announced only to the reviewers and the presenters and took place in Schenectady about once every six months.

In that capacity I heard a few absolutely stupid weapon system proposals and several very advanced ideas. The winnowing was accomplished and of course the decisions were made in Headquarters, but it soon became known that the door to any GE development money was in Schenectady in a back room of the Lab. This was the same lab that gave me a bad review when I was a young test engineer, but all that was in the past.

* * *

I received an assignment that became my most fascinating task in GE. This was surveying the European market for non-NATO electronic components and equipment. We knew the nature of the NATO equipment, which mainly was of US design.

The question was what were the Europeans doing on their own. and what could we sell them.

The fascinating aspect of this task was to learn how each nation, Sweden, Germany, France and UK viewed their military role as dictated by their culture and socio-political milieu. A lot of study went into the ancient and current history of each country as well as their recent political statements and actions. Then came the visits to each country. There I first tapped a US source of information by visiting each embassy and asking for the Naval or Military attaché. To this person I described my task and asked what they could tell me on a non-classified basis about the countries' view of its own military. Typically this opened the door to a fund of knowledge that the person was pleased to share on what would be a relief from continuing paperwork.

A typical example was in London where the Naval attache said, "They have four all-singing-all-dancing aircraft carriers." I looked puzzled and he explained, "It's a theatrical term meaning the cast is capable of any action required by the stage director. In the Brit Navy, they have fighter and attack aircraft, helicopters and marines. But, you see they don't have a need for any of them. They are there to project power over a British Empire that no longer exists." I began to get the picture and said, "presumably if they are projecting power, they will want up-to-date equipment?"

"True, but they are finding that to be expensive. The new Labour government is likely to cut back a bit. However, you might wish to go down to the manufacturer at the Isle of Wight. Devilishly good aircraft search radar." Later I did, It was. They were using GEs ceramic tubes. In the US we didn't know about this, our British Rep didn't think it was worth poking into. He would rather have lunch with the managing director. I began to see how business was done in the U.K.

\* \* \*

In Germany a totally different picture emerged. Here the army was king and the Bundeswehr, which I once mistakenly referred to as the Wehrmacht only to be told, "ist nicht Wehrmacht, ist Bundeswehr". I carefully avoided saying, "you could have fooled me". They were wearing the same field-gray uniforms and the same black short field boots.

However, their approach was totally modern and in some ways made US equipment look ancient. Their view of infantry communications was that it should be capable of direct open transmission from company level to corps level both ways. The US viewed this as open invitation to complete blocking of the radio band with everyone talking at once. The Germans depended upon discipline and training to make it work. What they wanted was up-to-date information on action at the cutting edge. As a result each company had a 125 Watt VHF transmitter – receiver with a short 1 meter antenna that the neighbors couldn't see. The US approach was a 30 foot tower at division level which could be found in the dark and required an hour to set up. We discovered in Iraq the problems of our approach.

\* \* \*

The practice in Sweden differed the greatest from that of the US. I repeatedly misjudged the tonnage of the Swedish Navy ships by a factor of at least 1/3. The reasons lay with the mission and equipment. They generally depended on very accurate fire control from interpretation of the enemies signals, not from their own emissions. Thus, there were many more antennas aboard than would commonly be the case as there were both outbound detectors and inbound detectors. Also the Swedes depended on high speed maneuver among the islands of the archepelago which required smaller more maneuverable ships.

Their avoidance of radar emissions came from their own use of the enemies emissions for fire control. A retired naval officer told me they could get fire-control data to about 10 meters accuracy if two Swedish ships intercepted an enemies radar on just one sweep. As a result, their own radar officers were limited to one 90 degree sweep every 15 minutes to prevent detection by the enemy. They need not have been so careful, the Russians were later found to be nowhere near the Swedish fire-control capability.

In contrast to the German army communication equipment, the Swedish army radios were from WWII. I questioned why and received a question in response. "How long would it take a front line Russian aircraft to overfly the inhabited portion of the Swedish coast?" I quickly did the math and said, "I make it 1 ½ to 2 minutes." My face turned red as I realized how stupid my initial question must have seemed to him. Blushing, I said," you're telling me they are to die in place so they have no need to maneuver or communicate?"

"It was not I who told you that. Now, let's change the subject."

\* \* \*

France presented a different problem. They were so enamored of their "Force de Frap" that they saw no other military need. In addition, the producers of military hardware were under some control by government ownership of their assets via the Banc de France. Thus it became difficult to separate rational planing from politics. I finally gave up.

On leaving France I returned to London, meeting a fellow GE employee who had a problem. He had a contract with a consortium of the governments of Iraq, Iran, Jordan and Egypt. The idea was to develop a plan for production of television parts and sets in the Middle East. He just returned from a visit to the four countries where each of them offered a bribe for favoritism in the outcome of the study. It did not take long to figure a response to this, "Andy, I think we should tell them that our load is such that we cannot undertake the job at this time and return their contract money." This seemed reasonable we had tea and sandwiches in the hotel lobby and pondered the future of television production in the Middle East.

* * *

Shari spent the summer in France. She had decided to major in French and arranged to live for a month or so in the Loire valley and the Brittany coast. A good choice representing the wide differentials in French culture at these locations. She had prepared me for my brief stay in France by tutoring a travelers version of French. This left me with very little vocabulary, but due to her work, a passable accent. This repeatedly brought a rapid-fire response when I asked a question in French. I would walk away and repeat the question to another person after a polite "merci" to the first one. Eventually I got a simple answer and silently thanked my daughter Chris at 13 became the "Pebble Pup" to my "Rock Hound". We studied the geological formations of upstate New York and played a game in which she named and described the geology she saw out the window as we rode in the car up to the boat on Lake George. I bought her a wet suit and made a weight belt for her featuring my own invention of a quick-release buckle It had a "do I really want to do this?" position in the release sequence. She and I snorkeled and Collie painted while Shari was in France for the summer. We were becoming a diversified international family.

# Viet Nam War, Selma March, Northeast Blackout

The year 1965 saw a massive acceleration of the Viet Nam War. In the early months, 3500 Marines were sent to Nam and soon after 4000 troops of the 101st airborne. Before year end, Johnson announced that he was increasing the U.S. military in Nam from 75,000 to 125,000 and the draft from 17,000 to 35,000. Previously the Pentagon had advised him that an increase to 400,000 troops would be necessary. The first march by the Students for a Democratic Society (SDS) took place in New York, protesting the draft.

Several Civil Rights marches in and near Selma, Alabama were led by Martin Luther King. Marchers and transporters were injured or killed by white supremacists and Klansmen. The Watts riots occurred in Los Angeles with great destruction of property and loss of several lives.

War broke out between India and Pakistan. Rhodesia lapsed into internal conflict. War was general in the continent of Africa. It seemed the whole world had gone mad.

The Early Bird satellite was launched becoming the first commercial communications relay station in space. The satellite Gemini-5 was launched with the first fuel-Cell power source in space. The supply was Built by GE. I would later be tasked with designing a control system to adapt it to electric automobiles.

The great Northeast Blackout occurred while I was leaving work. The darkness made the shutdown of power evident. I turned on the car radio and could not find a local station. The only thing I could hear was WLW in Cinncinatti, Ohio. My first thought was that "the balloon has gone up" and we are under nuclear attack. A quick tune across the radio band brought relief as there was absolute quiet, not the noisy frying background hiss that would accompany a nuclear attack. Breathing a sigh, I started the car and drove home to find all of the northeast U.S. and part of Canada disconnected from their electrical power sources, a state that would not be remedied for 13 days.

* * *

I was asked to serve on a committee to study the state of development of integrated circuits or ICs (not yet called chips) and recommend whether GE should attempt to make a business of this new development. The committee was well staffed with top people from The Knolls Research Lab, The General Engineering Lab and of course the Electronic Components Division and users of ICs. Competitors at that time included Fairchild Semiconductor, Texas Instruments and GEs' universal competitor RCA.

To those on the inside of this development the sky was not the limit, it was only a way station on the path to a gigantic market. Thus the consensus on potential market was "beyond belief". In fact the market later proved to be larger than any of us could imagine, with ICs used in radio, television, computers, cell phones, military equipment and countless types of appliances by the 2000s. We chickened out with a guess of "over $2 billion".. We were short by a factor of several hundred.

Nevertheless, we did forecast a market in GE products of radio, TV, computers, jet engine controls and military hardware. We also pointed out that GE had an initial jump on the technology wagon with work on a new type of IC called metal-oxide-semiconductor (MOS). Today, MOS is the only type of IC in production, but then it was just a hope on the horizon. RCA was the nearest technical competitor on MOS, but no devices were in production. The committee recommendation was a unanimous "go for broke NOW"

The committee was astounded to learn that GE top management after studying the report felt that there was plenty of time and we could always buy our way in if we so desired. My estimate was that Texas Instruments was spending over $1 million a year on development with no intention of letting anyone buy in. We all took this decision with a sour taste in our mouths. The only consoling thought was "maybe next year they will see the light as MOS progresses in development.

To make a long story short, three years later I was again asked to serve on the same committee for the FOURTH TIME. My letter of refusal stated that it was now too late to enter or buy into a market led by RCA, Fairchild and Texas Instruments. In any event, why should one expect any decision different from the three made before against the unanimous recommendation of the committee. That would be shortly before I left GE in anguish over its' top management's lack of foresight.

* * *

GEs Nickel-Cadmium Battery operation transferred to the Electronic Components Division and my boss, immediately dreamed up a way for us to serve our new associate. I was assigned to design product models using nickel-cadmium batteries, which were a neat product that could be recharged several hundred times and had a very high energy density. They were until recently the energy source for laptop computers.

However, Gus wanted very mundane products, flashlights and cigarette lighters. I felt insulted. A top engineer in very advanced product areas and he wanted me to design flashlights! After a little thought and a shot of scotch, I settled down and made some sketches – a camping lantern, a hand-held flashlight with offset head and a new idea – a novel mower consisting of an electric motor driving a shaft with a stainless steel wire attached at a right angle. The device would have a plastic handle on a rod long enough to permit a person to walk upright and clip grass at foot level. If you are thinking "weed whacker", that's exactly the idea.

A model of the weed cutter was built using a small surplus electric motor and small nickel-cadmium batteries. It worked very well. My boss showed it to GEs' small appliance division who immediately decided that it was "too dangerous for home use". There went GEs' chance for a patent on the weed whacker and I took on the less exciting flashlight area. designing and building three flashlight models. One was a camping lantern, fluorescent about 7" wide by 4" tall by 3" deep. It had a polished aluminum reflector, clear plastic grill and black aluminum outer case. Estimated selling price was $24.95 based on a manufacturers cost estimate. Small Appliance Division proclaimed "No one will pay $25. for a flashlight" Within two years a lot of people were paying up to $29. for camping lanterns. Ah well. Collie was absolutely taken with this lantern. We used it happily on the boat for several years.

The second flashlight aimed at utility workers who had to repair pole-top equipment at night. It had a light bulb with its own built-in reflector (standard GE product). The lamp was mounted on a tilting fixture supported by a small battery box about 5" x 7" by 2" that formed a base that could sit on the ground or a truck hood. The lamp cast a beam with a rectangular cross section that would illuminate a cross-arm from ground level, leaving the workman's hands free. Small Appliance didn't think there was a large enough market. I gave the model to my uncle, an avid fisherman he found it very useful on his boat for illuminating the masthead or a dock. Ah well.

The third flashlight was a tiny unit in a plastic case shaped to fit the hand with an angled lamp housing that pointed at the ground about four feet in front of someone holding it. This aimed at hikers, campers and night walkers of any stripe. Collie loved this one and used it for several years. I had given up showing product models to Small Appliance and hoped to go on to other things.

* * *

This was the year we bought the boat "Seacat II" and donated our old boat Seacat I to the Boy Scouts of America for use by their Seascouts. The owner had kept Seacat II in a dockyard at New Rochelle, NY under the name "Honeychile". The boat was an odd one, it had registration as a United States Vessel and so its registry numbers were burned into the steel forward bulkhead with a welding torch. The entire hull was steel and came from a model made by a well known naval architect, Crocker. He did a contract for the Navy to try out ideas for speeding up small launches. His ideas were successful. At 32 feet length and steel hull, Seacat II was not light, but could rise up onto a planning attitude and do about 18 mph. Collie fell in love with the light yellow interior and the gleaming stainless steel rubbing rails. The girls saw it as a "guy magnet" and for me it was the ultimate diving platform.

We cruised on the Mohawk River and then up the Hudson to Lake Champlain where we docked it for the summer and enjoyed that wonderful waterway. Shari was my first mate in bringing the boat back to Schenectady for winter storage. She cooked the meals and we went out on the town at an overnight docking stop – just two sailors on liberty.

We survived the Northeast Blackout better than most, experienced and equipped for outdoor living plus having two fireplaces and a good store of firewood. The cats were puzzled when the heating lamp didn't light in the packing crate where they lived in the garage. We did take them in one at a time to let them warm up and know the world hadn't ended. We were becoming a resourceful and self-confident family.

# CONTRASTS AND THE AUTOMATION
# OF CLOTHES WASHING

The year 1966 saw marked contrasts in several fields.. The Supreme Court made the "Miranda" decision that a person arrested must be read their rights and Congress passed the Freedom of Information Act requiring government agencies to furnish copies of unclassified documents upon written request. It seemed personal rights were on the path up. In contrast Mao Zedong initiated the Cultural Revolution in China, purging and reorganizing the communist party of intellectuals and professional people.

On the European scene, France resigned from NATO and later signed a contract with Russia to develop nuclear energy. I recalled the self-centered stance of the French I experienced in the survey of non-NATO military electronic equipment. NATO moved its headquarters from Paris to Brussels.

Charles Whitman stood on the balcony atop the tower at the campus of the University of Texas at Austin, killed 13 people and wounded 31 with a 30-06 hunting rifle before being killed himself. Many times I had stood on that same balcony and admired the campus of U.T. below. I did not know that my high school classmate, Bob Pape, a doctor in charge of the emergency room at an Austin hospital, was down at street level treating the wounded and exposing himself to sniping.

On the entertainment scene, the Beatles recorded "Sargent Pepper", John Lennon met Yoko Uno and Walt Disney died. The number of U.S troops in Viet Nam exceeded 200,000 and the bombing of Hanoi began.

* * *

Following our fiasco with GE's Small Appliance Division my boss made a contact with Major Appliance Division for what looked to be an excellent opportunity. I got the task to produce a model of an automated clothes washing machine controlled by results rather than a fixed time schedule. This was a welcome step up from designing flashlights!

I went to Louisville, KY where the division was headquartered to meet the washing machine people. Apparently they liked the idea as there were three people from engineering and one from marketing at our meeting. The lead engineer explained the idea of automating the washer based on results and then nodded to me. My first statement was that we thought the total time for a load could be shortened if the cycles were switched on and off based on results rather than a fixed time schedule. The leader turned to the end of the table and asked, "What would Mrs. Jones think of that?" The reply was that Mrs. Jones would love it as she thought the cycle took too long as it was. This puzzled me. I'd done my homework and memorized the organization chart for Major Appliance Division and there was no Mr. Jones or Mrs. Jones there.

Mrs. Jones was a puzzle, but not a show-stopper, so I continued. "We could also provide a control of speed on the rotor during the wash portion of the cycle." This produced the same question to the same man, "What would Mrs. Jones think of that?"    "Mrs Jones in the U.S couldn't care less, but Mrs. Jones in Italy would love it. She could go from *andante* to *pronto con fuerzo* in the turn of a knob". Now I was thoroughly confused, there were two Mrs. Jones and one was in Italy and spoke Italian.

The leader caught my puzzled look and explained, "We in engineering won't touch anything that has not been shown by market research to be something that the typical housewife really wants. The fellow at the end of the table is the curator of all our market research. It's combined into a customer model that we call 'Mrs. Jones".

I had to hand it to them for their discipline and the unification of market research, two principles experience had taught me to respect.. Their position in the major appliance field spoke volumes, its' basis now visible. I left Louisville with a warm feeling. The tasks were to develop a variable-speed rotor drive and controls to sense the point of diminishing returns on dirt removal in the wash cycle and water removal in the spin cycle. This was real engineering!

* * *

It's one thing to have a task and quite another to have a concept for accomplishing it. The variable speed rotor drive had already been invented so this was a question of how to control costs. I gave this task to my associate, George Wolf, newly added to our team, and took on the other two myself.

In a conversation with our marketing manager, Harold, I got the idea for the sensor of dirt removal. He was a former U.S. Navy pilot and told of landing on a strip close to a surf which created a mist of salt spray over the runway. He said, "When I turned crosswind for the final approach, I could see the runway just fine, maybe a little misty with salt spray. The sun was at my back. When I turned into final the sun was off my left side and the runway just disappeared!" He took a wave off and on the second try saw the runway slowly disappear in a glare of sunlight as he turned, but he had enough of a lineup to risk going lower and as he got closer to the ground the glare from the sun diminished and he made a good landing. He stated, "That glare of light is the 'Tyndal Effect' where sunlight reflects most strongly from suspended particles at right angles to the light."

Maybe this key could lead to a good sensor of dirt removal. I built a block which water could flow through. It had two light sensors and a light source. One sensor measured the light going through the water and the second measured the light reflected at right angles. By taking the ratio of the right angle light to the straight through light, this should give a direct measure of the suspended particles. The measure was independent of the color of the water or the starting amount of dirt. It worked like a charm and produced a very accurate measure of the suspended dirt independent of other factors. With the sensor problem licked, I passed on to George the design of the circuit to compare each measure to the one before and shut down when the difference was insignificant.

Now the remaining task was to conceive a sensor to measure water removal during the spin cycle. One thing that could be measured was the size of the water globules coming off the outside wall of the tub. These would be large droplets at the start of the cycle and go to a fine mist toward the point of diminishing returns. What I needed was a recording of the signal from these different sized droplets hitting a sensor that would be between the inner spinning tub and the outer fixed tub. Then I could figure a circuit to do the control job of shutting off when the droplets got to the mist stage.

I had all the necessary material at home to make this recording. Out in the front yard, the setup included the waterproof microphone from a Navy Sonobouy used to track submarines, a tape recorder on the driveway and a hose nozzle that was adjustable from coarse to fine. With this setup I started the nozzle at coarse and slowly changed it over a couple minutes until it was down to a fine mist falling on the microphone. When I went over to turn off the recorder my neighbor and family physician, Bill Brown, was standing there. "Art, what in hell are you doing? I've watched this from my front window and I just had to come over and find out." I explained the whole thing to Bill, who simply shook his head and said, "you engineers work in strange ways.".

When the signal from the tape recording was viewed on an oscilloscope down at the lab, the needed circuitry of the control became evident and its' design was no big deal. When tried on the washing machine, it worked beautifully.

George had finished the design of the variable-speed rotor and the point-of-diminishing-returns-circuit so we now had Fred integrate these into the washing machine and found that indeed, we had reduced the cycle time without sacrificing the quality of the operation. The machine was shipped back to Louisville for evaluation. The engineers were pleased, but I have not seen any of these features on a production washer.

\* \* \*

Late in the year my boss, noting that GE made the fuel-cell power supply for NASAs' Apollo space vehicle, decided that I should design a control to permit its use on commercial vehicles to charge GE nickel-cadmium batteries. This would create an electric car running on compressed hydrogen and oxygen. I was not in love with that idea because of the safety issues of compressed oxygen and hydrogen in a system maintained by garage mechanics and filling station workers. However, I was willing to try to build in the necessary safety guards. Then he went one step further and demanded that the design be finished in the next three weeks. I had an approved vacation time for this period so that the family could spend it on our boat on Lake George enjoying the marvelous fall colors of the maple trees and the clear blue water. That made no difference to Gus, who said the deadline stood. I replied that I would do the design on a picnic table on an island in the middle of Lake George. He said nothing. I never found out what the hurry was.

I did the design on a picnic table and incorporated a compressed cylinder of Argon which acted as a purge of the gaseous hydrogen and oxygen if there was a fire or mis-connection in the system. To me a fire seemed quite possible as grease in the oxygen lines would lead quickly to combustion. We could trust NASAs licensed aircraft mechanics, but garage mechanics aren't that careful about oil and grease.

After reviewing the design, my boss called me in and lectured me about being afraid of oxygen. I readily admitted to that and went a step further, "I'm also afraid of compressed hydrogen. I was raised in the oilfields and I've seen the results of a hydrogen gas explosion. That and the oxygen are why I put in the Argon purge system." He simply snorted at that and our meeting was over.

A few weeks later Gus Grissom and another astronaut were burned to death in a Mercury spacecraft capsule on the ground. It came out that the stupid design had used full pressure oxygen while still on the ground. A break in the capsule wiring had initiated the fire in a pure oxygen atmosphere. I heard no more about being afraid of oxygen. I also heard no more about the fuel-cell control, but the electric automobile was definitely in the future.

* * *

The family was growing up. Shari was now a junior in high school and Chris was a freshman. Both had boy friends, Chris's, Dave, became my diving buddy. We made a good team and were members of the Schenectady Aquaddicts, a scuba diving club that owned its own air compressor and promoted under-water hockey as well as dives in the numerous lakes of up-state New York.

The entire family and Dave went on a club dive to York Beach, Maine taking our Siamese cat Mu Ying with us. She always accompanied us to the boat and this was just a driving trip further away. Dave and I dove in water that was close to 32 degrees as there had been an offshore wind all night, blowing the warm surface water out to sea and bringing the cold bottom water up to shore. It was a splendid dive as tiny shrimp filled the water. They were transparent and only a half inch long, nearly invisible in the clear ice water. I caught a lobster which we broiled and ate that night with Mu Ying getting the little lobster feet. She indicated she would go on that diet when we got home.

Shari's boyfriend, Steven, asked her to the senior prom. He was a grade ahead of her at high school. They were a lovely pair in tux and evening dress. Collie and I beamed. She was now painting steadily in her downstairs studio and doing excellent work. She studied for a week under John Pike at Woodstock, NY where she produced her greatest painting of pine trees in snow. That painting now hangs over the fireplace in my house on Oceanaire Drive. As a family, we were beginning to find our own personal ways.

# A Year Of Conflict
# Throughout The World

The year 1967 proved to be one of conflict in many spheres. The six-day war was fought between Israel and its' Arab neighbors when Egyptian and Syrian forces were found massed to invade. Israel demolished Egyptian ground and air forces and Syrian air forces, occupying the West Bank, Golan Heights, Sinai Peninsula and Gaza strip. An Egyptian surface-air missile sank the Israel destroyer Eilat in minutes.

China and Russia massed forces at their common border and China tested its' first hydrogen bomb. There was extensive warfare in Congo and Nigeria invaded Biafra.

The Viet Nam War saw heavy marine actions in the Mekong Delta and north of Saigon. President Johnson stated, "We are making progress". Two months later the Tet Offensive by North Viet Nam drove the U.S. back to the edge of Saigon. Defense secretary McNamara resigned in disagreement with Johnson. The Peoples Republic of China started giving military aid to North Viet Nam and shot down U.S. aircraft violating PRC air space. The crews were killed or interned.

Race riots started in Detroit with 72 dead, 342 wounded and 1400 building destroyed. The riots spread to Milwaukee, shutting down the city for 10 days and later spread to Washington, DC.

The European Economic Community, EEC was formed with the U. K and Ireland applying to enter. De Gaulle vetoed their applications.

In space it was a terrible year with U.S. astronauts Grissom, White and Chaffee burned to death on the ground and Russian cosmonaut Vladimir Komarov died when the re-entry parachute of Soyez 2 failed to open at re-entry.

To me it seemed that the world had gone mad. The Eilat sinking opened a new page in naval warfare and the six-day war completely unsettled the mid-east. I thought the final curtain was going up when roused from deep thought on a flight from Washington, DC to Schenectady. Passing over New Jersey I saw a huge flame rise through the cloud layer below like a yellow sword. I read the next day that a natural gas pipe-line explosion had sent a plume of fire several hundred feet into the air. Thank God it was only natural gas.

On the plus side, Thurgood Marshall became the first African-American to join the U.S. Supreme Court. The U.S. X-15 aircraft set a speed record of 6.7 Mach. The first ATM machine was installed at Barclays Bank in Enfield England.

\* \* \*

My boss, having bombed out on his idea converting the Apollo fuel cell to power an electric automobile was still thinking of saving petroleum in the face of the Middle East conflicts. I was tasked with demonstrating a small electric automobile using a golf cart and GE nickel-cadmium batteries. The golf cart was delivered to my lab and Fred and I set to work adapting it. We built a battery holder to house the NiCads in place of the conventional lead-acid batteries. The cart was licensed to drive on New York roads so that we could test it.

I was unhappy with the accelerator pedal on the golf cart. It was essentially an "all or nothing" control appropriate to a golf course, but not suited to town driving. Fred and I tore into it and I made a new accelerator profile that permitted slow easy starts and low-speed maneuvering. There was an unused second-floor area next to our lab which would serve well for test driving of the new vehicle. We built a charger and parked the cart on the second floor with the front bumper against a brick pillar of the building. One morning Fred unplugged the charger, stepped into the seat and without thinking floor-boarded the accelerator with the switch in the "forward" position. The NiCads furnished much greater torque at low speed than the original batteries. Fred discovered this when the brick pillar refused to move and the rear tires tore out tiles from the floor and shot them across the room. He was embarrassed, but in a way I was elated and anxious to try the vehicle on the street.

When we were ready to drive in town, I already had 32 miles of driving experience executing figures of eight at various speeds on the blank second floor. I have yet to be challenged for my claim of longest driving record on a second floor. When we finally took the cart out for a test, it was all worth while. People found it exciting to watch the smooth, soundless, blistering acceleration from a stop. One pedestrian shouted from the sidewalk, "My God, what is that? Where do I get one?" It was real fun to drive a midget sports vehicle that could do 0 – 30 in 3 seconds!

Sporty as it was, I thought we needed one additional thing – a way to fast-charge the NiCads. Say maybe 30 minutes instead of the standard 8 hours. To do this we needed a measure of the charge state of the cells that are connected in series to make up the battery. They would not all be the same as over time, some would self-discharge more than others. The problem was that if we over-charged any one cell at the 30-minute charging rate we risked an explosion and at the very least, ruined it chemically. Then, came the flash of light. If we could arrange one cell, of the total of 40 cells to definitely have less discharge than the rest, then we could charge the whole battery until the test cells' voltage jumped up at the full-charge state. At that time, we could go to an 8-hour charge rate to finish the battery or use it as is with maybe 90 – 95% charge for the whole collection of cells.

Then came the invention. If the cart was wired so that the motor ran off of all cells and the auxiliaries (lights, radio, instruments) ran off of all but one cell, then that one cell would always be the one most charged. By monitoring it, we would know when to stop that huge current of the 30-minute rate and not overcharge any of the cells.

This arrangement was not hard to construct and within days, we were ready to try the idea with the new high-rate charger that we had built. Its' current was so high that we had to make a new connector for the vehicle to handle the current and be safely usable by a tired moron. I am pleased to see that the connectors for todays' electric cars closely resemble that pattern.

With permission from the Mohawk Golf Club (my boss was a member) we arranged the experiment. The high-rate charger was installed in their cart shed. Fred and I would drive at high speed around the course and then recharge for 30 minutes and repeat the drive. The Mohawk course was up and down hilly and exciting to drive at 30 – 35 mph, but the real excitement came at the end of the day. We had completed 108 "holes" or 6 trips around the course which normally required an 8-12 hour recharge after each 18 hole round. We had done it with five 30-minute recharges and looked like we could continue all night and tomorrow if necessary. The cells of the battery were not hot, but Fred and I were shot. We called it a day.

We had a test bed vehicle and a new fast-charge scheme and it worked! The next week I received a teletype from GE the battery department warning us not to ever charge their cells at the 30-minute rate. I replied that their teletype was a week late. A year later, after I had left GE, I received a letter from GEs' attorney asking if I would agree to a contract to review the patent application for a fast-charge scheme usable on Nickel-Cadmium batteries. I gave them a fair rate and did the job. It was my first patent.

* * *

Shari graduated from Niskayuna High School located in the town where she was born even though she lived in three other towns between those two key events. She and I made trips and had discussions as to where she would enter college. She preferred NYU in New York City and I leaned toward a smaller school in Vermont, so of course she went to NYU. The whole family, including the Siamese Mu Ying, drove with her to the dorm in downtown Manhattan. Mu Ying, who had starred in a high school play that year, was oohed and aahed over by Sharis' new room mates then all of us but Shari returned to Schenectady.

* * *

Chris and her boyfriend David continued their courtship with her as a sophomore at Niskayuna High. and David in High School across the river. We all spent the weekends on the boat at Lake George with David and I diving, Shari and Chris fishing and flirting. David and I caught and filleted yellow perch for

Mu Yings' breakfast. She considered this a great treat and waited patiently until they were filleted and served, the freshest breakfast in the whole state. However, she was no wimp. One night as we sat at the campfire ashore, a raccoon discovered a loaf of bread we left on the picnic table and tried to steal it Mu Ying made a lunge for him. He put the loaf under one arm and tried to run for the woods. Mu Ying was right behind him until the end of her anchor line that was tied to a large rock. The raccoon was so afraid that it dropped the loaf and disappeared.

Collie sketched constantly at the Lake when she was not cooking dinner. The black and white sketches contained color notations and filled several notebooks. Sometimes it was years before the sketches turned up in a painting, sometimes it was only the next week.

With the girls going their own ways, Collie and I had a standing Friday night dinner date at a local restaurant. Our favorite waitress confided in us once that we really seemed to have "the make" on for each other. This was reasonable as I didn't wear a wedding ring owing to my work with high-current electrical equipment. When she learned that we had been married for 21 years, we got a big smile and an extra serving now and then. The family was making headway on their independent personal paths.

\* \* \*

# A Year Of Massive Change

The year 1968 saw abrupt changes in both domestic and international affairs. It became a year of significant change for both the United States and the Dickerson family. In January the North Korean Navy captured the USS Pueblo in international waters and towed it into port in North Korea where it and its' crew were held for trial. I was furious at the ineptitude of Navy command's rules of engagement that would not permit US Navy aircraft to attack the small North Korean ship while it towed the Pueblo into port. I was appalled at the Captain of the Pueblo who surrendered and allowed boarding, "because I feared my men would be wounded". He could have put the crew below the waterline and gone to flank speed which would have prevented boarding. What had the Navy come to? The nuclear submarine USS Scorpion sank at sea off the Azores with nuclear missiles aboard. The cause is not clear today.

In Viet Nam, the Tet offensive began. It led to Viet Cong attacking the U.S. Embassy in Saigon. Two months later the My Lai massacre took place when a U.S. Army unit is ordered to kill all civilians in a Viet Nam village. What had the Army come to?

In retrospect, my brothers' steadfast refusal in 1955 to build highway one into Saigon from North Viet Nam seemed prophetic. He had been black-balled from the industry he had served, but he was on the right side. What had U.S. Industry and government come to?

Martin Luther King was assassinated in Memphis, Tennessee. Riots broke out for days in American cities. Students at Columbia University in New York, protesting the Viet Nam War, took over and closed the University for several days. President Johnson signed the Civil Rights Act then announced he will not run for re-election. The Republican Convention in Chicago nominated Richard Nixon for president. Johnson also removed the United States from the Gold Standard which required U.S. debt to be backed by a reserve of gold at Fort Knox. Democratic presidential candidate Robert F. Kennedy is assassinated at the Ambassador Hotel in Los Angeles. "Quo Vadis America?"

President Johnson, citing progress at the Paris Peace talks; declared cessation of "all air, naval and artillery bombardment of North Viet Nam". It would be another 7 years before such progress brought American evacuation from Saigon by helicopter.

On the positive side, Rowan and Martins "Laugh In" debuted on TV and Yale University elected to admit women.

* * *

At work my beginning effort on an electric automobile powered by NiCad batteries blossomed into a GE electric car in which an acceleration and hill-climbing package would use NiCad batteries with the main power coming from conventional lead-acid batteries. This was a neat idea and I was tasked with designing and constructing the acceleration package which would permit the NiCads to be recharged rapidly from the lead acid batteries during normal operation. A new idea for switching automatically between battery types was tried and proved to be both cheap and effective. The car featured a body styled and built in Detroit which would look neat and modern on the road today. With the acceleration package, it did 0 to 60 mph in 6.5 seconds, all together a neat automobile.

One day, Bruce Laumeister, the promising young GE executive in charge of the project was asked to surrender the car keys to a man from GE headquarters. The car was driven away and never seen publicly again. It was, of course, simply coincidental that Edsel Ford was then on the board of directors of GE. I filled out the patent application papers for the NiCad recharge circuit, but it was never pursued.

\* \* \*

It was at this time that I learned something of the background in my GE career during the past eight years. The "brass ring" or immediate goal for anyone in a manager of engineering position was to become the General Manager of a profit center or department of GE. It was considered "de rigeur" to request the permission of the boss of an Engineering Manager before interviewing him or her for the General Manager spot. It turned out that my boss had received requests to interview me for that hallowed spot five times in the last five years. He had denied that permission five times.in a row and I had not learned of it until now. I had done good work for him and although the permission was his to grant or deny, five times in a row was entirely too much.

Fate works in strange ways. While mulling over this situation I received a phone call from a prior boss who had moved on to Hughes Aircrafts' Industrial Division. He said, "Art, there's a job here at Hughes that has your name on it. It's an exact fit to your experience and skills. Could you come out and interview for it?" He outlined the job and I had to agree, I would be a good candidate for it. It would be interesting work and best of all, I would be free of my boss. We agreed on a date and I applied for a vacation week "to go diving with a friend in California". Just so that I wouldn't be lying, I did pack a duffel bag with my diving gear and took it with me on the trip.

* * *

The interview at Hughes turned out very well. The job and I did fit well. The only problem was pay scale. I was demanding more than Hughes imagined that job to be worth. On the other hand, they had never hired anyone to do that work. I suggested we both needed a day to think that over and that I would go diving in Newport Beach so that I could truthfully say that I had dived in California. The following day, the pay issue was found to be OK and the application was filled. Being an honest sort, I called my boss to say that I was leaving GE to go with Hughes and was giving 30 days notice to complete any lab work and bring my patent notebook up to date.

When I returned, my key did not open the office door. A phone call from the finance manager set me straight. "Art, I've been asked to pack up all your belongings and transfer them to your house. The keys have been changed on your office and the lab. I'm frankly not sure he can do this, but you are off the payroll as of last week. I'm sorry to have to bring this to you." I thanked him for his honesty and friendliness, then hung up.

A going away party was arranged which my boss pointedly did not attend. For that I was thankful. After I received the going away gifts, I took off my solid gold GE cuff links and gave them to my Assistant Engineering Manager with the best hopes for his career. For the finance manager, I endorsed my dividend check on GE stock back to GE and gave it him so that the GE president could meet his goal of $8.00 earnings per share at least on a limited number of shares. It was a warm and friendly goodbye.

* * *

In retrospect, the logistics of selling a house in New York, buying a house in Los Angeles and moving a family of four across country seem too simple to believe. That is in part because the 1968 housing market was not in problems and in part because I was exuberant about a new career at a new company and happy to shuck out of a career that had become loathsome. In that latter point, I was not alone. several people left GE in 1968 in rebellion against policies that belied the older gentler GE. I recall the policy delivered orally so that it would not appear in print, "don't bother giving raises to people over 40, they won't quit and go elsewhere. Put you money on the younger folks you might loose to competition." I recall thinking, "You stupid ass – I'm over 40 myself." It marked the shift in GE management from the "doers" who built a profitable technical giant to the "undoers" who sold off any business that failed to meet their 7/22 criteria. This resulted in GE eventually selling virtually all of the company operations which I had participated in. I'm glad I was not around to see that directly.

* * *

We put the Schenectady house on the market and I went to locate a house in Los Angeles. This was a drill Collie & I had been through before. We could even transfer floor plans by phone long before Fax. In LA it took only 1 day to narrow down to the San Fernando Valley. Although I liked the beach areas up toward Malibu, they looked too expensive and I opted instead for buying as high as I could in the San FernandoValley using the 101 and 405 routes to get to work. In two more days I had located a nice place with swimming pool, virtually no lawn, a nice garden area and room for Collies studio. She OK'd the floor plan and I made an offer after we had an offer in Schenectady. It all went like clockwork. Before the week was up, I was back home and discovering that I could spend a few days on the boat in Lake George. The boat proved to be the only moving problem. It was a fine boat in good shape, but the middle of the summer is no time to sell a boat. It was arranged to haul and stow the boat, leaving it for sale with the yard owner. Collie and the girls were angered that I was also leaving the dinghy. In ten years they had learned to handle it like another arm and abandoning it proved my cruelty. But the point was that LA had only the Pacific Ocean and that was no place for an 8 foot dinghy. They saw the point, but with sad hearts.

\* \* \*

We sold off my car and kept only Collies' new "Golden Fox" station wagon, which was driven out to LA for us by a contract driver lady who was heading west. We flew to LA and holed up in a motel until our furniture was moved into the new home. It all fit and we were then Californians.

Shari elected not to continue college. Chris checked into a new High School, one of the best in the state. Collie sorted out her new studio and began painting and enjoying the swimming pool. We were delighted to find that we had a dichondra lawn that didn't need mowing and a native queen olive tree with huge green olives.

I checked in at Hughes and began to learn a new company style far different from GE. The first blow was that Hughes top management didn't understand money. This was a shock as my job was to evaluate purchases of new business entities. I consulted with the Chief Financial Officer, who was delighted to find a person who understood money. Now he had someone to talk to. We got along like old buddies while I tried to master a new culture. California proved to be a strange world.

* * *

# A Year Of Consolidations

It is strange how events in our family seemed to track the character of events on a world scale during the year 1969. The preceding year had been one of massive change and this year saw a breathing spell in both world and home affairs.

Richard Nixon became the U.S. President and Charles de Gaulle ceased to be the ruler of France. In Lybia an obscure Colonel Moammar Ghaddofi took over the country in a coup. At the time, none of these events seemed of vital import, but time would show that each event changed the political climate and track of its' country or region.

The Viet Nam War continued with the infantry battle of Hamburger Hill and the surfacing of the My Lai massacre. Nixon tried behind the scenes diplomacy with North Viet Nam while secretly bombing Cambodia. Chris's fiancée David was now a Marine grunt who boarded ship three times in the Pacific to invade Laos while Nixon loudly proclaimed that the war was strictly confined to Viet Nam and anyway, he was reducing troop strength in Nam. Chris suffered an emotional crisis in which her psychiatrist proved totally useless. With steady home care, she was able to continue in high school after a brief absence.

The space programs of both Russia and the U.S. showed the progress made since the ascendance of Sputnik 12 years earlier. The Soviets launched Soyuz 4 and 5, which linked in space and performed a crew transfer between the vehicles. The U.S. Apollo program rolled ahead doggedly with Apollo 10 successfully testing the complete moon landing mission and Apollo 11 actually landing the lunar module on the moons' surface while a worldwide audience of 500 million watched on TV.

The forces of China and the USSR battled intermittently at the Chinese border. The joke of the period was that the Soviet Premier was awakened by his assistant at 0200. The assistant said, "I have good news and bad news. Which do you wish to hear first?" Kruschov replied, "In Russia always the bad news first."

"The bad news is the Chinese have landed on the moon." Kruschov sighed deeply and asked, "The good news?" The assistant replied, "All of them."

* * *

The vice-president in charge of Hughes' Industrial Electronics Division slightly changed the nature of my tasks and asked that I visit and familiarize myself with the five profit centers reporting to him and then to suggest ways in which their operations might improve. This was tricky as he did not inform his managers that I was doing reconnaissance and reporting to him. Actually, that was not necessary as they were all very sharp and pretty well knew at the start why I was there. The surprising thing was their wide range of reactions to this ploy. In Torrance, at the Microwave Tube Department, I was greeted like an old friend and folded right into their inner circle. This was possibly because I had been associated with GEs' microwave tube operation which they respected as a competitor. More likely it was because the V.P. had previously been the manager of that department and already knew where all the skeletons were buried. I could not possibly add to his store of knowledge and was therefore safe.

At the Oceanside plant, the manager had been a previous direct competitor with me personally ten years before when he was at Sylvania. He viewed me as a fierce competitor and was uneasy with this new relationship. When that became evident, we had a close heart-to-heart talk in which we set the ground rules for our relationship. That conversation took about three hours, but set a solid basis for our dealings. He did his accounting on a totally different basis than any other Hughes department. Coming from GE, I could not understand why this was allowed, but went along with the local practice. Each of us held rigorously to the agreement. When he later became assistant V.P. of the division and therefore my direct boss, we got on well with strong mutual respect. His department was well run with an iron fist and was a credit to Hughes.

At Newport Beach there were two departments, the Semiconductor and the Connector operations. The connector department was so ineptly run as to be incredible. Once while sitting with the V.P. reviewing operations with the manager and financial officer of the Connector operation I committed what with the V.P. was a gross error. I found in the financial records in front of us a fraud that was beyond belief. My tongue flew loose and I said, "Jesus Christ you didn't -----." I won't describe the fraud, it was complicated, but not brilliant as was seen by being picked up on first sight. I learned that day that if I found a major management error, I was to tell the V.P. so that he could do the cursing. That was a lesson I did not forget.

The other Newport Beach department was in a field where I was familiar with GEs' competing work and so had to be careful not to disclose trade secrets with which I'd been entrusted at GE. That was handled in a straight-forward manner which was appreciated by the Hughes people.

The basic question presented by the Hughes V.P. was whether they should take a license from RCA on a technology being pursued by RCA, Hughes and GE. This was a field where the potential market seemed to me to be so huge that all else should be abandoned if necessary to pursue it. My recommendation was definitely for the RCA license, but more strongly that all Hughes available R&D funds should be put behind this technology. That technology would in a few years completely replace transistors as they were known in 1969. It is today the basis of all integrated circuits or "chips" whether they are in your iPad, automobile, household appliances or military weapons. Hughes was too timid and didn't take the RCA license, putting only a modest sum into R&D. I learned later that this was probably a correct decision for Hughes as they did not have the marketing guts to stand up to Texas Instruments and Intel who eventually overshadowed GE and RCA.

The fifth operation, located in Los Angeles, designed and built digital controls for machine tools. Hughes had started early in this field, building on its' skill in military controls. However, the top management of the operation was not mentally or physically up to pushing this promising product. Fortunately, the chief engineer was a very bright guy with good experience. My message here was that the redesign they were undertaking should carefully observe the technology coming up at Newport Beach, because I felt it would sweep everything else out the door on both technical and economic bases. We agreed that the machine organization should be such that the new technology could be put in place with a minimum redesign cost should it sweep the field. Fortunately this was done and when the great new sweep came, Hughes was able to adapt it readily. Unfortunately Hughes had to buy the product from Texas Instruments rather than its'own Newport Beach.

\* \* \*

In the family area, Chris graduated from high school nd achieved very high SAT scores on her college entrance exams. She and David were married when he returned from Viet Nam and she became a Marine Corps wife at Camp Le Jeune. Sherry entered the insurance business in the adjusting field and proved very effective in telephone conversations and negotiations. Her imagination served her well in seeing solutions where others saw only problems. Fortunately she could also see problems where the scale of a miscue might drive all solutions off the field. She once told me of a request to insure a shipment of $500 million in gold bullion flying across the Atlantic from Africa to South America in a single aircraft. We talked for two hours, laughing at all the ways we could steal the shipment or dump the shipment and collect the insurance. It was a clear example of the first principle of risk management – "don't go there". The company decided not to insure.

Collie continued painting and went to a painters' school in Oaxaca, Mexico. I bought a 17 foot fiberglass boat to go to the offshore islands for scuba diving. When you have a boat, you collect a lot of diver friends. I collected a 250 pound Turk as a diving buddy. He was one of the few who could out-swim me underwater. He was not trained in deep diving, but made a great spear-fishing buddy. Together we harvested a 35 pound halibut which provided a lot of frozen meals. The family was developing its' own paths in a new and different world.

\* \* \*

# A World In Conflict As We Become Californians

The major events of 1970 chiefly concerned space, the Viet Nam war, Africa and the middle-east. In April, during the Apollo 13 mission, an oxygen tank of the fuel cell power system exploded, causing an immediate return to earth with all but a few power systems shut down and the crews' lives in extreme danger. This was the same power system that my GE boss had me design an adaptation for electric autos and then roundly labored me about being afraid of oxygen when I incorporated an Argon purge system as a safety feature. Fortunately the crew made it home, but it was close. China launched its' first satellite, showing a growing technical capability in space and later performed a nuclear weapons test at Lop Nor. The Soviet Union landed the first roving vehicle on the moon from the Luna 17 spacecraft and also achieved the first landing on Venus with communication back to earth.

President Nixon ordered the invasion of Cambodia. Fortunately Chris's husband was back in the US by that time. A student demonstration at Kent State University against the Cambodia invasion went awry when National Guard troops under an inexperienced platoon leader fired into the students, killing 4 and wounding 9. I recall seeing the video of the firing ordered by a frightened Lieutenant and wondering where and why they got that quality of officer. In New York construction workers attacked 1,000 students protesting the Kent State shooting and in Washington, D.C., 100,000 people protested the Viet Nam War. In the second day of war protests at Jackson State University in Mississippi, state police fired into demonstrators killing 2 and wounding 12. What had this country become? The US Senate repealed the Gulf of Tonkin Resolution and US troops were removed from Cambodia. President Nixon initiated both EPA and OSHA operations. At least some things went right.

The Aswan Dam was completed in Egypt, but the Israelis fought Palestinians in Lebanon and the Popular Front for the Liberation of Palestine hi-jacked four flights to New York from Frankfort, Brussels and Zurich. Fighting broke out between Arab guerillas and Government forces in Jordan. Syrian forces crossed the border of Jordan. The congress gave President Nixon authority to sell arms to Israel. The US again sold arms to Pakistan. There seemed to be no reasonable actions in the middle east. I was both puzzled and angry that the U.S. might somehow become involved directly.

* * *

In Culver City, headquarters of Hughes Aircraft, I saw the first and only indication that Hughes was personally involved in the company. My job in the Industrial Products Division required understanding of the thinking and action patterns of Hughes top management so that the Division would not be blind-sided at the corporate level in any proposal we might make to buy or start a new business. In the annual review of Research and Development proposals from all Divisions, I sat listening to a general Manager, Sam, propose further development on a moving map display for the instrument panels of commercial aircraft.. This was a neat idea, which would keep the pilot in touch with his geographic position and point up safety hazards like tall towers and power lines.

Pat Hyland was the CEO of Hughes at that time. He was the inventor of the "Bendix Compass" used on all US military aircraft in WWII and later head of Bendix. Pats' interest in aircraft navigation and safety clearly stood out in his earlier support for the moving map display project. Thus, it was surprising to hear him interrupt during the map presentation to say, "Sam, we're not going to do that." Sam misinterpreted, thinking a detail of the project was being canceled. He said, "OK Pat" and went on with the presentation only to be interrupted again by Highland, "Sam we're not doing this project." This time Sam got the message, gathered his notes and sat down. To myself I said, "So that's what it looks like when Howard Hughes runs his company!"

\* \* \*

The new business side of my job proved fascinating. One assignment was to look at a new computer product being offered to HAC. I visited the inventor and saw the product, a TV screen rotated 90 degrees so that it formed a portrait pattern instead of a landscape format. In front of the screen was an IBM Selectric typewriter. The inventor demonstrated by striking a key and a moment later the appropriate letter appeared on the TV screen. It was not instantaneous, as each letter was being drawn like script on the screen, but the form was clearly that of a font like "Times Roman". This proved fascinating (remember, this was 12 years before the IBM PC appeared on the market. The term word-processor was far in the future).

The inventor explained that each key code generated by the IBM keyboard was stored in a small computer device and given a specific location on the TV screen. The screen was scanned exactly as if it were a TV picture. However, at each letter location a signal was injected which wiggled the electron beam so that it drew the appropriate letter in full white illumination. If there was no letter, the screen remained dark. The neat thing was that a separate set of keys allowed any letter space to be located and then striking a different key on the keyboard allowed a replacement of the letter on the screen by the letter struck on the keyboard. The new letter also appeared at that location in the memory of the little computer device. Thus, editing could be readily performed. When the editing was complete, the stored script could be typed out on the electric typewriter. Incredible, my secretary would absolutely love this.

In the mind of the inventor, the market for this device would be law offices, where editing was frequent and proof reading absolutely necessary. He figured it could be made to sell for under $4000. I did a quick mental math and figured that if it saved 10% of a legal secretaries' time, it would save $1200/year and thus pay for itself in 3 years quite apart from the shorter time it would permit a document to be produced. This looked reasonable. The inventor reached his present status on venture capital funds and they had negotiated ownership of 30% of his patent to bring it this far. He thought the V. C. s were eating him alive and that Hughes might pay cash for the remaining rights that he held. I had to agree on the VCs voraciousness, but the question was what about Hughes?

I pondered this one. Clearly he was onto something of value in a part of the business world and if the cost could be brought down, a greater part of the business world and maybe even government offices. In short, the potential market was large. There was no question that Hughes had the technology to development this product and probably cut its production cost. However, the immediate need of the inventor aside from cash was marketing and more precisely, marketing to the business world. In that area Hughes had nothing to offer and was not interested in developing any such marketing force. If you were marketing weapons in Ryhad, Arabia, they could handle that with expertise, but lawyers' offices? No way.

I developed some trial numbers for the market and the profit and tacked on the inventors' price for entry so that there was a specific deal to discuss. Meeting with the V.P. of Industrial Products, I laid out the proposition and concluded that if he wanted, I'd be happy to start negotiations, but that personally I felt it was a bad fit because of the lack of marketing skills and my estimate that HAC top management would not want to develop that capability for one product. He tilted back his chair and gazed at the ceiling for a full two minutes, then pulled forward and said, "You're right, it's an interesting deal, but not for HAC. I don't even want to present it to Highland."

I conveyed this to the inventor with regrets and wished him well. I later learned that he had to fall back on the VCs and they wound up with 95% ownership of the worlds first word-processor rig. I was remotely angry at the greedy V.C.s who personally benefitted from new technology while virtually bankrupting the creator.

\* \* \*

Not everything was negative at Industrial Products. One fascinating and novel product combined the Division's machine tool control capability with its' high power lasers to form a computer-controlled laser cutting machine. The material that sparked this idea was the heavy wool used in mens' suits. At the outset, a problem arose. The energy of the laser made the initial cut faultlessly, but then the smoke and debris from the cut flew up in the air it began to absorb the laser light, limiting the cutting speed. After some thought, we tried a two-dimensional cutting bed that consisted of a steel structure like the bottom half of an egg-carton except that the compartments were only ¼" square with a hole in the bottom. A vacuum was applied to the underside of this bed with the laser above it. Thus, when the cutting began, the debris and smoke were sucked underneath and away from the laser path, permitting full power to be applied to the cloth. This worked like a charm and soon it was possible to cut 6 layers of cloth simultaneously at a computer-controlled speed of over a foot per second. All of the tracks necessary to cut pieces for a given sized suit jacket and pants were stored in the computer and six sets were cut at once. There was no marketing problem, as the first purchasers were the machine tool people that were already customers of Hughes.

* * *

Shari married Robert, a fellow Marine and friend of Chris' husband David. So now we had two Marine son-in-laws. Chris enrolled in college to major in marine science. She also became pregnant and I loaned her my blue Navy flight jacket to wear on boat trips out to Catalina. It fit her fine with the developing mound of her waist, but was badly oversized elsewhere. To her credit, she made the boat trips and avoided being seasick to the great consternation of her instructor. David enrolled in college to major in engineering. Collie continued painting although her attention was being drawn to a house up on the hillside below Topanga Canyon. We both enjoyed our swimming pool and the crab, fish and scallops from scuba diving. I learned to make Greek olives from the big ones on our tree in the garden. We had become Californians.

\* \* \*

# WE MOVE IN A YEAR OF MANY TRENDS

Early in the year 1971 Los Angeles experienced a 6.4 level earthquake located in the north San Fernando Valley at Sylmar. The quake found us with two houses in escrow, one that we had bought on the hillside at the Valley end of Topanga Canyon road. The other was the one we had sold to the builder of the new house in a trade arrangement. A conference with the builder reached the agreement that each of us would restore one house to its' condition before the quake and act as if it had never occurred. For us this was new overhead plumbing to replace a pipe fractured in the slab. For him it was repairs to plaster and complete certification of the slab and masonry walls. We moved in to the new house where Collie had a painting studio off the kitchen with a view of the San Fernando Valley.

\* \* \*

On the world scene many trends were evident. The first Intelsat was launched and initiated commercial satellite communication. The first microprocessor, fore-runner of to-days' personal computers and a multitude of residential controls, was Introduced by Intel as the Intel 4004. It was a 4-bit processor (16 words) as compared to to-days processors of 32 bits (4.3 billion words). The first e-mail was sent over the ARPA-Net, named after the Advanced Research Projects Agency, which funded the internet development as a means for scientists to communicate there experimental results. U.S. oil production peaked at 4.5 million barrels of oil per day.

The UN seated the Peoples Republic of China to replace China (Taiwan). The Indo-Pakistan War began. South Viet Nam, with U.S. aid, invaded Laos. In Washington, D.C. 500,000 people marched to protest the war. With our two Marine Corps son-in-laws at home, we were less personally concerned, but strongly opposed to the War. Nixon set 1972 as a target date to remove another 45,000 U.S. troops from Viet Nam. Polls showed that over 60% of U.S. citizens opposed the War. It continued.

The Pentagon Papers were published by the NY Times and the U.S. Supreme Court ruled that the publication was not a crime. Nixon took the U.S formally off the gold standard and imposed a 90 day fix on prices of commodities in the U.S. D.B. Cooper performed the only unsolved aircraft high-jacking in history when he leaped from an airliner with $200,000. in cash during a severe rain storm. .The voting age was lowered from 21 to 18, which automatically allowed Chris to vote, but there was no election.

* * *

For my career this was a year of monumental change. Shortly after we moved into the new house with Collies studio and the view of the Valley. My boss, who had set up the offer that moved me from GE, was fired by Hughes Aircraft. He had been in charge of the connector operation at Newport Beach and had very unwisely moved some capital equipment to a suppliers' location. This was Government supplied equipment and Hughes management may have been slow to understand money, but they were very quick to see any potential problem with government assets.

The immediate effect was for me to receive his company supplied car as a form of compensation. I had been on "Incentive Compensation" at GE which was a form of bonus based on GEs' operational profit. Hughes as a major supplier to the U.S. Government was restricted in the bonus area, but found other ways to compensate their executives. Special investment opportunities were set up independent of the company, but restricted to a list of Hughes management. I had already participated in one of these with the weird arrangement of signing the papers in the parking lot of a local Hotel. Something I would never have done in New York, but here I was assured by top Hughes management that it was a good deal and the man I was meeting was legitimate. So, in the parking lot I became a part owner of a new apartment complex that would be built near the ocean in L.A. with docks and boat access to the Pacific.

It was neat to have my secretary on her own initiative drive my car over to the Hughes garage to be washed, serviced and filled with gas. However, I missed my Mustang convertible and felt very conservative driving a black Buick sedan.

\* \* \*

There were further changes in the Newport Beach operation after my boss was fired. The boss of the semi-conductor products operation was removed for technical incompetence. I now believe that was crafted by his engineering Manager who felt that he would get the job. He failed to understand Hughes top management philosophy. They held the top technical job in a profit center as a key responsibility, but totally different from nominal manager of that operation. However, at the time I saw no connection between the removal of the boss and the engineering manager who I knew reasonably well.

My boss asked if I would be interested in the vacant job as manager of Semi-conductor products at Newport Beach. This presented a problem. On the one hand that was exactly the job that I was aiming for in GE when I worked there. Thus, I understood the business and its customers and competitors and felt that I was up to managing it and that would be both challenging and fun. On the other hand, Collie was taken with her new house and studio and we had a swimming pool installed, where we could watch the lights of the Valley while paddling around at night.. We both enjoyed the place. The semiconductor job would be a 1 ½ hour drive each way unless we moved to Newport Beach. Collie and I drove to look at houses in the vicinity of the new job. They were nice, but she was in love with her new place. So, if I took the job, I'd be driving at least 3 hours per day or I'd be taking a room in Newport and driving home for the weekends.

My boss arranged a meeting between the Engineering manager and I to talk privately about the operation and how we would wok together if I were to take the job. This did not go well. Now that I was a contender for the managers' job, I saw a completely different person in the Engineering Manager. He was as technically brilliant as I had known him before, but my visceral reactions were telling me that I could not trust him. This reaction was not minor, it was deep and in my view meant we could not work together.

The next day I met with my boss to tell him that I couldn't take the job in Newport Beach. He said that his conversation after the meeting disclosed that the Engineering Manager said, "We can't work together. Art's afraid of me." I replied that in a sense that was correct as I could not trust him and was afraid that we would simply not be able to work together.

My suspicion was prophetic. The man was later asked to sign an agreement which would be adverse to him. He returned the agreement with his signature the next day. It was later found that he had not signed the agreement as presented, but had used a scissors and a Xerox machine to remove key passages and then signed the mutilated document. He was fired when this was later discovered.

* * *

One of the Hughes activities which I had been tasked with observing for Industrial Products Division was a new product development at Hughes Research Labs in Malibu, CA. It comprised two technologies. One allowed the interruption of a direct electric current. This was becoming important because of progress in High Voltage Direct Current transmission of electric power. HVDC as it was known, permitted cheap and stable transmission of electricity over long distances. Alternating current transmission was limited to around 200 miles before the cost of stabilizing the system made it impractical The driving force was that new cheap sources of electric power were very remote from the urban locations where the electricity would be used.. An example of the economics involved was the HVDC receiving station at Sylmar, CA where the earthquake was centered. This station gets its energy from a generating station in Dalles, OR on the Columbia River 1150 miles away. AC transmission simply could not deliver that energy over that distance, the reasons are technically complex, but trust me on that. The dollar savings of the HVDC system that delivers electricity to Los Angeles was in 1971, $128,000. each hour or about 6 cents per kilowatt-hour. The utility was selling this power for around 8 cents per kilowatt-hour, so that saving was massive.

The problem was that there was no way to interrupt a DC current and so protecting and controlling such a system presented problems. The Malibu development had raised the interruption capability from 1.5 Amperes to around 1000 Amperes. There would be a viable product at about 3000 Amperes.

The second technical development also aimed to serve HVDC transmission. This was a replacement for the large and unreliable mercury-arc rectifiers that were at the heart of the HVDC systems. The two technologies were based on completely different areas of physics and so there were two separate technical teams pursuing the developments. A $1 million test facility had just been completed at Malibu to permit testing and validation of the products resulting from these technologies. There was a three-headed problem at Malibu: one, no one there understood making and running a business in technical products: two, the new facility presented safety problems at a completely new level. You could be killed 6 different ways there, all new to the Malibu facility: three, the two technical teams were in revolt against their manager.

My boss had a simple question, "Would you be willing to take over the management of the two technical teams and bring that work around to a set of products for the electric utility field?" The vice-president of Hughes Research knew me from my liason with his two technical groups. He was willing. I asked for a chance to consider it overnight and on the following day said, "Chris, I'll be delighted to do it." He then made a generous offer, "Art, you can stay on my staff while you do this if you want to. I've talked this over with George, the Malibu V.P. and he's agreeable either way. You can be part of his organization or mine."

I was surprised. To me there was only one way to do it. "Chris, if I go there, I must be totally in charge. The troops won't believe me or trust me unless I'm part of their organization. Further, the things that need to be done will require my total control. I have to be part of George's organization or it won't work."

Fortunately both Chris and George saw this and so I changed security ID from a "90-badger" (Industrial Products Division) to a "30-badger" (Hughes Research). I had an opportunity to use this shift at the introductory meeting with my new organization in the auditorium at Malibu. After my overview talk, I asked for questions, one of which was, "If we get these developments fully tested, what will we do then?" I gave that one two beats and then said, "What's this crap about 'if'? It's a question of 'when' we get these developments fully tested. The answer is then we'll market and sell them to the electric utilities." This show of command presence drew applause from all the technicians and engineers. I noticed that the senior scientists were sitting on their hands.

The next day I started on the safety manifesto and before the end of the week it was complete. Practice in the test facility was totally prescribed and the troops were for the first time exposed to the phrase, "Instant and irrevocable discharge from employment" as a result of breaking key rules. Some of the troops asked the personnel department, "can he do that?" They were assured, "In matters of life-and-death safety he certainly can."

* * *

We settled into our new house, only a 20 minute drive from my work at Malibu. Collie began to spend more time painting and I enjoyed several laps of swimming in the morning before breakfast. We got to know our neighbors and threw a party on the fourth of July to watch the fireworks in the Valley from our hillside perch.

Chris' son Travis was born and we occasionally baby sat him at our place for Chris and David, both of whom were now in college. The wild coyotes killed and devoured our black and white cat in the front yard, one of the problems of being so close to nature. I found their trail and the next night in the stillness before dawn I took my .30 caliber rifle and climbed the hill to station myself on their track. In the stillness I discovered while climbing that my right knee creaked loud enough to rule me out as a coyote stalker. I was now 45 and beginning to feel approaching age physically if not mentally. I unloaded the rifle and gave up night hunting for coyotes.

# A Year Of Progress And Setbacks

The year 1972 was a mixture of social and scientific progress interspersed with political setbacks. The discovery of DNA recombinant molecules opened the field of molecular medicine which has changed the field of medical practice substantially. The U.S. announced the start of the Space Shuttle program which supplied the International Space Station until its' closure in 2011. The HP-35, first hand-held scientific calculator, went on sale for $395. I was happy to buy one and benefit from its arithmetic power. The 15 millionth VW beetle made it the largest selling vehicle since the Ford model T and highlighted the penetration of German and Japanese automobiles into the U.S. market at the expense of the "Big Three" U. S. companies. Our Ford of the late 60's had enough design flaws to warrant this progress. Pioneer 10 became the first man-made spacecraft to leave the solar system in inter-spacial discovery. The Soviet Luna 10 un-manned spacecraft landed on the moon, retrieved soil samples and returned to earth, somewhat mollifying the Soviets over the U.S. moon landings, of which Apollo 17, the last, which also landed and returned in 1972. The first successful video game, Pong, went on sale. Seventy nations signed an agreement to outlaw biological weapons.

On the political scene things were not so bright. Pakistan, having surrendered to India in the 1971 war announced they would start a nuclear weapons program. Riots in Ireland and bombings in England marked the high point of the UK internal conflict. The Watergate break-ins occurred. Nixon and Haldeman were taped discussing how to use the FBI to harass the DNC. However, Nixon won the 1972 election in a landslide over George Mc Govern. The finale would not play out until 1973.

In Viet Nam, A spring offensive invaded the DMZ of South Viet Nam. The North Vietnamese walked out of the Paris peace talks and Nixon resumed bombing of Hanoi and Haiphong. Late in the year, Nixon withdrew all U.S. ground combat troops from Viet Nam.

* * *

In the research program at Malibu, it became evident that the two basic products, DC interrupter and a DC rectifier valve would not be large enough in sales to support the necessary personnel for development and marketing during the early years. Accordingly, two new markets were opened. The first was in support of the research efforts in the U.S., England and Germany on the development of nuclear fusion power generation. In these applications it was necessary to control large DC currents and the DC interrupter was a promising tool. The second market was the military, where the DC rectifier could be used as a modulator to control the pulses of very high power radars. Both of these markets were successfully entered. A research contract was obtained with the Naval research labs in Washington DC to develop switches for fusion generators.

In later years supply contracts would be signed for units in Germany and England. However, the first year saw an event which warmed my heart. The principal investigator for the Navy contract told me that the Navy was in town and wanted to have lunch with us to discuss the contract. This seemed unusual as the contract was not so big as to warrant an on-site visit. However, I told myself that whatever they wanted to do was ok as a meeting. The PI and I drive to a good local restaurant and he led me to one of their meeting halls. When the door opened, there was the entire membership of my operation standing and applauding. The PI said, "It's been exactly one year since you took over and we all wanted to thank you for that year. Sit down and have lunch on us." Suddenly all the effort and the hours of off-duty thinking and planning seemed totally worthwhile – I was in love with the whole crew.

* * *

Safety continued to be a prime concern for a facility where one could get killed in six different ways, electrocution, smoke inhalation, heavy metal poisoning, explosion, acid spray and radiation. I took to spending my lunch hour wandering the facilities and leaving notes to the facility operators wherever I found an OSHA violation. for example, "There is a cardboard box blocking the access to the disconnect switch on the north wall. Move it!" This had two effects, first it cleared the hazard, but second it planted the message that concern for safety came from the top and one might be inspected at any time – safety was a full-time concern. The week finally came when I encountered no OSHA violations for 5 days running. The message had been received.

Safety also involved techniques of operation. For example, in closing the main switch on our DC supply, the largest battery bank outside the Navy's submarine service, the technique was to grab the handle and then turn away so that the switch was behind you, then shove the switch closed suddenly. This paid off when the switch was closed against an accidental short circuit. The switch was destroyed and the operator lost a pair of pants the seat of which was sprayed with molten copper from the switch blades. We bought him a new pair of pants and awarded them with a handshake and commendation for following procedures. The message got through.

* * *

At year end the salaries of the entire operation were reviewed and I found what I considered a gross imbalance. The senior technicians, all of whom had at least a bachelors' degree in science and twenty years technical work experience, were paid less than a newly graduated Phd. This reflected the snobbishness of a management by all Phds over a period of several years. The prior management completely overlooked the position of the three senior techs as supervisors of the junior techs and in fact the backbones of day-to-day operations. They were viewed as "non-Phds" and therefore in a lesser class.

I had the final word on salaries although the verbal announcement to each employee would come from their respective senior scientist/section head. I held a discussion individually with each section head and explained that I wanted to up the rate for the senior techs significantly and proposed no raise for a few of their techs that I viewed as marginal. There was opposition to this, but finally agreement was achieved. The unexpected boost to the senior techs produced a distinct sense of pride throughout the tech fraternity. The senior scientists clearly saw that low performance would not be rewarded and began to agree with this approach.

Not everything was milk and honey in the operation. I discovered problems with the manager engineering who did not sufficiently consider safety in his design of facility arrangements. Also the manager marketing was overly ambitious and wanted a product line that he could supervise on his way to replacing me. He did not know that I always developed someone to replace me, but not prematurely. These matters would have to be settled in succeeding years. For the present, they were simply noted.

\* \* \*

Both daughters were married and living with their husbands. Collie and I were enjoying the house overlooking the San Fernando Valley all to ourselves. We had installed a swimming pool where I swam laps every morning and we both enjoyed soaking in the evening while viewing the lights of the valley. We made friends with our neighbors on each side and settled into being part of our new neighborhood.

Collie enjoyed her studio just off the kitchen, where she could paint with a view of the valley. I took up the hobby of wine making and made several bottles of champagne according to the French Methode. This proved to be fascinating as a process and enjoyable on the porch before dinner. We were settling into our new location.

\* \* \*

# The Year Watergate Unravels And Yom Kippur War Brings The 1973 Oil Emergency

The good news was that 1973 saw relations initiated between the Peoples Republic of China and the U.S. Roe –v- Wade was decided in the Supreme Court overturning state laws banning abortion.

For calibration of technology timing, a patent was issued for the ATM and the first handheld cell phone went on sale. Skylabs 1 – 3, the first U.S. space stations, were launched. Initial science experiments aboard were biological.

Watergate began to unwind with McCords admission of guilt in the break-in. He named Attorney General Mitchell as the lead boss. Ehrlichman and Haldeman, Nixon assistants resigned. An 18 minute gap in Nixons recording of White House conversations was found. The "Saturday Night Massacre" occurred when Nixon demanded the Watergate prosecutor be fired and the Attorney General and Assistant A.G. resigned rather than carry out the order. The third in line did not resign. The call for Nixon's impeachment began at year end. Voters began to wonder what they had done when they re-elected him the preceding November.

\* \* \*

The Yom Kippur War began in October. It was the 4th and largest Arab-Israeli war. Syrian and Egyptian forces attacked Israel in the Sinai Peninsula and the Golan Heights. The Syrian air-force was quickly destroyed and the Egyptian army isolated at the Suez Canal. The war ended six days after it began.

Arab oil-producing countries embargoed nations supporting Israel, initiating the 1973 energy crisis. OPEC doubled the price of crude oil. Long lines formed at U.S. filling stations and signs reading "out of gas" appeared at many locations. The president announced that federal policy would make the U.S. "oil independent". Four decades later each successive president has voiced that same message and no coherent U.S. energy policy had yet appeared.

\* \* \*

At the Hughes Research Labs work continued on the two fundamental high-Voltage DC devices and efforts were undertaken to add related products to broaden the dollar sales and thus support the staff necessary to the basic endeavor. This side effort was successful in part, with orders from England and Germany for high current DC interrupters to be used in nuclear fusion research.

A new idea arose from the people on the electronics staff. This was an electronic data recorder that would make a continous recording of events beginning 30 milliseconds before it was keyed on. This would permit an accurate record of any precursor conditions ahead of a major failure in high energy equipment. The concept was very simple. An electronic device kept a temporary digital record 30 milliseconds long. Data was continually fed in at one end and the output simply spilled over and ceased to exist if it was not used. Thus, the output was always 30 milliseconds behind real time. A tape recorder was connected to this delayed output. It could come up to speed in less than 30 milliseconds. It was keyed on when an outage occurred and of course it began to record events that occurred 30 milliseconds before the outage occurred.

The first market for this equipment was the same High Voltage DC power transmission systems that would use the HVDC rectifiers. Thus, we would be upping the $ sales to the same customers we would have to serve for our primary products. One unit was designed and built and then installed at the HVDC link that supplies Los Angeles from the generating station at The Dalles, Oregon on the Columbia River. The unit did its job. However, it eventually had a negative effect on the Hughes program as it attracted the attention of General Electric, the original builder of the Dalles plant, to the fact that Hughes was serious in pursuing the HVDC valve replacement for the GE-supplied units that were giving some trouble at Dalles. This would eventually bring the Hughes program to a halt. (see year 1977) when GE made an offer to The Dalles that it could not refuse, but which was dependent on them saying they did not have a use for the Hughes product, which they had initially endorsed. Their initial endorsement had caused several million $ of funding to go to Hughes from both the Department of Energy and the Electric Power Research Institute (EPRI). However, in 1974 the recorder did its' job.

Installation of the voltage and current measuring equipment to feed the recorder also put Hughes briefly in the position of having built the worlds' longest fiber-optic data transmission link. This link, which was an electric insulator, safely carried the current measurement data from the high voltage level (150,000 volts) down to ground level at the instrument room.

The position of world's first did not last long. Hughes gave me $90,000. to pursue fiber-optic data link development. For once I gave back money as I'd learned that Nippon Electric Company (NEC) had a budget of $2 million for the same work. I said, "I'm a good manger, but I can't play 90 K against 2 million and win, so we just better not do it." I think it was the first time Hughes management had received back the funds they had allocated for a research program. They could have been insulted, but instead they took it well. We continued to build fiber-optic links, but were definitely out of the Worlds First competition.

* * *

Collie and I continued to enjoy our hill-top house with the view of the valley. Chris and David were in San Luis Obispo, enrolled in Cal Poly. Sherry and Bob were in Los Angeles where she worked in the insurance business and he as an electronics technician in commercial instruments. With the exception of high gasoline prices, the world seemed to be settling a bit. We were becoming a dispersed family.

* * *

# A Quiet World Year And In Malibu A House Cleaning

Compared to the immediately preceding years, 1974 on the world scene was comparatively quiet. There was continuance of "The Troubles" in Ireland and England with bombings in Ulster and Monaghan killing 33 and wounding 300 in Ireland. Bombings in Birmingham, England killed 21. No settlement appeared in sight. India tested a nuclear warhead and became the 6th nation to join the "Nuclear Club".

On the positive side, the return of the Skylab 4 crew after 84 days in orbit set a new record. The Rubik Cube puzzle was invented and achieved almost instant success as a game. The universal Product bar-code was first used on the sale of a package of Wrigleys' chewing gum in Ohio.

President Nixon resigned as the Watergate affair reached crisis proportions and Gerald Ford assumed the presidency of the United States. Voters heaved a sigh of relief that this embarrassing episode was over.

* * *

In Malibu, it proved to be a year of house cleaning in the personnel department. The first to go was our salesman. He was the contact man for the Electric Utility customers. The contacts for military and nuclear fusion research were handled separately. The peculiar aspect about him was that he had an active imagination and any idea that occurred to him he regarded as a stroke of genius which did not need to be checked out for feasibility. I first discovered this when I had to Visit the Schweitzer & Conrad Electric Company in Chicago to explain to a kindly, elder Mr. Conrad that Hughes was not really in a position to purchase his company as he had been led to believe by the salesman.

This was a sad visit. Conrad was a founder of the company which manufactured high voltage switches for the electric utility companies. His children were not interested in taking over the company and his partner, Schweitzer had died. So he needed a buyer for his company as he had reached an advanced age and wanted to retire gracefully.

Superficially this appeared to him to be an opportunity made in heaven. However, he overlooked that the products of S&C and Hughes went to entirely different applications. Also the technologies were as far apart as one could get. However, perhaps the most important thing was the difference in management culture. S&C viewed its hourly employees as part owners of the company. "They've been with us since the beginning" as Conrad put it. The Hughes philosophy respected the hourly employees, but faced the necessity to adjust employment levels to the level of government contracts. They did this well, but the two philosophies would not mix. Further, Hughes just did not buy outside companies. If they were to buy S&C, it would require approval of the V.P. of Industrial Products and the president of Hughes. I knew both of these men well and was confident they simply would not go along with it even if the $ figures looked good.

The salesman gave no consideration to any of this and simply viewed his idea as a brain storm of brilliant proportions. He and I had a talk of some length regarding his job definition.

Later in the year the salesman was sitting in on a conference I was having with the General Manager of English Electric Company. I had carefully introduced a topic and led up to the question of whether English Electric would be interested in a joint bid. Before he could reply to my question, the saleman jumped in and changed the topic to an idea that had just occurred to him. I said, "shut up." The Englishman simply smiled and the carefully prepared opportunity was lost.

Later that day I sat down with the salesman and told him that he was ineffective in his job as it had been outlined to him and that I was firing him, but would give him 60 days continuance so that he might search for another job. He accepted this quietly. I did not see him again.

* * *

The next event concerned the chief engineer. I thought that my continued placement of safety at the highest priority for two years would have gotten through to him, but somehow it did not. This was despite my publishing of procedures and many notes to him personally after my noon-time facility inspections. He always took the indicated action, but there was no learning and the offense would occur again.

Finally, he made a change in a new design for the facility in which he intentionally reduced the level of personnel safety. His reply was, "I thought it would please you as it would be less costly." Clearly I could not get the message through to him. I told him that he was fired for errors in performance and that I would give him 90 days to find a new job in recognition of the long hours he had put into his work. He replied, "You can't fire me!" I recommended that he see the personnel manager. I believe he was told that the 90 days was actually rather generous.

He did find a job at my alma mater, the University of Texas in Austin. The University never bothered to check his reference with me. Had they done so, I would have given him good marks as an electrical engineer, outstanding marks on record keeping, but poor marks on attention to personnel safety.

I was able to hire a very experienced chief engineer who served admirably until the operation was disbanded in 1978. He then became the chief engineer for another Hughes operation. Never during his tenure was there the slightest question of the supremacy of personnel safety as a design consideration.

\* \* \*

The final house-cleaning event concerned a junior technician. He had been working on one of the High Voltage DC interrupters for over a year with no problems and then he noticed the yellow and pink radiation warning sign on the device. It had been there all along, but suddenly it became threatening and he said, "I won't work on that and expose myself to radiation poisoning." He laid down his tools and walked away. When I heard of this, I took a radiation meter and went to find him. We went back to the device and I showed him that the radiation level was less than 1/10 of that considered to be harmful after a year of exposure. I asked, you've been here a year, you see how this place operates, do you think for a moment that I would tolerate a damaging radiation exposure?" He did not answer, but simply said, "I won't work on it." I looked directly at him and said, you will be here tomorrow morning and pick up your tools and work. If you do not, you'll be fired.

He did not. He was fired. In a hazardous environment, there must be no question of obeying the direct order of the responsible person. This could place the life of others in danger if one element of an emergency procedure is omitted. For example, if there was an explosion and fire in the main test facility (this happened over 50 times in 7 years) the test director would yell "abort" and the person on the control panel would hit the red "abort" button. The test director would be rushing through the interior facility door to direct the control of the fire. The abort button would remove the high voltage from the facility, protecting the director and his assistant. Actually, protection was redundant. Just opening the facility door should remove the high voltage, but some times switches don't work properly and redundancy is essential. So is instant reaction to a direct order.

\* \* \*

Not everything that year involved personnel actions. A new product idea grew out of the high current DC interrupter work. The market for this product was limited to High Voltage DC (HVDC) systems in electric utilities. There were few of these and although the future for HVDC looked promising, the fact remained that there would always be fewer DC systems than AC systems. The new product was an AC Fault Current Limiter. The DC interrupter was used in conjunction with a conventional AC switch to insert a resistor into an AC line very rapidly when a short circuit occurred. The heart of this scheme was an electronic device which monitored the AC line current and when the start of a current rise occurred it would quickly simulate, in high speed time, the pattern that would occur if it was a short circuit. If the ensuing actual current followed the high-speed simulation, a short circuit would be assumed and the protective resistor inserted using the very high speed action of the non-mechanical DC interrupter.

A patent for the sensing and high-speed simulation circuitry was issued to Hughes under my name. The initial tests worked well and the idea was broached to American Electric Power, headquartered in New York, but operator of many generating plants in the Midwest. They liked the idea and a contract was negotiated for development and installation of the device in Ohio. Development of the electronic control and the interrupter-mechanical switch combination continued through the year. It was necessary for the simulation and comparison be completed in less than 4 thousanths of a second in order to start the resistor insertion effectively. This proved to be achievable and a further invention occurred for a continuous self-test scheme for the fiber-optic data transfer system that brought the information on line current from the high-voltage level down to ground. A patent was also issued in my name for this scheme. work on the hardware development continued.

* * *

Shari and Bob were divorced and Shari continued in the insurance industry. Chris and David continued their studies at Cal Poly. Collie and I rented a motor home and explored the Owens Valley up to Bishop. This is a beautiful section of California, with small lakes and streams available for fly-fishing.

I experienced a stroke which resulted in the loss of hearing in the right ear when the blood supply to the 8th nerve was blocked. The loss of feeling in the ear canal caused me to give up scuba diving as I could not tell if my ear drum was pressurized or cleared. This ended a decade of enjoyable oceanic experience in both the Atlantic and Pacific.

At our home in the valley, the neighbors' dog began a continuous night time barking which I think was prompted by the coyotes up on the hillside. They tried as best they could to stop him, but nothing seemed to work. We started to look for another place, perhaps one where Collie could have a larger studio.

We also gave thought to a location to which we might retire and settled on San Luis Obispo for its beauty and climate. We found land in the Los Osos Valley and made a bid with the condition that water had to be located on the property. The driller had his own "dowser" who located a spot half way up the hill at the back of the property. The well was drilled and when the driller informed me that he was at 87 feet, had found no water and had run out of money, we folded and gave the escrow back to the seller. Some months later I noticed a pump at the well site and concluded that the driller and the seller were friends. We were a family dispersed and planning for the future.

* * *

# A Year Of Worlds' Firsts

The year 1975 saw significant "firsts" and a few significant "lasts". Francisco Franco ruled himself out as the head of Spain which replaced him with the monarch Juan Carlos. Spain gave up its' last colonial holding, Western Sahara, bringing to an end the Spanish Empire that rose in the 14th century. Franco died later in the year. The Viet Nam war ended when North Viet Nam occupied Saigon. Memorable films showed helicopters taking off from the roof of the U.S. Embassy in Saigon to ferry Vietnamese who had been working for America to safety on Navy aircraft carriers. The Cambodian War ended and genocide by the conquering Kmer Rouge began. The next week Kmer Rouge forces captured the U.S. merchant ship SS Mayaguez, which was reclaimed by the U.S. Navy and Marines at a cost of 38 dead.

The "firsts" were prophetic. The Altair 8800 was introduced, beginning the era of microcomputers, PCs and I-pads. Bill gates coined the company name Microsoft which was copyrighted the following year. Margaret Thatcher became the first female Prime Minister of England. Ronald Reagan, Governor of California entered the race for the 1976 presidential election. Work began on the Trans-Alaska Pipeline. A Russian and an American vehicle docked together in space when an Apollo and a Soyuz were temporarily joined, pointing toward the International

Space Station of the 80's. Perhaps most prophetic, the worlds population exceeded 4 billion souls. In the following 36 years it would climb to 7 billion and concerns would arise as to the capacity of the earth for human inhabitants.

* * *

In Malibu it was a year of great accomplishment. We had a contract with the Electric Power Research Institute (EPRI) to build and demonstrate a high voltage DC (HVDC) circuit breaker using our proprietary plasma-based DC interrupter. EPRI was a pooled operation supported by the U.S. electric utility companies to promote and monitor research that would be of use in utility operations. At the time there was no HVDC circuit breaker and this was seen as limiting the spread of this promising method of transmitting electric energy.

The function of a circuit breaker is to assist in clearing a short circuit on a transmission line or feeder. Imagine a "Y" shaped line with the source of energy at the stem of the Y. The two arms of the Y represent two independent loads or users of that energy. In normal operation, energy flows from the stem, is divided between the two arms and there used by customers of the utility. In AC systems there would be a circuit breaker in each arm of the Y. If a short circuit develops in one arm, the circuit breaker disconnects that arm so that the other arm may continue to function normally. When the short circuit is removed from the disabled arm, the breaker then reconnects it to the source so that both arms can receive energy. The function is exactly what the name implies, it "breaks" or opens a circuit in an emergency situation, then recloses it when the emergency is past.

The absence of an HVDC circuit breaker meant that operation could only occur on a single generating point and a single receiving point. For example, Los Angeles receives a significant amount of electric energy from a generating station at The Dalles in Oregon on the Columbia River. There might be merit in dropping off some of the energy at San Francisco, but without a circuit breaker this would not be possible. As a result, the line was built with a single load connection at Sylmar in the San Fernando Valley. It was this station at Sylmar that would be the demonstration point for the HVDC breaker. The second connection was ingeniously provided by using the other wire of the transmission line to send energy back to The Dalles.. This was the line in which the breaker would be installed and the short circuit applied. Hopefully the short could be disconnected on one line without interrupting the flow of energy into Los Angeles on the other.

EPRI insisted that the demonstration breaker not look like a finished product as their rules prohibited supplying money just for product development. I often said that we met that requirement magnificently. The breaker was built on a flat-bed truck. It measured the full width and length of the bed and rose about 10 feet above the bed. It was not designed nor built to be weatherproof. It looked like a large scientific experiment being transported by truck – which was exactly what it was.

We had the capability to test the breaker at Malibu under laboratory conditions, but this did not include the uncertainties of being connected to 1100 miles of transmission line. The unit had been tested satisfactorily at Malibu before it was driven to Sylmar to be installed for test. The connections to the transmission line were at the highest point on the unit and comprised a corona-ring shaped like a doughnut about 2 feet in diameter atop a ceramic insulator around three feet long and

one entire session of its' international technical meeting in San Francisco to papers on the breaker and its' test. Hughes personnel were authors along with one LADWP engineer of all the papers in the session. Completion was greeted with a long round of applause. I felt elated, but nothing approaching that moment when the PA announced, "Congratulations, you did it."

\* \* \*

Chris and David broke up, Chris moved out while David and a Cal Poly student cared for Travis. Chris continued her employment at Atascadero State Hospital. Shari continued in the insurance business as a claim adjuster. Collie and I bought a Recreational Vehicle with large picture windows, so that Collie could sit inside and paint on site if the weather was bad. The vehicle proved excellent fun with trips to the Owens Valley and to Baja Mexico as well as around the California dessert. Life was becoming fun except for Chris' problems at Atascadero State Hospital with violent inmates. She was fast and well coordinated, but the technicians had to travel in pairs for protection. Life was becoming varied.

\* \* \*

# A Year Of Technical Progress And Political Change

The year 1976 saw technical progress that foreshadowed events of the next 35 years. The Cray computer, the worlds first super computer, was announced by the Cray company. This would dramatically change the depth of data processing in science, military intelligence and industry. The U.S. space program progressed with Viking 1 and Viking 2 landing on Mars. Viking 2 produced the first close up color photos of the surface of Mars. The space shuttle Enterprise was rolled out in Palmdale, California. This design would lead the U.S. effort in space until their retirement 36 years later with the U.S. then depending on Russian launches for crew and supplies transfer to the International Space Station. The first laser printer was introduced by IBM and Jobs and Wozniak formed Apple to produce the first competition to the IBM PC personal computer. These two machines would lead Americans into the internet, e-mail and Facebook, changing dramatically interpersonal communication on a world-wide basis. Howard Hughes, a pioneer of technical companies, died.

Turmoil existed worldwide in the area of politics. North and South Vietnam united in the Socialist Republic of Vietnam. The U.S. military considered deeply what had been accomplished in the Vietnam War. Twelve bombs planted by the Provisional Irish Republican Army exploded in London. Rule of Northern Ireland was transferred to Britain via the English Parliament. The Soweto Riots in South Africa began, leading eventually to a change in the government of that country. In the U.S., the 200th anniversary of the Declaration Of Independence was celebrated. Conrail was formed to transfer to the U.S. Government control of 13 U.S. railroads in the North East which were in bankruptcy. Jimmy Carter was elected President of the U.S. He was the first president from the deep south since Civil War days. Annapolis admitted the first female cadets in its' history.

\* \* \*

The High Voltage Systems Operation at Hughes Research experienced its' first major setback. A metallic return transfer breaker (MRTB) exploded while undergoing test at The Dalles, Oregon. The contract to design and build this unit was a direct result of the successful test of the worlds first HVDC circuit breaker at Sylmar, California the previous year. The Dalles and Sylmar are the two terminals for the West Coat DC intertie. In addition to the overhead high voltage cables on towers, there is also a metallic underground cable which establishes the ground potential for the system and carries any imbalance of current between the positive and negative cables on the towers. The system operators desired the ability to open or "break" this connection if the current resulting from the imbalance became excessive. Hence the need for a Metallic Return Transfer Breaker or MRTB. It offered the operators a chance to see a unit designed for outdoor continuous operation at a lower price than a full-up HVDC breaker.

The voltage rating for the MRTB was about one tenth that of a full-up HVDC breaker. There was a switch available from Germany that was rated to perform the mechanical part of the breaker operation while our proprietary plasma switch did it's interruption. The German unit was much less expensive than our high voltage design that had been proven at Sylmar the previous year. Naturally we incorporated the German unit at the suggestion of the operators to reduce the cost.

The completed MRTB was in a weatherproof metal housing about 8 feet by 10 feet on its base and 8 feet in height as a base for a high-voltage bushing that added another two feet. Neil Marshall, our chief engineer was in charge of the test for Hughes. Neil was very thorough and took a complete set of photos prior to initiation of the test which was under the control of the station operators. These would prove essential in the later analysis of the test.

The test began with the intertie operating, the MRTB buttoned up in its' metallic housing. Then an imbalance was created causing a current to flow though the MRTB. There was an immediate explosion, blowing the door open and releasing a shock wave onto the observers. Examination showed that the German switch had exploded, scattering parts inside and outside the 8X10 enclosure. Clearly the test was a failure.

One of our technicians at the site was German trained and thoroughly schooled in German discipline. Trusting his thoroughness to any work, I asked Neil to assign him the task of collecting all the fragments of the German switch so that we might reconstruct it and determine the cause of failure. The technician even searched the gravel yard outside the enclosure and saved pieces as tiny as the size of an English pea. All were packed and brought back to Malibu for reassembly. This disclosed a defect in the molded plastic housing which held the oil insulation for the switch. This was the initiation point of the explosion and once the housing was ruptured and the oil blown out, the switch failed to function.

One mystery remained, the oscilloscope trace recording the test failed to show any rise in voltage across the switch during the test. Reference to Neil's enlarged photos solved this puzzle. The input switch for the subject channel was seen to be in the "off" position. This would not have stopped the test or hindered it, but would have been a puzzle without his photos. Attention to detail triumphed against a failure prompted by a defect in fabrication. However, the failure put an end to our hopes for a saleable product in the HVDC breaker field. The operators decided they would live with what they had.

\* \* \*

Although the future looked bleak for breakers in the utility market, the same technology was receiving a welcome in the scientific field of nuclear power generation. Here it was desired to switch on and off a high voltage beam of electrons which was injected into a magnetically contained plasma. Orders were received from both Max Planck Institute in Germany and Princeton University in the U.S. Work began on both devices which used different technologies. In order to assemble these large devices, we needed more floor space. A building formerly used by PG&E in downtown Malibu was rented and served this need well.

Work also continued on the contract with American Electric Power Company for an AC Current-limiting Breaker to be installed at their plant in southern Ohio. This device required a new design for the mechanical switch used in the Sylmar test of the HVDC breaker. The new unit would use a torsion bar to supply the force to hold it closed instead of the coil spring used in the HVDC device. We had learned that we were at the theoretical limit for coil springs and the torsion bar approach offered room for improvement. The first unit was constructed using a Craftsmen 1/2" wrench extension purchased at Sears. It worked surprisingly well. Also required was a higher current capability for the proprietary plasma interrupter tube. This was presenting a problem.

\* \* \*

The RV purchased in1975 was becoming a source of enjoyment for the family. Collie and I drove to Baja California and to nearby locations in the Mohave Desert for camping and rock hounding. Shari and I took a jaunt down in Baja to Bahia de Los Angeles and Marmol, enjoying snorkeling and gathering shellfish from the ocean for our supper. Chris continued employment at Atascadero State Hospital and became a licensed Psychiatric Nurse. Collie continued to paint in her new studio. The only problem on the scene was the dramatic increase in taxes on our home by the Los Angeles County. Over a period of 3 years the taxes had increased by a factor of 500%. This raised the prospect that we might need to down-size our living accommodations. That would be in the future. For the time being we were finding our individual niches and enjoying them.

# A Year Of Indicators For The Future

The year 1977 presented in nearly every field seminal events that were precursors of the long range future. In the technology area, the Commodore PET computer was announced. It was the first all-in-one personal computer. The Apple Company was formed and the Atari 2600 computer game was announced. These simple fore-runners opened the field of personal computing which blossomed into the internet, ipads and personal communications we enjoy in the 21st century. I can recall saying, "who could possibly use 128 kilobytes of memory in a personal computer?". How wrong could I be? Last night I had a download to my computer 1000 times greater and it only took a few minutes.

In the social area there were also forerunners. The "Lady Marines" were abolished and future ladies would be inducted directly into the Corps. The same thing occurred for the "Waves", where future lady inductees would go directly into the U.S. Navy.

Not all social events showed progress. The 1977 New York Blackout proved markedly different from the similar cases in 1965 and 2003 in that looting and vandalism were widespread. The blackout was found to be caused by lack of standard procedures and management in Con Edison. The looting was a symptom of anguish in the lower economic part of the society.

The movie Star Wars opened giving a target for our attention on the future of society.

In the political area, Anwar Sadat of Egypt became the first Arab leader to visit Israel's leader Menachim Begin to search for a answer to the Palestine-Israel problem. They came close, but that one has yet to mature. The nuclear non-proliferation treaty was signed by 15 nations including the United States and the USSR. It has held with the signers, but the non-signers have developed their own weapons.

In the general technology area, the first stealth aircraft flew. It was the Lockheed "Have Blue", the forerunner of the F-117 that would prove effective in the 1990's. The USSR launched the Soyuz 24 which docked with the Salyut 5 space station. This was on the road to the International Space Station, an accomplishment in which I would play a small part, but that would be in the future. The first telephone conversation over fiber-optic cable occurred in 1977. I recall briefly holding the worlds record for longest fiber-optic data link in 1975, but losing it to others before the end of the year. Technology progress is expensive and my $90,000. budget was not in the same league with my Japanese competitors' $1,000,000. budget. The last natural case of smallpox occurred and was hailed as a medical accomplishment.

* * *

In my operation at Malibu, there were forerunners, but they were negative and would not mature until year end. We developed several small products with good success, but our main effort was on two products the AC Current limiting breaker for American Electric Power and the HVDC rectifier valve for the Pacific Intertie at The Dalles, Oregon.

The operators at The Dalles, Bonneville Power Administration (BPA) wanted our valve to replace the mercury valves made by General Electric which were very unreliable. We worked closely with the Chief Engineer of BPA after achieving the assurance of the general manager that BPA was definitely interested. We had a contract with the Department of Energy to develop the valves and were proceeding on it.

One day I was asked to meet with the Hughes Vice President of Industrial Electronics. It would be his operation to which my group would transfer if the products became successful. He was my former boss at Hughes, so I had no qualms of meeting with him. We sat down with a third man John, whom I also knew as a former manager in the Industrial Electronics Division. What he had to say was a major blow. John had visited BPA's General Manager and flatly asked if they were still interested in the Hughes valve. In General Electric he would have been skinned for visiting another managers customer and questioning the product, but this was Hughes Aircraft. The problem was that he came away with the story that there was no longer an interest. This was a horrible prospect as there was no other HVDC application in America then. This was our only starting point. I said that there must be a misunderstanding as we were working closely with the BPA Chief Engineer who seemed to want a trial of the Hughes valve. I agreed to call him, which I did and he confirmed their continuing interest, but said he would check with the General Manger and call me back. When he did there was clear embarresment in his voice and apology in his words. Officially, BPA was no longer interested. I searched for an answer and learned that General Electric had offered to supply a solid state valve of new design for trial at no cost to BPA. This was no small matter, probably a $2 million gift. It was not clear why the

General Manager neglected to tell his chief engineer and the tone of voice indicated considerable anguish on his part. I felt crushed.

This was clearly the end of the road for that development and possibly the end of the road for our electric utility products. The lesser products we had developed for the military and the Fusion Energy fields were simply technical spin offs to add more dollars of sales to support a basic technology. Now the basic product was pulled out and it was doubtful whether the secondary products could support the technical effort by themselves. I had a team honed to a smooth competent operating group and now the rug was pulled out from under the program.

I received a call from the Department of Energy saying that they wished to close the R&D contract based on a lack of interest at BPA. I traveled to Washington and with sadness but firmness negotiated the many details of closing the contract and made copious notes of the proceedings. These would prove of great value in the next year when DOE decided to investigate their own closing of the contract.

* * *

On the other major product, the AC Current Limiting Breaker, we were technically hung up at a current level of 5000 Amperes. It didn't matter that when we started the world record for this type of current interruption was 1.5 Amperes and that we had raised that to 5000 Amperes. we needed 6500 Amperes to have a saleable product. Great effort was put into this and yet the 5000 Ampere limit continued. We began to understand the basis of the limitation. I finally called a meeting of all out physicists and technicians to review what we knew and had experienced. Then I presented the question, "Does anyone see a way out or a thing we should try?". The silence was apalling. This was a noisy and flamboyant group with great imagination and quick-fire verbal response. When the silence reached a minute and a half I knew there was no way out, thanked them and dismissed the meeting.

I gave it one week for any late ideas to surface. None did. So, I did what I had to do and asked for a meeting with my boss to inform him that we had lost both of our fundamental products within months of each other. He was saddened as he too had great aspirations for these developments, but he set up a meeting with the new president of Hughes Aircraft. We sat down with him and reviewed the story. He asked one simple question, "Why are we doing this?" The answer was that we had hoped to make money. His decision was that the program should revert to a plasma research effort and abandon the effort to diversify into the Electric Utility market except for minor products that could be picked up by existing operations of the Industrial Electronics Group. Although this meant the end of my program, I had to admit that it was a sound management decision.

\* \* \*

I later talked with my boss and asked that I be allowed to continue on until I could see to the placement of the 40 or so engineers that I had hired for the program to supplement the 30 physicists and technicians that were originally part of the Research Lab. The engineers had no future at the lab and correct placement required that I be available to discuss their attributes and performance with possible hiring managers. He readily agreed to this and I added that if the placements went rapidly that I would like to stay on the few extra months until my Hughes pension was vested. To pay for this I would make R&D proposals for my own work and thus pay my way when I was no longer needed as manager. I suggested that my #2 man should be the manager of the continuing R&D operation. He was both a PHD physicist and an excellent manager. All of this was acceptable.

I called a meeting of my people and explained the situation, stressing that there would be no rush for the exits and that I would assist in all ways that I could to get a good placement for those who would be transferring. This of course broke up the team spirit between the imported engineers and the resident researchers. A spirit which had required such effort to develop, but it was best to be straight-forward. The placements went very well. Not one of my men took a downgrade in position or pay and in two cases they were actually promoted.

* * *

Collie enjoyed her studio at the house on the hilltop and decided she wanted to go back to school to complete her bachelors degree. She enrolled in CSU Northridge and was apalled at the load of studying. Shari moved to New Orleans with a boyfriend and found work, continuing in the insurance industry. She also developed a taste for oysters, which were readily found in New Orleans. Chris found a new boy friend in San Luis Obispo and continued as a psych-tech at the Atascadero State Hospital. I inherited a bluepoint Siamese cat, "Chukee" that came with the hilltop house. Chukee regarded herself as the chief cat and accompanied me each morning down the driveway to pick up the newspaper. During this trip she would fill me in on the nights events with a continuing meowing discourse. While I was managing the placement of my people, she became known as "the management consultant" for her continued "advice".

\* \* \*

# A Year Of Great Change

It was a year of great change for me personally. So great that it is divided into two chapters. And on the U.S. and international scene changes also were underway that foreshadowed the future. The year saw the birth of the worlds first "test-tube baby", an accomplishment which has become common in the 21st century. Both the U.S. Senate and the British Parliament began broadcasting their meetings on radio. Unfortunately this was only a superficial effort toward transparency.

In China, Deng Xiaopeng reversed the Mao era of anti-intellectualism by removing the ban on publishing the works of Aristotle, Shakespeare and Dickens. He also initiated the period of "Chinese Economic Reform". These efforts eventually led to the current position of China as a leader in world economy and elementary-high school education. Unfortunately less successful was the signing of the "Camp David Accords" between Egypt and Israel leading to the Nobel peace Prize for Anwar Sadat and Menachim Begin. The promise has not yet been fulfilled. I must admit that at the time I was optimistic for the Camp David accord and pessimistic for Chinas' change. How wrong can you be?

Russias' Cosmos satellite broke up and scattered burning debris across Canadas' Northwest Territories. This led to more attention on satellite design to cause breakup into smaller pieces on re-entry so that burnout well above the earths' surface would occur.

The world was shocked at the Jonestown Event where 914 people committed suicide at the command of their leader. Similar events have not re-occurred, but belief in the imminent end of the world does indeed repeat from time to time.

President Carter postponed construction of the neutron bomb, which would kill people but leave buildings unharmed.

* * *

For me the year began with a detailed analysis of the feasibility of my desire to end my career teaching engineering. It soon became evident that I would have to both teach and practice engineering in order to survive economicaly. The movement to academia would mean a 60% reduction in pay. Part of this could be made up by down-sizing from the hilltop house plus the tax protection promised by Prop 13. If I took a pension from Hughes Aircraft an additional amount would be obtained, but there would still be a sizable gap. I talked with USC, where I would be teaching and asked for Thursdays off to permit consulting work. They were agreeable. Now, for tax and insurance reasons I needed to form a company. A quick check with possible utility customers indicated this should be a full "C-Corp". Thus I formed "Bluepoint Associates Ltd." recognizing my bluepoint Siamese "Chukee" as the earlier management consultant. The company would be dissolved in 2013 after been profitable 36 out of 37 years.

* * *

My agreement with Hughes was that I would bring in research contract money for myself to cover my salary for 6 months until my pension was vested. This started with two proposals each based on a sole-party invention. One was a scheme to locate an insulation breakdown point in buried high voltage cable. The second was to detect an arcing downed conductor in overhead medium-voltage distribution lines. Both proposals were funded by Electric Power Research Institute (EPRI), a consortium of the U.S. electric utility companies. I had not expected both proposals to be funded, but that was alright. I worked full time until I began teaching in the fall and then only on Thursdays. This worked out very well as the basic design was complete before my work shifted to one day a week. Thus the one day was just to review the construction work and later to perform the basic operational tests. The designs proved operational with good results and led to field tests in 1979.

\* \* \*

The preparation for teaching at USC proved very difficult. I was enrolled as a full-time student to bring my math up to snuff and to cover new technical fields that had developed since my graduation. Indicative of this latter group was "Modern Control Theory" which simply didn't exist until a decade after I graduated. It didn't matter that at GE my first assignment was with Hal Chestnut who would become the father of Modern Control Theory and later the president of the Institute of Electrical and Electronic Engineers. My problem in 1978 was that I was not experienced with the detail theory and the math that was required for analysis and design using this technique. The work was exhausting, but five years later I would be lecturing at Cal Poly using Modern Control Theory applied to Semiconductor Integrated Circuits which had not existed before 1970. The speed of modern technology is astounding.

* * *

If technology progressed at "Warp Speed" management did not. When I went to enroll as a retread student at USC I was pleased to see that a Digital Equipment Corp type 70 computer (about the size of a large refrigerator) was receiving the hand entered data on students as they were registered in the gymnasium. Well, I thought that's modern management, they've got the little machine down here linked into the big IBM computer at its fixed site on campus so that registration is speedy and consumes little human effort. I commented on this to another USC prof who set me straight, "Art, you give management too much credit. The DEC-70 is just for printing out the receipts for the students. It's not linked to anything although it could be. The registration data all has to be hand-entered again into the central IBM machine using the students hand-written inputs. I was learning more than modern math.

* * *

Collie and I found a smaller house with swimming pool and a fenced yard that would keep the cats off the street. We moved in and she began her studies for Northridge and I at USC. It was weird and mentally taxing to be college students in our 50's, but we were dedicated and pored the effort into it. I worked at Malibu on Thursdays and on Saturdays drove the camper over to the hilltop house we were selling to turn on the sprinklers and water the lawns and trees. While the sprinklers ran, I studied in the camper. It worked out pretty well. Shari and her New Orleans boyfriend broke up and she moved in with us temporarily. It was nice to have her at home again while she worked for an insurance company downtown in L.A. Chris left Atascadero State Hospital, completely burned out from the attacks by inmates. She married and moved to Northern California. The family was in the midst of life-style changes.

* * *

# A Year Of Pointers To The Future

In both the world scene and private life events of 1979 were fore-runners of the future. In the middle east, Shah Mohammed Reza Pahlavi fled from Iran and wound up in the U.S. for hospitalization. Iran declared itself an Islamic Republic and insurgents trapped 90 hostages in the U.S. embassy in Tehran, 53 were American. The insurgents demanded that the U.S. return the Shah. This was poignant as one of his family was a student of mine at USC. In Morocco 200 insurgents occupied Mecca's Grand Mosque. They were eventually ousted by French commandos who were given special permission to enter the city because they were not Muslims. In the ensuing fight, 250 were killed and 600 wounded. Saddam Hussein became the president of Iraq. I was incensed at the movements of revolutionaries evident in the near east. The fact that many of my USC students were from this area only added to the emotion.

Jimmy Carter signed off on secret funds to be given to anti-Soviet agencies in Kabul, Afghanistan. Later, the USSR invaded Afganistan. Later, Russia would give up on Afganistan and we would try our turn.

The U.S. and China formed full diplomatic relations. China instituted its' "one child" policy which limited families to one child each.

Margaret Thatcher became the first feminine Prime Minister of England. To the father of two daughters this was a welcome progress for women.The eradication of Small Pox was certified, the worlds first medical victory over a disease. The world premiere of "Star Trek" opened minds to space beyond the earth. The USC students were enthralled with the prospects of space that "Star Trek" brought to mind.Chrysler received U.S. funds for loan guarantees. It was seen as "too big to fail". In retrospect, 1979 appears as a forerunner of the 21st century.

\* \* \*

The year presented a monstrous work load to me. I was teaching a full load at USC and also carrying a large load as a re-tread student. My Thursdays were taken up with work at Hughes Research in finishing the development of a novel equipment to precisely locate short circuits in buried electric cables. Weekends were spent in either study or watering the landscape at the hilltop house we had up for sale. Fortunately the RV provided a place to do both study and control of watering which required a 5-hour regimen.

The work on the short-circuit locator went well until we reached the point where a high-voltage test of the device was required. The work was not in my high-voltage test building, but in a sort of truck garage that Hughes rented from SCE for my work and some ion-propulsion work. This meant that I had to perform a 150,000 volt "soak" test, where the voltage was applied to the equipment for 5 minutes to insure it would stand up in field usage. The problem of safety was severe as we were not working in the test building with its' well-trained crew, but in an off-site building with other workers that were not trained in high voltage safety.

I obtained a long roll of red and white tape and surrounded the test area with a strand of it much as the police cordon off a crime scene with yellow tape. I announced the procedure to both groups in the building. Unfortunately one member of the ion-propulsion crew was in the restroom during my announcement. He returned to the work space when we had the 150,000 volts turned on. He was in a hurry and started to lift the tape and enter the high-voltage area. I had the "deadman switch" in my hand and was ready to dump power when he lifted the tape, but this dump procedure was unproven in this building. I shouted, "Freeze. Stop right where you are". I believe he had some experience with the police because he instantaneously froze in place. I explained that he had to stand there outside the tape for the remaining 3 minutes of the "soak" and then we would slowly dump the voltage. He turned white when 150,000 volts was mentioned, but he did as told. The test was passed and the conventional dump cleared the voltage so that the "dead man switch" did not have to be used in an unproven setup. I inwardly cursed myself for not testing it before starting the soak test.

The equipment worked fine at the test building and a field test was arranged for the short circuit locator at an electric utility in New Jersey. The utility granted 3 hours to perform the test. My replacement went back with the equipment, set it up and called for a start of the alloted 3 hours. The utility sent a lineman to connect it. This was not finished for 2 1/2 hours. Then the lineman sat down to eat his lunch. When it was pointed out that we only had 3 hours and he had used up 2 1/2 of it he stated, "I have an hour off for lunch and I'm taking it now." A plea to the manager of the site produced no results. "He has a right to an hour for lunch and you've used up your 3 hours. That's the end of it. Pack up and leave."

Thus a year of work went down the drain and a fine piece of equipment was never tested on line because a lineman needed a full hour for lunch and a utility manager felt he must do things exactly as he was told. This attitude was found to prevail through much of the utility companies. My anguish did nothing to change utility management practice.

* * *

Teaching at USC proved a totally new experience. I enjoyed the interaction with the students from the U.S. and China especially, but the students from the near east were a problem. To them, there was no difficulty in lying. They felt they could tell fantastic tales and should be believed. I quickly learned to count the number of exams I handed out and count those turned back before releasing the students. A favorite trick of the Saudi students was to not turn in the completed exam and then claim that the teacher had lost it and he should receive an "A", saying "because I worked all the problems correctly." Once when my count of exams turned in was one less than those handed out I turned to a group of Sauds and said, "I'm short one exam and of course I will discover who it was. Tell him he is dead in this class." The next day he withdrew.

The Chinese students were at the opposite pole. They were brilliant, dedicated to becoming engineers and possessed of a fine sense of humor and of honor. The humor was demonstrated one day when I was lecturing a course in control theory. The math resulted in a three-dimensional plot featuring "poles" and "zeroes" as the points of interest. When lecturing three dimensions on a two-dimensional blackboard I discovered early the need for colored chalk to distinguish the third-dimension representation of the poles, which rose like towers into the + portion of space and the "zeroes which were semi-circular pits that descended into - space.

This day I had my hand full of colored chalk and thinking to establish participation by the students while standing facing the blackboard I asked, "What color shall we use for poles and zeros today?"

A female Chinese voice answered, "Blue for the poles and pink for the zeroes." It took only 5 seconds to realize that miss Chinese had played a marvelous joke on the professor by giving sexual orientation to the mathematical concept of "poles" and "zeroes". I turned around to see if I had lost the class. All that I saw was rapt attention except for one lovely young Chinese face grinning from ear to ear and with figurative canary feathers at both ends of the grin. I returned to the blackboard and the lecture in three dimensions. The canary eater not only had a sense of humor, she earned an honest "A" in the course.

\* \* \*

Collie continued her studies at Northridge and obtained her much-delayed batchelor degree in art. The hilltop house finally sold and my labors decreased by 5 hours each week. However, my student courses at USC became more complex. It was a standoff. Our Abysinian cat Nefertiti simply would not stay in the side yard which the other cats at least tolerated. She learned to spring up and down on a tree limb and thus catapult herself to the roof of the house and from there down the front porch to the street. This gained freedom, but she was killed by a car in the street. At least she had her freedom briefly.

\* \* \*

# FROM LOS ANGELES TO
# SAN LUIS OBISPO

The year 1980 saw significant advances in technology which heralded the socially interconnected world of today. The Global Positioning System (GPS) which appears in a majority of new automobiles today was announced in January. I was aware of the technology in 1968 when a young naval officer that I had recommended for Annapolis told me when I asked about surveillance accuracy that he could distinguish between his ship and another of the same class tied up alongside. That meant about 50 foot resolution.

I never expected to see this released to the public in my lifetime.

Later in the year Digital Equipment Corp., Intel and Xerox introduced "Ethernet" a means of communicating digitally at speeds of 10 Megabits/S. The modem that connects my computer to the internet today uses Ethernet code 35 years after its introduction. That' is a long lifetime in todays technology. Also during the year "Pac-Man" was introduced. Still the largest selling computer arcade game. The broadcasting network CNN was launched and still today is a leader in news programs.

Jimmy Carters administration encountered varied problems. He signed the congressional bill to bail out Chrysler for $1.5 billion. He also signed "proclamation #4771" which established the first peace-time draft of men 18 - 25 years of age for military service. This was in response to Russias' invasion of Afganistan. In Iran, Operation Eagle claw, aimed at rescue of the U.S. hostages, came to a sad end when two aircraft collided in the desert, killing 8 men and reducing the force below that required. Reagan was elected at year end.

Elsewhere on the world scene significant political events occurred. Israel and Egypt established diplomatic relations. In Poland the movement "Solidarity" was recognized following the successful strike by workers at the Gdansk shipyard. The Iran - Iraq war began with an attack by Iraq aimed at "eliminating the Iranian regime". I was saddened by this back-and-forth motion with no discernable progress in an area where America derived a huge percentage of its oil. OPEC met and decided to increase oil prices by 10%. They could and did in what was thought once to be a "free" market. Nature could not be left out. Mount St. Helens erupted violently and film/tape recordings provided the world with a view of natures violence.

\* \* \*

My teaching and student days at USC drew to a close in June. My commuting time had increased to 3 hours daily as Los Angeles traffic stifled on freeways. Early in the year there was an announcement of an opening at Cal Poly for a teacher in the Electrical Engineering Department. I was on to this like a catfish on a ball of worms. Not only was Cal Poly "numero uno" in my particular field, but the prospect of 30 minutes commuting instead of 3 hours was enchanting. I sent in my application and was asked to come up for an interview. Saul Goldberg, a Cal Poly Prof had brought his class down to Malibu when I was running the High Voltage Systems operation. I gave the class a lecture on what we were doing in DC interruption and Saul kindly said at his departure, "If you ever decide to go into teaching, let me know". Now I was doing just that. I went to the campus an hour before the appointed time just to look around and see the place come alive. It was impressive. A pretty grounds with new buildings and an active student body including zero middle eastern people. I liked what I saw and on completion of the interview knew that I truly wanted to teach here. Then began the waiting to hear their decision. There were 87 applicants for the job, indicating the reputation of Cal Polys EE department in the academic community. Finally I got the news. I could come in as an Assistant Professor, but that was probably all they could offer as I did not have a Phd and thus advancement was unlikely. That made no problem for me if they could let me have Thursdays clear to do consulting work. On that basis the handshake was made. Collie and I started our planning for a shift from LA to SLO.

\* \* \*

I was still working Thursdays at Hughes on one of the two research projects for which I had brought in funding when I stepped down as manager. This invention was a detector for downed distribution conductors. These conductors operated at voltages from 2 kilovolts to 15 kilovolts in residential or commercial areas. When they broke and fell down they were a major safety hazard. The scope is evident from the fact that in 1980 there were 194 wrongful death suits active in the

U.S. from downed utility lines. The usual downed distribution conductor was hard to detect as the arcing into the earth or driveway or sidewalk was small and not noticed by the short-circuit detectors at the distribution center. Without going into the technical background, the idea was to detect the presence in the line current of a third harmonic of the power line frequency (about 1 1/2 octaves above for those musically oriented). This frequency occurred when there was a small arc to ground on the utility line and was detectable at arc levels well below that of a short circuit. Initially this was pure theory, but simulations bore it out and a prototype device was built and tested at a utility in Ohio. The tests were excellent and a contract was signed to provide 25 devices to Southern California Edison for installation and test on their system.

In the process of moving to SLO, I lost track of this activity and so was surprised a year later to learn that SCE removed all the devices. At a technical conference I ran into the SCE engineer who had been in charge of the project. He was no longer with SCE and told an interesting story when I asked what had been the problem. He said the devices had worked very well with prompt detection of a few conductor drops during a wind storm and no false alarms. SCE management noted this and felt that such good results that they might be required to install the device throughout their system. The cost seemed to be greater than any loss from wrongful death suits and so they decided to table the whole thing by removing the trial units. He apologized for his management saying that he opposed the removal, but the decision was bigger than him. Again the utility management doctrine was displayed.

After a brief spat of anger I decided the issue was bigger than me too and that I lacked the wherewithal to take on the utility industry. The funding for the project had come from the Electric Power Research Institute (EPRI) which was a joint creation of all U,S. utilities. I could certainly not count on any support from them. I put my emotions on the back burner and went ahead with my teaching career.

\* \* \*

My departure from USC brought two real heart warmers. The students of the Electrical Engineering department gave me their 1980 award as most valuable instructor at a dinner hosted by the IEEE student president. This brought many warm handshakes and best wishes from both the students and from me for their future careers. The second heart warmer was a much smaller dinner of the Chinese students who wished me the best of fortune in my move to Cal Poly. I made a gift to each of them of an empty bound log book in which they could keep their personal account of their career. We parted with mutual best wishes for the future.

\* \* \*

I graduated with an MSEE from USC that summer. My thesis was on an invention which detected the location of short circuits in buried three-phase transmission cables. This was the device for which the test at a New Jersey utility was terminated because a lineman had to have his lunch on time. A test at Malibu on a short section of cable had proved that the idea worked, locating the short within 1 meter. This test and the background math analysis of the problem constituted the thesis material.

On graduation and completion of my teaching schedule at USC, Collie and I took a vacation to a Colorado backwoods inn where she attended a watercolor painting session by Tony van Hasselt and where I would simply collapse. Each day brought sleep until 10 or 11 and then up to have breakfast and sit in on the watercolor class. After dinner I would only last until about 10 and was then back in bed. Only once before in my life had I been that far gone. Fortunately after 4 days of sleep came resurrection. It was a reality check on the effort that a year and a half had taken in teaching, studying and working all simultaneously. However, I was on the way to Cal Poly and it was all worth it.

* * *

Collie and I looked for a house in San Luis Obispo. I wanted a place with some land around it as that seemed a good investment as well as providing a view which we had not had since the hilltop house. Also, it seemed the town was growing eastward toward Arroyo Grande. These thoughts led us to the Edna Valley where we found a place with an acre of land and room to build a studio for Collie. Shari recommended a contractor in SLO that had done good work for her when she was an insurance adjuster in LA. He turned out to be ideal. I drew the plans after incorporating all of Collies ideas. She would have 450 square foot studio with builtin storage and bookcases and a waist-to-ceiling glass view of the Edna Valley. The ceiling went along under the roof rafters resting on two long wood beams from which hung four double lamp fluorescent fixtures each with both a blue and an "warm" bulb to achieve a close to daylight color throughout the room. Construction went very well and Collie delightedly moved in to spend six hours each day painting. I set up a shop in the garage and an electronics lab in what had been the prior owners photo darkroom. This would help with my Thursday work.

Chris moved to SLO to take up a job with a bank. Shari remained in LA and became a superintendent at the apartment house where she lived, acting as "aunt Shari" and "mother" to the children of her first husband and his second wife. The family was finding its own ways.

# A New Life In San Luis Obispo

The year 1981 continued the trends visible on the world scene in 1980. Technology continued its' frantic advance while activities in the middle east grew in intra-mural hostility. This mode lapsed over into U.S. politics.

Early in the year the Israeli Air Force destroyed the Iranian Osirak nuclear reactor, under the assumption that it was producing material for an Iranian nuclear weapon program. Iran president Banisadr was deposed as a result.

Later in the year the Israeli Air Force bombed Beirut, Lebanon. The United States imposed an embargo on the shipment of aircraft to Israel. The embargo would be lifted later in the 1980s. A car bomb destroyed the Israeli embassy in Beirut. It was thought that Syrian intelligence planned and conducted the action.

Anwar Sadat was assassinated in Egypt during a parade of members of the Islamic Jihad. I felt this was a world loss as the one person driving toward peace between Israel and the Middle East countries was now dead. Hosni Mubarik assumed the leadership of Egypt, a role he would play for over 30 years until deposed by popular revolt during the "Arab Spring" of 2011.

Outside the Middle East, politics continued in a mixed pattern. Within minutes after Ronald Reagan assumed the presidency, succeeding Jimmy Carter, an agreement was signed and the American hostages held by Iran for 14 months were released. Within months Reagan along with two officers and James Brady would be shot by John Brinkley. Reagan's humor did not fail him. As he was wheeled into the operating room, he turned to the staff and said, "I hope you are all Republicans".

In France Francois Mitterand and Giscard D'estang faced a runoff for the Presidency after the spring election. Mitterand won. I could not help a small pleasant feeling. I was in France in 1964 at a trade show and spotting D'Estang approaching (he was then the economics minister) I stepped into the aisle to say in my best French, "Bon Soir Monsieur D'Estang." He spotted the U.S. flag over my head at the General Electric booth and pointedly crossed the aisle so that he would not be troubled with speaking to an American. I recalled thinking, "You egotistical bastard. We pulled your ass out of the hands of the Germans twice and now you snub us." My face held it's fixed smile. I had learned to be a politician myself.

In the technical area results were mixed. The walkway of the Hyatt Regency in Kansa City Missouri collapsed and fell on the people standing in the Atrium beneath, killing 114 of them. The inquiry showed marginal design, outright alteration during construction and sloppy inspection. I recall thinking "They call you Civil Engineers? What a misnomer. Please get your act together all along the line before people think all engineers perform like this!"

On the plus side, The space shuttle Columbia returned to land on earth after it's manned space mission becoming the first recoverable and re-usable spacecraft. IBM introduced the IBM PC. I bought one of the first, so early in production that when it went in for repair two years later they could not find a technician who had worked on that model. It cost $5000. and

I was happy to pay that. In 2011 I would buy a laptop with 20 times the speed and 100 times the memory for $500. I had learned how to program in higher order languages in 1964 and was now able to write my own programs. Particularly those to analyze and design solar power systems, which was becoming my sub-specialty.

The feminine cause saw progress with Reagan appointing Sandra Day O'Connor to become the first woman on the Supreme Court. The Synod of the Church of England voted to permit women into the higher orders of the church. As the father of two daughters I was pleased.

Medicine saw mixed occurrences, in Los Angeles the first case of AIDS was documented and no cure existed.

* * *

At Cal Poly I was given the test for "Newbies" to see if I really wanted to teach. This was done by scheduling one upper division lecture at 0800 in the morning and one freshman basics lecture at 1800 in the evening with three three hour labs. This virtually insured that I would eat lunch with the other professors and not eat dinner at home on Monday, Wednesday or Friday. I soon learned to consume a can of Chef Boyardee's "Whatever" for dinner along with some crackers and a cup of water.

It was not as bad as the scheduler might have thought. I had taught both the upper division and the freshman courses at USC so this was not new territory. Further, I had rewritten USC's labs for the lab courses I was assigned, so there I was up to date also.

* * *

My Thursday consulting work began to include proposal preparation for solar photovoltaic power systems that convert sunlight into usable electricity. This involved analyzing the available sunlight, the best tilt angle to get good year-round results. Also it involved the conversion of the direct-current (DC) electricity from the solar cells into alternating current (AC) electricity for connection to the utility grid or to local appliances. That conversion from DC to AC required a power electronic device called an inverter. This was to become my sub-sub specialty for the next 30 years and result in three patents for what would be known as "Dickerson Inverters".

The consulting work on photovoltaic or PV systems was fascinating. It was all new and there were no texts in the field. I carefully saved my analysis and proposal materials and saw that they might become the basis for a textbook. This was both challenging and fascinating. I had been co-author of a textbook in 1952 which was the first to apply statistical analysis techniques to the design of electronic equipment. That had been fun and the text had been well accepted, used by both IBM and the Air Force.

I began to lay out the structure for a text. This was essential as a start, for there were no texts and thus no guides. Much of the spare time in 1981 was spent in forming this structure and doing the research to fill in the necessary parts. For example, it became necessary to write the equations for the apparent position of the sun during each hour of the day and each day of the year. This had to be incorporated into a program in XBAS which would run on the IBM PC so that students could do their own design analysis on the PCs that were becoming available on a time-share basis at schools. It was also necessary to write a chapter on batteries for energy storage to supply loads when the sun was not up. My daughter Crystal helped here by doing the title research in Science Abstracts B, the standard log of technical papers. I would select those that I wanted and she would get the Cal Poly library to order them for me. Soon the battery chapter began to take shape.

\* \* \*

My student ratings were good for the first trimester and I graduated from "Newbie" status and began to eat dinner at home again. However, I now started to teach through the entire curriculum for electronic engineering. Fortunately this involved only one new course in each trimester. However, I began to understand why Cal Poly held the esteemed position it did in the Electronic Engineering field. The curriculum was superb. It went far beyond that of USC and attempted to produce a practicing engineer at the bachelors degree level. This was fast becoming impossible for two reasons. First, technology was exploding. There was always new material that had to be incorporated. Sometimes this meant a new course. At the least it meant additions and alterations to existing courses. Second, the Cal State system insisted on a broadened base of non-technical courses. I must agree with that stance. Engineering is not just technology and certainly life is not just technology. However, the result was to cram more into the available classroom hours than was permitted for a bachelors' degree. Specialization was the best short-term answer and so several sub-specialties of electronics engineering evolved. However, I'll leave that to a future chapter.

\* \* \*

Collie's studio consumed her time for six hours a day, but the view of the back yard and the Edna Valley led her to the idea that she had to have a second rose bed. This was done in a large kidney shaped arrangement that received yellow, orange and deep red rose plants. I was not to be out-done in the gardening area and decided that with the good fertile soil I should try vegetable gardening. A cedar fence was built around the lawn and rose beds of the back yard. In the outside space I began to grow vegetables. This started with hills of squash, yellow crook neck and zucchini. Then corn and later Japanese eggplant and asparagus. The latter two were because they were somewhat expensive and I wanted to learn from their growth how to select and buy them and also how to prepare them. This turned into real fun with a new recipe for Japanese eggplant as a finger-food oer'deurve and varied ways to microwave asparagus.

Chris had great fun doing library research for me and began to consider herself an expert on lead-acid batteries. Shari continued her work as an insurance adjuster and landlord in Los Angeles. She met, fell in love with and married Jerry, a fireman. They continued to live in Los Angeles. The family was finding special, individual goals and pursuits.

# A Year Of War And Weird Economics

The year 1982 presented several wars, weird economics and some glimpses of the future as the role of computers expanded. I was particularly struck by the experiences of the British Navy in the Falklands' War. This began when Argentina invaded the Falklands Islands which were the property of Britain. Margaret Thatcher was determined that this would not go unpunished and sent a sizable naval force to support an invasion by marines. The Brit Navy was somewhat behind in defense against both aircraft and missiles. They paid for this dearly through loss of six ships, five by missile attacks from aircraft and one, HMS Sheffield by an Exocet surface-to-surface missile. The Sheffield was particularly striking to me as it was a new design in which the superstructure was all aluminum to reduce weight and thus limit the ships heeling during a turn. The Exocet struck the superstructure and started a fire which melted the aluminum preventing the crew from fighting the fire. The fire burned for six days before the ship sank. This ended the idea of aluminum superstructures. The Brit nuclear submarine HMS Conquerer justified its name by sinking the Argentine cruiser General Bellano. Finally, British Marines conquered the Argentine forces and achieved a surrender. Leopoldo Galien, the military dictator of Argentina resigned.

War also began again in the Middle East when Israel invaded Lebanon to unseat the PLO. They captured Beirut, but the UN censured Israel and sent a UN force, including Americans to occupy Beirut.

Foreshadowing the entry of computers into the lives of individuals, the first PC, the Commodore-64 appeared on the market and the first emoticons entered the American consciousness. Sony announced the first CD player, named unimaginatively the CDP-101.

In the medical arena, there was contrasting news. The first artificial heart was implanted in a man named Barney Clark who lived for 112 days. Seven persons died from consuming Tylenol pills that were injected with potassium cyanide. These Tylenol murders forever changed the way medicine was packaged.

There was a severe recession and gas prices fell on a world surplus of gasoline. The recession cut back briefly on outside consulting causing my company, Bluepoint Associates to suffer a loss for the only time in its' history. The released time went into supplementing my textbook on Solar power systems.

* * *

In one sense it was well that the consulting work fell off in 1982 as I began teaching both the grad course in Solar Power systems and a new course in semiconductor devices. Both required a considerable amount of preparation. I had used semiconductor integrated circuits in design for at least five years, but teaching a course in their fundamentals required a deeper understanding and preparation. Thus I was studying semiconductor physics while using my new IBM PC to write programs for design of systems in the Solar course. These involved the hourly movement of the sun both in elevation and in azimuth to permit students to calculate the electric yield from a given solar panel position and tilt. Added to this was a set of tables of sunlight intensity for different locations in the United States. These formed the basis for homework problems which the students worked out using time-shared main frame computers. In later years the students would have their own PCs to work from, but this was still early times.

The new courses went well and the student evaluations were good. In the spring I was delighted to receive an award from Applied Magnetics as Outstanding Professor. The student response made all the work worthwhile.

* * *

Collie and I were well settled into our new house and had planted vegetables to supply our dinner table. We had four hills of squash, both zucchini and yellow crook-neck plus a long bed of mustard. The squash flourished and we soon had a surplus that we gave to friends. One of the male members Collie's Thursday Painters group complained to me that she handed this large zucchini to him and said, "you can stuff this". We learned a lot about stuffing zucchinis. The crook-necks were also prolific and we discovered multiple ways to prepare them including fried, grilled, roasted and stuffed. We and our friends were eating well from a garden planted in soil that had once been the bottom of an estuary. Shari continued in the insurance business in Los Angeles and was skilled enough to begin teaching insurance adjusting. Chris was raising her daughter Jessie and working as a teller for a local bank. The family prospered.

# PROGRESS IN SPACE, PROBLEMS IN NUCLEAR POWER & LEBANON

The year 1983 saw progress in space from the surface of the earth to the end of the solar system. The first civilian use of GPS (global positioning system) was authorized and the spacecraft Pioneer 1, launched in 1977, left the solar system. This was significant to me as I had picked up my best mechanical engineer from the Voyager project when its design phase closed in 1975. He did excellent work on the high speed mechanical switch, but had to leave at the same time as I when our project closed down in 1978. Another Hughes manager called my secretary and asked if there was a mechanical engineer available for transfer. She assured him there was and he said, "If Art hired him, I want him." It was one of the best compliments I ever received.

It was also the year that the first Space Shuttle, Challenger flew and in the same year sally Ride was on Challenger for STS-7 as the first woman in Space. On Challenger for STS-8 was Guion Bluford, the first Afro-American in space. Later, Vanessa L. Williams became the first Afro-American to be named Miss America.

Three nuclear power plants suffered significant failures: Kursk in Russia had a fuel rod failure, but was shut down with minimal radiation escape, Embalse, Argentina suffered a total loss of coolant, but was contained, Salem, New Jersey experienced an accident and the auto shutdown failed -- it was wrestled to a stop manually. It would be 3 more years until the Chernobyl catastrophe set back nuclear power on a world wide basis, but the leaves were in the wind.

Lebanon was a hotbed of conflict. In April the U.S. Embassy in Beirut was truck-bombed with 63 killed. Later two truck bombs destroyed the French Paratroop and U.S Marine Corps barracks in Beirut with 241 U.S dead and 58 French. killed. U.S.Navy Lts. Lange and Goodman were shot down by Syrians on a bombing raid over Lebanon. Lange died immediately, Goodman was imprisoned, but later freed when Jesse Jackson went to Lebanon and pled for his release. Jackson was running for Democratic Presidential candidate and appealed to them as a possible future U.S. president. Later in the year Lebanon, Israel and the U.S. signed an agreement for Israel to withdraw from Lebanon.

* * *

At Cal Poly my instructors role was changing. I had been teaching upper division courses to Juniors and Seniors long enough to attract several to enroll with me as advisor for their senior project. This is a six month course in which the student undertakes to design, build and demonstrate a device of his or her own choice. The advisor meets individually with the student for an hour each week to monitor the progress of the work, answer questions and offer suggestions. Some of the Senior Projects were truly advanced and the work was nearly always exceptional. One project was to build equipment to track and download from a Navy satellite the image of cloud cover over the U.S. and then to alter the gamma of the image (increase or decrease contrast) so as to better show up the cloud cover locally. The main design work was the device to download the image and manipulate it. I contributed a receiver that I had for the reception of the satellite signal and the project prospered with the two students (it was a rare joint project) happily grinding out modified cloud cover images. One day they could not get an image and so summoning courage they called the Navy and asked if there was anything wrong with the satellite. The officer hummed and hawed and then said, "Wait a minute." The minute turned into five and the the voice said more politely, "There is something wrong with the satellite. Thank you for alerting us." Needless to say the students were pleased with themselves. I thought a grade of A was in order.

* * *

Sometimes a student would ask the instructor if their was an unused idea around that would make a good senior project. This happened once and I tried out the student on an idea that I was intellectually pursuing as part of my interest in solar power systems. Off-line systems used lead-acid batteries to supply power when the sun was down. This made a need to measure the state of charge of the battery, so that it would not be run down completely, damaging the plates. The conventional way was like dead-reckoning navigation, an electronic record was kept of the time of current flow into and out of the cells since the last time the battery was fully charged. An estimate of the present state of the battery was then made based on the timed sum of these ins and outs. This was terribly inaccurate if there was a long time over which the tracking was made after the last time the battery was fully charged. Unfortunately in a solar system that could be weeks. It was known that the state of charge could be measured by knowing the temperature of the liquid electrolyte and the terminal voltage when the battery was supplying a moderately high current.

My idea was to draw a moderate current for a short period, about 1/100 th of a second and measure the voltage with a short instrument timing pulse of about 1/1000 th of a second in the middle of the current draw.

What the student would need to do was design, construct and test a simple electronic circuit to do this. This student had taken my course in the design of solar power systems and was eager to do something in that field. We conceived of measuring the electrolyte temperature by embedding a thermal resistor in the lead clamp that secured the cable to the wiring. The other end of the post that this clamp fitted on was immersed in the electrolyte and so became a thermal dip-stick. The electronics were not really complicated. He did a good simple design, built it and we started the tests on a battery and charger that I then had in a small lab room where Cal Poly was kind enough to let me do some research.

It would make a good story if we had problems to overcome, but that was not the case. It worked the first time and we got data at various states of charge and also different temperatures. When the calculations were made, we were reading state of charge to an accuracy well under 10%, an precision unheard of by conventional means. The student was overjoyed and of course earned an A. He then did his masters thesis on the same measurement scheme, including simple electronics to do the math of combining the temperature and voltage readings to get the state value. A very good job.

* * *

Collie decided she needed another rose bed, so the back yard began to disappear, but the view from her studio was superb. I expanded my vegetable gardening to include Japanese eggplant and Chinese snow peas, bot supposedly hard to raise, but the excellent soil of the Edna valley produced fine results. The eggplant was so prolific that I had to invent a recipe to use it up. I still make oer d'oerves from a fried slice of Japanese eggplant with wasabi mayonaise and half of a cherry tomato on top. Shari and Jerry became apartment managers in Los Angeles. Chris raised Travis (11) and Jessie (4) while working as a bank teller and single mom. She discovered the effect of food coloring on Travis's ADHD and eliminating it calmed him a little. The family was diversifying

# A Year Of Catastrophe
# And Political Upset

The year 1984 saw two major catastrophes. A famine occurred in Ethiopia which by year end had resulted in deaths over 1 million. Well meaning attempts by the United Nations were simply too late in the drought and famine cycle to stem the terrible human loss. The second catastrophe was industrial and should have been avoidable with reasonable safety management. The Union Carbide chemical plant at Bhopal, India leaked a deadly chemical, methyl isocyanide into the surrounding city. By year end there were over 1 million deaths, I saw these as a terrible inability to forecast and reach agreement in the Ethiopian case and criminal negligence in the Indian instance. In both cases deaths exceeded 1 million. We should certainly do better than this.

Political assassination in India led to riots and killing. Prime minister Indira Ghandi was murdered by two of her Sihk guards. Riots began in New Delhi where normally quiet Hindus killed between 10 and 20 thousand Sikhs. Rahjiv Ghandi replaced her as prime minister. In Beirut, Lebanon the U.S. Marines were sent home. Later in the year a car bomb at the embassy killed 22 persons. Ronald Reagan was re-elected in a landslide over

Walter Mondale. The killings by religious militants appalled me. This was the very antithesis of religion.

* * *

At Cal Poly my activities took an additional path which would prove interesting over the next three decades. My grad course in Solar Photovoltaic Power System Design had proved popular and had led me to recognize the absence of new ideas on inverters for Solar power systems. The inverter is a power electronics device that changes the direct current put out by the solar cells to alternating current usable in the electric utility connection. That function, so simple to describe is anything but simple to accomplish in practice. The first solar inverters were re-treads from the emergency power systems that used batteries as a backup to large computer installations allowing seamless operation in the event of failure of the utility source. Seamless to a computer means less than a millionth of a second. Clearly it is not addressable by starting up a backup diesel generator -- inverters were needed. These emergency inverters were applicable because they had the right power capacity. However, they lacked the controls for performance in emergencies required for solar power systems. Also, they were designed to operate indoors in an air-conditioned environment, not outdoors where the solar array field would be. In short, there was a need for new equipment and the design problems looked sweet.

The inverter function is to convert a power source with constant value to one with values on a sinusoidal basis, both positive and negative and matching the frequency of the utility system. This requires a lot of fast switching back and forth. Switching means power loss. If the switching could be reduced the lost power would be reduced and the efficiency would increase. Some computer simulations were done and indeed it looked like a solar cell field with two positive values and two negative values would when properly switched make a significant improvement in efficiency.

I was doing some work for Sandia National Laboratories during the summer and broached this idea to them. The first result was complete silence and I thought perhaps I had committed a social error. Then their question was, "Are you in a position to make some hardware to demonstrate this idea?" That was moving ahead of me -- I hadn't checked to see if Cal Poly would go along with this. My response was, "Let me see what I can do with Cal Poly."

I discovered that Cal Poly at that time was really not geared to handle research contracts. All contracts had to go through The Foundation which had rules on what an employee could be paid based on their normal salary with the Foundation taking a cut for the Cal Poly Presidents slush fund. As an Assistant Professor, my pay was miserable even before the cut. I talked this over with Bill Horton who was then the Dean of the School of engineering. "Bill, I've got a Catch 22 situation. I have a chance to bring in some research money from SANDIA and hire a few students to work on Saturdays, but the foundations rules cut my pay to a level I haven't seen since 1951. Is there any way that I can get a pay level that I negotiate with the contractor?" Bill laughed bitterly and said, "I think so, give me a week." At the end of the week the rules had been changed and I had the agreement from the EE department to use a small room (about 8 foot square) as a working lab exclusively for this project. I was able to get two very good students lined up and thus made the proposal to SANDIA. They bought it and wanted to start immediately. There would be no reduction in my teaching load so life took on a concentrated nature with nighttime computer work and Saturdays with the students on hardware.

In about three months we had a bench version of the inverter which proved the concept. This had required not only the design and construction of the inverter, but the construction of a power source that mocked the four-voltage solar array. The students were absolutely delighted to be working on a practical job that was cutting-edge in nature.

SANDIA was delighted and wanted a proposal for a weatherproof 6 kilowatt demonstrator inverter to be installed at their lab in Albuquerque. A proposal was made Cal Poly had its first research-level hardware contract in the solar field, the students and Art were being paid a respectable rate and the Foundation was happy with its cut.

# A Quiet Year On The World Scene

The year 1985 was relatively quiet compared to those recently passed. However, three events were forerunners of the current concern for atmospheric contamination and earth warming. A British antarctic survey team discovered the ozone hole over the south pole which was the result of pollution in the atmosphere. Concern was that it might grow and allow greatly increased levels of UV radiation to reach the surface of the earth with bad effects on human health. Bangladesh suffered a tropical cyclone and ocean surge that drowned 10,00 persons. A foretaste of surge effects in low-lying areas with dense populations. Forty one tornadoes struck Ohio, Pennsylvania, New York and Ontario killing 76 persons.

Progress continued in the area of medicine where the first heart transplant patient survived long enough to leave the hospital. DNA was used in a criminal trial for the first time and the FDA approved screening of blood donations for infection from AIDS. It was welcome, but came too late for one acquaintance who died from a transfusion and the resulting disease.

In the theater of old and new, Microsoft released Windows 1.0 which would forever change personal computing and the the highway U.S. 66 was de-commissioned taking with it memories of the depression and journeys west to find a new life..

* * *

A proposal had been made to SANDIA for a 6 kW inverter in the new "Dickerson Inverter" configuration. I didn't invent that name, but had not opposed it either. The job started in earnest with the same two students and before completion in 1986 would involve two more. The small technician shop in the EE department had sheet metal forming equipment which allowed us to make the custom-fitted weatherproof housing for the inverter. The students had not experienced sheet metal work before and were fascinated with the techniques and results. One of which produced creases on the outer cover to shed rain over the inner cover which permitted forced cooling air flow.

Not all of the design was electrical. The unit was spray-painted outside on the lawn where the next mowing would remove the droppings. It began to look professional. The students participated in the heat transfer analysis and design. This is an essential task in power equipment but is often overlooked in technical courses. It involves the design of the heat sink that allows transfer of heat from metal to the forced cooling air. The volume and speed of the air flow and the resulting temperature difference between metal and air need to be calculated. Also needed is a calculation of the temperature rise if the fan fails and the resulting time until the over-temperature control shuts down the unit. The students got a mini-course in mechanical engineering of heat transfer. They were fascinated to see the flow of theory into practice. By year end, the mechanical aspects of the inverter were complete and work was well underway on the electrical assembly and its electronic control.

\* \* \*

I had been promoted to Associate Professor in 1983 and now with four years experience on tenure track, I was up for for consideration of tenure and full professor. My only problem was The Doctor, a tenured professor. I had made the mistake of incurring his enmity the first week that I was at Cal Poly in 1980. At a faculty meeting I was asked to review my curriculum vitae so the faculty would know my background. I had just started when he interrupted to make some comment about my long industrial

experience and short teaching time. I let him wrangle on and then my testosterone fueled former-manger self took command. I could see he was trying to put me in a low class and so, forgive me, when he stopped I said in a calm voice, "Please pardon me for speaking while you interrupt." This brought a peal of laughter from the other faculty and undying hatred from him. Now he was the class scheduler and he accosted me in the hall saying, "I'm going to give you a new class you have never taught and your poor student ratings from that will stop your bid for tenure." I was astonished at this brazen attack and miss-use of power. Later that day when when I was in the mail room with a tenured faculty member, he walked in and I presented him with a written paper of his statement and asked that he sign it. He refused, saying, "That is not necessary." I then turned to another tenured faculty member and asked if he would witness that The Doctor had refused my request to sign a paper. He said, "Sure, I heard that.". The Doctor repeated that it was unnecessary and left.

The tenured faculty man asked what that was about and I showed him the paper with the Doctor's threat. He thought for a moment and then laughed out loud.

When the vote on tenure came up it was unanimous except for one. I learned later that The Doctor had even proposed a rule that no one retired from industry could receive tenure. That was voted down. So I received tenure. The curious thing about The Doctor's threat was that he assigned me an upper division course in digital design, observing that I had mainly taught analog design at both USC and Cal Poly. Digital design was his major subject. He did not know, but I was thoroughly experienced in digital design at Hughes Aircraft and held two patents in that area. The course did require extra preparation time, but I was never lost in it and the student evaluations were excellent as I could cite and use many practical examples as problems. Sorry 'bout that, Doctor.

* * *

Collie continued to paint from her studio and from our RV which became known as the rolling studio. Favored locations included the beach at Montano de Oro and roadside spots of the California back country. She held a one-person show of watercolors and acrylics at the San Luis Obispo Art Museum. It was well received and the sea-scapes and verdant landscapes were praised.

Shari continued her insurance work and began to teach insurance adjusting at night. Chris continued her work as a relief teller, but came to me one day with a story that chilled me. Banking was now on the computerized system and she said, "Dad, there's something going on. Yesterday $25,000. came into my records without me knowing why and then just as mysteriously disappeared later in the day." My advice was simple, "Make a written record of this and if it happens again go to your supervisor. If you don't get a satisfactory explanation start looking for a job with another company." She did just that and a year later the company went bankrupt, but she was out of it.. The family was meeting reality in its many forms.

* * *

# Nuclear Disaster, Terrorists, Computers & Space

The year 1986 was filled with major events across a broad spectrum. Many forecast the future and it was not bright. A major event was the meltdown of the Soviet nuclear reactor at Chernobyl which killed over 4000 people and caused over 350,000 to be resettled. The reactor was eventually cast in concrete costing the lives of many workers, but still deposits of nuclear material were later found in every country of the northern hemisphere. Unhappy with western reporting, I fired up a WWII spy radio, looked up the frequency of the Kiev radio station and tuned in. The first words heard were *"Chernobyl Disastrasche"*. Despite central control, they knew they had a big one on their hands Wind currents carried the radiation products over the entire northern hemisphere and changed the nuclear policies of Germany, Sweden and others. Unfortunately it did nothing for Fukushima, Japan.

Things shone brighter in the computer area. Microsoft made its' first public offering of stock. Those who went on board were handsomely rewarded later. The first role-playing computer game, "Dragon Quest" appeared on the market, but so also appeared the first virus, "Brain". Many more of each ilk would follow. I was appalled that a human being would invent computer code to inhibit and destroy the work of other computer users.

In space there was also plus and minus. The USSR launched the space station MIR with many shortcomings, but stealing a march on the U.S. More problems occurred with the disintegration of the "Challenger" spacecraft 73 seconds after launch. The death of all crew members is is chiefly remembered for Christa Mc Auliff, a school teacher riding as assistant crew member, to dramatize the space program for school children. I remember it for the loss of Ron McNair whom I knew at Hughes Research Labs. He was a fine man and good physicist. Navy divers recovered the command module with the bodies of all seven crew members.

Terrorist activities spanned the world. In Berlin a disco bombing killed 3 and wounded 230. The disco was a hangout for US troops. Lybia was thought to be at fault. U.S. Navy planes bombed both Tripoli and Benghazi with the death of 15 and unknown number of injuries. Two Lybian jets were shot down when they arose to attack the Navy planes. Members of an Islamist group, Abu Nidal, highjacked Pan Am flight 53 with 358 persons aboard at Kirachi . The same Abu Nidal group on the following day killed 22 persons in a synagogue at Shabbot services. In Oklahoma, a USPS employee "went postal", shot and killed 14 employees and himself. In Washington it was discovered that the US sold weapons to Iran and channeled the resulting funds to finance an anti-communist group in Nicarauga. This became the Iran-Contra affair. Col. Oliver North had shredded the papers associated with the actions.

* * *

A full load of lectures, lab courses and senior projects continued. One fascinating project came from a student who was an amateur astronomer and wanted to take long time exposures on camera film using his telescope. To do this he needed a two-axis motor drive to cause his telescope to track a star in the field he was photographing. He came in with his project completely designed and I felt like a passenger riding in his car. He proposed two servo-mechanism drives, one moving up and down, the other moving left and right. He proposed two light detectors each of which had a focused image of the tracking star. Each detector was connected through a drive mechanism with a stepping motor and a high-ratio gear train so that one impulse to move resulted in only an infinitesimal movement of the telescope. This was not a novel approach, but it was surely sophisticated for an undergraduate. We discussed oscillation of the system and the instability that always lurks in the background of servo-mechanisms. To my surprise he had already thought of this and had done the calculations and design necessary to achieve stable operation.

When he had completed design and construction we did a test on his telescope with me using a penlight to simulate the tracking star. I moved it up and down, left and right to see if the telescope tracked. It did track with great precision and excellent stability. Both the student and I were delighted. Clearly he got an A grade with a handshake and back slap.

* * *

Work continued with the team of four students on the Solar Power inverter for Sandia. The team include two students then working on their masters degrees and a young woman and man finishing their batchelor' degrees. The young lady screamed the first time that she witnessed a direct current arc, but bravely overcame this sensitivity and learned to live effectively.with small fireworks. When she graduated her father came to me and said, "I sent you a young girl and you have returned to me an engineer. Thank you so much". It was one of the better moments in my teaching career.

\* \* \*

A curious end came to the affair with The Doctor regarding my tenure. I did receive tenure and so attended the tenured faculty meeting that discussed curriculum, promotions and department policies. At the end of the first meeting of my attendance the department chair asked if there was any new business. I held up my hand and he said, "Art, we're kinda late, could you postpone that to the next meeting?" I readily agreed. The nature of the business has skipped my mind, but it was not pressing. The Doctor apparently thought I was going to bring up his hallway threat to defeat my tenure through scheduling a new class. That was certainly not my intent. The tenure issue was now for me a thing of the past. However, he was greatly relieved to see the postponement. The following month exactly the same thing happened with him more red-faced and upset. I readily agreed to a postponement and, God forgive me, was beginning to enjoy the game. At the third meeting The Doctor announced that he would be teaching at another school the following year. I pleased and when my turn came up for new business was able to introduce my trivial topic which was quickly settled. The Doctors puzzled expression told me that he didn't know whether I had excused the transgression after his announcement of departure or never intended to bring it up. I maintained a poker face.

\* \* \*

Collie continued to paint 8 hours a day and also grew closer to the San Luis Art Center. She gave a lecture and watercolor painting demonstration there. It was well attended and featured an overhead mirror with Collie facing the audience and painting a watercolor on a flat horizontal desktop. That way she could talk directly to the audience over the painting while they could see the painting develop in the overhead mirror. The audience applauded vigorously when she finished.

Chris continued in her banking work and the raising of Travis and Jessie. Shari and Jerry continued their apartment management and insurance work in Los Angeles. The family was embarked on its' individually chosen paths.

* * *

# On The World Scene A Relatively Quiet Year

The year 1987 a quiet year compared to the near past. President Reagan had to admit that in the Iran-Contra affair he had allowed it to descend into arms for hostages bargaining. His reputation recovered when in Berlin he shouted, "Mr. Gorbachev -- tear down this wall!". It would be two years before the wall was knocked down, but the move was started. The Unabomber exploded his second vengence bomb in a computer store.

The software Windows 2.0 was released, setting Microsoft on the path to annual up-dating of the windows program. The first PC version of Photoshop was released, permitting users to manipulate and print photos and drawings. The first Simpsons cartoon series appeared.

Iraqi aircraft released two Exocet missiles which struck the U.S.S. Stark, killimg 57 navy men. Iraqi planes also dropped mustard gas bombs on four residential areas of Sardasas in Iran. This was the first known military use of chemical weapons on purely civilian targets. Terrible! But compared to some preceding years relatively quiet.

\* \* \*

Along with the usual teaching load and senior projects, the work on the 6 kilowatt solar inverter proceeded to completion and first tests at Cal Poly.. In the summer the unit was driven in my car to Sandia National Labs for on line testing. Owing to a separate contract, I would work the entire summer at Sandia after the inverter tests. The tests went well except for one unexpected event. A necessary function of the inverters electronic control was to synchronize it closely to the AC voltage of the system it was supplying. Unknown to me, Sandia used a peculiar means to update time on its electric clocks when they were too slow. This involved sending a 300 cycle signal on the power line just after noon each day. The number of additional cycles was such that the clocks would be correctly updated down to the correct second.

I was sitting beside my operating inverter at noon one day when it began to vibrate terribly at 300 cycles trying to follow the clock setting signal.. This only went on for a few seconds, then everything was back to normal. When your technical child is taking a critical exam and suddenly throws a fit, it gets your attention. I mentioned this to the Sandia engineers. They laughed then set me straight on their clock updating scheme. No harm was done and it was actually a positive indication that the inverter was doing its best to follow the AC voltage and didn't break anything while doing it.

* * *

When the inverter tests were complete Sandia asked that I design for them a battery charge control that would permit a solar panel to charge batteries considering their temperature and not over-charging them. Over-charge greatly reduces the life of a battery. The point where over-charge is reached depends on the temperature of the batteries electrolyte. Thus, the control must shift the solar voltage to match that of the battery and control the process, stopping when full charge is reached. This seemed like an interesting project and I fell in with it quickly. When the circuit drawings were complete they furnished a technician to layout the printed circuit board and construct the control. I was delighted to be left out of that tedious task. When the unit was done, test began. The control, I'm happy to say, worked just as designed and did a neat lob of controlling overcharge. Sandia was impressed that the design incorporated a tiny plug in "Personality Module" which permitted different voltages of battery and solar panels to be accommodated. The module was only an inch long by half an inch wide and a quarter inch high. It plugged into a standard integrated circuit socket on the printed circuit board, permitting an easy field change of charging properties.

* * *.

One thing Sandia was not happy with was that the "Model 2" inverter required two different voltages from the solar array field. They felt that this was a complication that would be troublesome when inexperienced crews installed the panels. It would be better if all arrays were the same number of panels, connected in the same way. I couldn't disagree with this and set to work thinking of ways to accomplish that simplification. Finally the idea came, but there was a question as to how well it would work. Circuit simulation programs were just appearing for PCs, but would not handle the complexity of a full scale three-phase inverter. That would be achieved in a few years, but in 1987 the only answer was to build a small model. Fortunately one of the ladies on the student inverter team was willing to undertake this not-so-simple task. She did a marvelous job of building it and we were both delighted to discover that indeed the idea and the model both worked as originally conceived. That lady went on to a masters degree and is now a lead engineer with Hawaian Electric Company, dealing with the proliferation of solar systems in Hawai.

Sandia was delighted with the new idea, which would become the Dickerson Inverter "Model 3". They signed a contract for a 12 kilowatt inverter. Work began in 1988.

* * *

Collies popularity at the San Luis Obispo Art Center led to her election as the leader of Opaque Art Group. She was at first honored, but later interest paled at the lengthy policy meetings and the need to organize and put on the various group functions. One year was enough. She did receive a brass plaque of appreciation which hung in her studio where she retired to paint 8 hours per day. Her output swelled with large watercolors of Central Coast scenes.

Shari continued her insurance career in Los Angeles and doubled as Apartment manager. Chris continued her bank work and briefly visited me in Albuquerque during my summer job there. We had a grand time visiting Albuquerque restaurants and the UNM library.

* * *

# Change In The USSR, Action In Iran, U.S. Drought

The year 1988 saw abrupt change on the world scene from the quiet of 1987. Soviet Premier Gorbachev initiated economic change through the program of *Perestroika* leading toward capitalism and the growth of the Russian Mafia. The soviets withdrew from Afganistan after 8 years of non-decisive war. Estonia declared itself sovereign and the USSR agreed..

The Near East was active as Iran declared the straight of Hormuz closed and mined the a navy frigate, USS Samuel Roberts. The U.S. responded with an action named Praying Mantis in which an Iranian frigate was attacked and several oil platforms shot up. An unfortunate accident occured when the USS Vincennes mis-identified an Iranian commercial airliner, flight 655 as an attacking military plane and shot it down. All aboard were killed. A truce was declared in the Iran - Iraq war after deaths over one million. Palestine declared itself an independent state.

Pan Am flight 103 crashed in Lockerbee, Scotland after a bomb aboard exploded. The person responsible was thought to be and later proved to be Libyan..

In the technology area, the first internet malware, Morris Worm appeared. The first transatlantic fiber optic cable started operation. I marveled that it was only 12 years since my operation at Hughes held the world record for longest fiber optic data link, all of 100 meters.

The U.S. experienced a severe drought estimated to have caused 17,000 excess deaths and $80 billion in damages. In the parched grass of Yellowstone park a fire started which burned 750,000 acres or 36% of the park area before it was extinguished.

* * *

At Cal Poly, work began on the 12 kW inverter "Model 3" which was destined to be installed in Phoenix Arizona. The work proceeded smoothly with surprising freedom of basic problems. A brilliant Chinese student, finishing his master's degree did the software design for the control which was complicated to meet all the requirements of safely interfacing with the electric utility and managing the moment by moment operation of the inverter in normal mode. He did a marvelous job on the software and the design of the microprocessor control, all packaged in a box 12" x 14" x 3" with a front panel display of mode. I always liked simple front panel controls and this one hit the mark. There were only two switches, one marked "on" and :off", the other marked "run" and "test". When a utility technician in the field later asked me to run him through the operation and he saw the front panel, he said, "With an hour or so I could master this".

In addition to the inverter work, a normal load of teaching and senior projects.occupied the days. One new activity was to act as Technical Referee to the Superior Court of California in the case of Escorp. - v - Stewart, Judge Hammer presiding.. I obtained this job by being on the list of both parties as trusted experts in the technology of the suit. Former students worked at both party locations. The judge found the technology formidable and wrote a series of questions to which he desired answers in order to decide whether Stewart was stealing technology from Escorp.

This was an interesting job as I did not wish to reveal confidential information from one party to the other. However, there were certain points of the investigation which clearly said to me that there was no theft. Also, the president of Escorp had failed to label his drawings "Confidential", so in my view he could hardly claim that confidential information had been stolen. I finally assembled enough facts that were non-revealing, but which to one skilled in the field indicated fundamental differences in the two products. The final report to the judge ran 19 pages single spaced. The Escorp software engineer agreed there was no theft and actually thanked me for the discreet, but conclusive statements. The Judge agreed and the suit was settled. I was told that was the first time a technical referee was used in that court

This year also saw publication of two technical papers, the first on the tests of the "Model 2" inverter at Sandia Labs and the second on the battery charge control designed for Sandia. A patent application was filed for the "model 3" inverter topology.

* * *

Shari and I took the camper on a trip north to the Owens Valley. There we ran into the smoke from the Yellowstone fire and also discovered that we had minor altitude sickness when we reached the trailhead to Mount Wilson so we decided to go back down to the town of Lone Pine. It was a fine, fun trip.

Collie continued to paint from her studio and did some private teaching of watercolor. She was active in the Thursday Painters, using the camper as her Rolling Studio. Chris continued her work in the SLO area. The family was enjoying themselves.

* * *

# Worlwide Political Turmoil
# & Firsts In Technology

The year 1989 saw great change in Europe, Asia and South America. The USSR began to come apart as a unified communist entity beginning with Poland recognizing the Solidarity party and holding elections. Hungary dismantled 150 miles of barbed wire fence on the border with Austria and opened that border. Lithuania, Latvia and Estonia formed a human chain holding hands and stretching for 500 miles to demand free elections which they obtained. Finally near year end the Berlin Wall fell as the border was opened between East and West Germany. President George H.W. Bush and Soviet Premier. met and indicated that the Cold War was over. Sheer joy prevailed in Berlin.

In China it was the year of the Tiananman Protest in which students unveiled a 33 foot statue of the "Goddess of Peace" and a single man stood down a tank in a demonstration of citizens versus communist goverment. On the reverse side Iran's Ayatolla Ruhallah Khomeini placed a death Fatwah and a $3 million dollar award for execution of Salman Rushdie, author of "The Satanic Verses" said to ridicule Mohammed.

In South America political changes occurred in Brazil, Chile, Argentina and Columbia. The one etched in my memory concerned the Takeover of Panama by Manuel Noriega. President Bush sent 1900 troops to protect U.S. citizens. This was not immediately announced. I was temporarily working at Sandia Labs in Albuquerque and one evening heard a section of 3 C-97 aircraft take off and circle to get in formation and then head East. I knew there were 3 C-97s at the AFB adjacent to Sandia, but all three out at one time seemed unusual. Then another three took off formed up and headed east. In succession a total of 12 C-97s formed up and headed east. I recall thinking "Wow, something big is up" as that number could transport 1800 men and their personal arms. Add another 4 and that could transport a complete battalion and its heavy weapons. I did not know until later that was exactly what happened.

In the technology area, the World Wide Web was conceived in Switzerland. The first 24 GPS satellites were put into orbit furnishing the basis for accurate navigation. Motorola introduced the first cell phone. It was also the year of the first flight for Northrup-Grummans' B-2 bomber, which is still the worlds most advanced. A severe geomagnetic storm caused collapse of the Canadian Hydro-Quebec power grid, putting 6 million people in the darkness and without heat for 9 hours. I had visited Hydro-Quebec while I was at Hughes Aircraft developing components for High Voltage DC transmission which were of interest to them. They had a full scale simulator in anticipation of a link to Quebec from the northern lakes.

The Exxon Valdez ran aground in Alaska's Prince William Sound, releasing 240,000 barrels of oil, killing extensive wildlife an spoiling miles of coastline.

* * *

In 1989 consulting work became varied and intense in addition to a full-time teaching load at Cal Poly. My log shows that 12,000 miles were driven on business in contrast to 2,000 miles driven on personal chores. The work included two trips to Albuquerque and one each to San Francisco, Los Angeles and Phoenix AZ.

The job as Technical Referee for the SLO Superior Court attracted another job as expert witness in a law suit defended by David Medvedov. The company he was defending was the manufacturer of the electronic control board for a printing machine. A technician in SLO repairing a machine replaced the control board and when the machine failed to start up he looked closely at the board. With his head only 8 -10 inches away, an electrolytic capacitor exploded driving its small aluminum enclosure can into his right eye. He did not lose sight, but the eye was damaged and the sight impaired. He sued the manufacturer of the control board. Medvedov's first question to me was, "What will cause an electrolytic capacitor to explode?". I replied, "In about 95% of the cases ot is because the DC voltage has been applied to it in the reverse direction, let me correct that to 98%". He then described the circumstances of the injury and asked if I would act as technical expert for him in the matter of the suit. I readily agreed and asked if he could let me examine the damaged control board. He did along with the aluminum case that had done the ocular damage. It was clear that that the capacitor had exploded. I immediately ordered six samples of the exact same capacitor in case tests or dissection was necessary.

The capacitor case was about the size of a type C dry battery and contained two sheets of thin aluminum foil and two sheets of fluffy paper. This combination was rolled together very tightly and inserted into the case which was then filled with salt water. Before rolling, one of the aluminum sheets had been oxidized and the other left plain. The oxide caused an electrical charge to exist on the one sheet relative to the other. If a voltage was then applied consistent with the polarity of this charge, a larger charge would build up and the capacitor would form its intended function of storing charge and become a temporary energy storage component. That's how its supposed to work. If the applied voltage is in the reverse direction, a large current flows and heats the salt water to form steam. The case is closed to prevent the escape of the salt water and when the steam pressure builds up, the capacitor explodes with a resounding bang, driving the case off of the plastic base that carries the wires from the two sheets to the outside world. It is possible that faulty construction could result in a short circuit between the two aluminum sheets which would produce the same end result, but this is very rare.

I applied reverse voltage to three of the purchased capacitors and it required from 8 to 10 seconds for the explosion to occur. The same as the technician described the accident.as occuring. Reverse voltage certainly looked likely. The question was whether the board could have been plugged in incorrectly, or was the capacitor wired in reverse connection. I examined to board and its receptacle. It had been correctly designed with an off center keyway that prevented it from being plugged in reverse. I had to inform Medvedov that it looked pretty bad for his client, but proposed we could do an autopsy on the fragments of the exploded capacitor still clinging to the board and determine absolutely whether the capacitor had been wired in place incorrectly. He was indeed a seeker of truth and readily agreed. The three attorneys and their three technical experts assembled. I explained that we could agree at the start which aluminum sheet was the oxidized sheet and then, by carefully cutting away fragments, could trace it to its connection on the board. This was agreeable so I took a pair of surgical scissors and began to cut slowly, explaining beforehand at each step what I proposed to do. This procedure continued slowly and accurately for about 15 minutes until the end of the sheets was reached. We all looked carefully and each simultaneously grunted when it was revealed that the capacitor had indeed been wired in place in reverse connection. The guilt clearly fell on Medvedov's client. I turned to him and said in sympathy, "I'm sorry, but that's the way it is." He smiled and said, "It's going to be a short trial if all the experts agree." He then polled the other two experts and found complete agreement.

Medvedov called on me later for a second different trial in San Francisco and would become my attorney in 1991 when I was sued for an accident involving an equipment which I had designed and built. Unfortunately he died in 2013.

* * *

A contract was signed for a 12 kilowatt inverter to be installed in Phoenix, AZ. I signed a contract with the Cal Poly Foundation to utilize myself and Poly students to build the inverter. This required stringing new wire in the race-ways of building 20 from the power room at the southern end all the way to a drafting classroom on the north corner. The students and I worked there on Saturdays and by late summer had completed and tested the inverter. This unit weighed several hundred pounds and so was shipped by truck to the Phoenix Star Center test bed, actually in Tempe, AZ. I rented an apartment there and set about the installation and test of that unit. It operated fine after minor changes to the cooling fan.

Unfortunately I had to inform Phoenix Power and Light that after our contract was signed that I had a further invention in the inverter area which would if successful make the 12 kW until obsolete. They were chagrined but left the unit installed at the Star Test Center as an example of their intent to follow new technology.

\* \* \*

I worked twice at Sandia National Labs on the battery charge control designed for them the previous year. They were interested in the new inverter invention and were instrumental in talking PG&E and Arco Solar into a contract to purchase two 100 kW units for test at PVUSA (Photovoltaic Utility Scale Array) in Davis, CA.

\* \* \*

Collie continued painting 8 hours per day and served as the chair of the SLO Art Center committee on Watercolor and Pastel. She also received a Best Of Show Award at the center. Shari continued her work in Los Angeles as an insurance adjuster and renewed her certificate to teach insurance adjusting classes. Chris divorced her husband, retaining custody of her daughter Jesse. Her son Travis had graduated from high school and was trying to work his way through Berkeley. The family was moving ahead in its separate specialties.

\* \* \*

# End Of The Cold War, Start Of Gulf War, Changes To Books

The year 1990 saw massive changes in the political venues of Europe and Asia. The Baltic states separated from the USSR, which declared itself open to multi-party elections. Michael Gorbachev was elected to a 5-year term. Gorbachev and George H.W. Bush signed a treaty eliminating stock-piles of chemical weapons and banning future production. Gorbachev received the Nobel Peace Prize. The first McDonalds was opened in Moscow. East and West Germany were reunited in a common currency and society. Checkpoint Charley was dismantled and the Berlin Wall fell.

In the area of science and publications, the scientist-based ARPANET was abandoned in favor of the public Internet. The Encyclopedia Britannica reached it's peak sales year of 120,000 copies and the number of librarians in the U.S. also peaked. The Hubble Telescope was launched to eventually become the worlds viewpoint of deep space.

The field of warfare was active. The U.S. invaded Panama. Iraq invaded and occupied Kuwait. The U.S. and many Mid-East nations sent troops and aircraft to Saudi Arabia, fearing an Iraqi invasion. The U.N. voted to require Iraq to remove itself from

Kuwait by January 15 of 1991. George H.W. Bush called up U.S. reservists.

* * *

The year opened with a full teaching load at Cal Poly. A new invention was had for a solar-powered battery charger. This resulted in a contract from Arco Solar to develop a weather-tight unit for the Canadian Navy to control the charging of batteries on navigation floats. This looked like fun. I could readily imagine the problems of the seamen in a small boat changing out the charge controller in high wind and a moderate sea. Students were hired to construct and test the sealed unit, the state of which was seen on light-emitting diodes visible through a transparent window in the water-tight casing. The students enjoyed this and the tests were good. A sample was sent to the Canadian Navy for test. It passed. Arco bid on the procurement only to find that Canada already had a Canadian supplier in mind and this exercise was just to show that there was competition. Ah well. At least the students learned something and in a way so did Arco solar and I.

There was a second contract with Arco Solar to supply two 100 kilowatt solar inverters for installation at PVUSA (Photovoltaic Utility Scale Activity) at Davis, California. A contract was let to Cal Poly for student help in construction and tests of the two units. These proceeded well with the students getting experience with a full-sized inverter, six feet tall by four feet wide by two feet deep. In the fall the two units were demonstrated for a PG&E and ARCO approval team in the courtyard of building 20 at Cal Poly. The tests went well and approval was received. At year end the two units were shipped to Davis. I took leave for one quarter to supervise installation and test, renting an apartment in Davis, anticipating a two-month period of test and modification that always occurs when a new device is installed on an existing system. That was optimistic as we will see in the next chapter.

* * *

Collie continued to photograph her rose beds and flower gardens. From these slides she painted eight hours per day and showed the results at the San Luis Obispo Art Museum. Shari continued to practice insurance adjustment by day and to teach it at night. Chris continued her work as a bank teller . The family continued their individual pursuits.

* * *

# Cold War Ends, Yugoslavian War Begins, Weather Worsens

The Soviet Union ceased to exist with the political exit of all the non-Russian members. A treaty was signed between the U.S and Russia to limit ballistic missiles and the U.S. called off the standing 24 hour alert for SAC bombers. The Cold War ended.

In a contrasting scenario, the Gulf War boomed as the UN deadline for Iraq to remove troops from Kuwait passed with no action. The U.S. initiated the air war and eventually sent 540,000 troops to the Middle East. The Iraqis fired SCUD missiles into Israel. The Iraqis evacuated Kuwait, but set fire to the oil fields as they left. Those fires would burn for over 6 months. The UN sent inspectors to close Iraqs nuclear and chemical weapon program, which they denied having. Records were found for the nuclear program and Iraqi soldiers tried to capture the inspectors. They UN threatened action and the inspectors and records were released. The Yugoslavian War began with scattered incidents in Croatia and Serbia.

The weather showed changes with the first cyclone in the southern hemisphere and a cyclone in Bangladesh killing 138,000 people. In one day there were 70 tornadoes in the middle U.S.

Technology began to show its' effects when the World Wide Web started operation and separately 4 Los Angeles policemen were indicted for beating Rodney King as seen on a video shot by a civilian from his portable camera.

\* \* \*

After 10 years of teaching, my CALPERS pension was vested and so when a strong push started for reduction in CSU faculty I accepted the offer of an additional record of one years service on my pension. I discovered later than this meant I could never again teach in the CSU system, not that I intended to, but it was a cold-hearted dismissal for one who received several awards for teaching performance. Ah well.

In my final year of teaching I was asked to teach EE-433 which was in the catalog, but had never been offered with a scheduled class. The intent was that I should do the work to lay out a syllabus and lecture schedule, choose a text and leave this in the files to ease the task of some future teacher. The subject, Advanced Analog Design was a cool one so I undertook the task. This added to the normal teaching load and the extreme effort to work with students to complete the contract with Arco Solar to build, test and install two 100 kilowatt solar inverters. It would be a busy year.

I took my "summer" leave in the first quarter and went to Davis, California to install and test the inverters. It was an incredibly cold winter.Several eucalyptus tries along the highway which had survived for decades were frozen and died. Fortunately I knew how to dress for cold weather after twice living in upstate New York.. My outdoor work was a surprise to the young engineers who were comfortable indoors. One asked, "How do you stand that cold?" He didn't know that I was wearing thermal underwear, Navy cold weather sweaters and a navy wool watch cap underneath my hard hat.

The inverters were installed and passed the PG&E acceptance tests which were extensive. It was found that the inverter efficiency was well over 95%, a record for that period. Unfortunately I had accommodated requests from ARCO solar to put some of their instrumentation inside my inverter cabinet and to incorporate one of their emergency shutdown procedures into the software of my control. As the test period progressed that would prove a problem. However, at the beginning the long term operation tests proved that some of the hardware protection schemes that I had provided were more problem than cure. Thus, some parts had to be removed to make operation more reliable. The test site proved to be more of a challenge than PG&E had intended. Other inverters on test were experiencing damage from over-voltage surges. I had been very conservative on this point and was experiencing no damage, but did have an occasional emergency shutdown. PG&E did not belive this, despite the fact that the feeder to which the site was tied supplied extensive large farm irrigation pumps that greatly distort the line voltage during startup. After some arguments PG&E agreed to install a recorder to make a record of line voltage surges. I watched the recording in real time and saw several surges exceed 200% for over 5 milliseconds. When I requested a copy of the results of the test, PG&E refused, but the argument about emergency overvoltage shutdowns stopped.

An argument then started about automatic shutdowns for an unknown cause. This was blamed on the inverter because, "That's where the signal came from.". I felt that this was a problem with Arco Solar-photovolatic arrays and that the signal "came from the inverter" simply because I had generously incorporated their procedure into my software. We finally agreed to rent high-speed recording equipment to determine the basic source of the problem. If it was the inverter, I would pay for the rental, if it was the array, Arco would pay. We installed the rentals and waited. Finally there was a shutdown and examination of the record showed that it was Arco's equipment. They paid and fixed the problem.

The matter of the Arco hardware in my equipment was not settled so easily. The full voltage of the solar arrays, 700 volts DC appeared on the top of the arco hardware on metal screws. These were only exposed when the weather-tight doors of the inverter were open. The doors were locked with a key available only to experienced people at the site. The ARCO technician on site was in charge of safety for the ARCO portion of the installation, including the inverters. He and I were making live measurements one day and he was not wearing his protective gloves. These gloves consist of a heavy rubber glove inside of a leather glove which protected the rubber from tears in usage. I called this to his attention saying, "Put on your gloves or I won't work with you." He gave me a look which said in effect, "Don't tell me what to do." It was a hot summer day with high humidity and we were both sweating liberally. He was measuring the 700 volt array potential inside the inverter on top of the ARCO instruments. Unfortunately the plastic probes of his voltmeter did not have guards that prevent the fingers from slipping over the end and contacting the metal probe end. I think what happened was that his sweaty fingers slipped down the plastic when he jammed the probe against the equipment terminal. This put him in contact with the 700 volts. He grunted and fell backwards knocking the door closed. I ran to him and did the first aid check. He had pulse, good. His face was a vivid red, there was evidently blood circulation. He was breathing noisily. He was temporarily safe, so I turned to shutting down the operation to make the area safe.

He had no broken limbs, so I drove my car to him and loaded him into the passenger seat and drove to the control room to ask the way to the hospital and request that they be called to notify them of an inbound electrocution patient. He got checked into the ER and I went over his insurance situation with the admittance people, then called ARCO Solar to report the accident. He seemed to be doing OK so I said good night.

I came in the next morning and found that in his view the inverter door had pushed him into the 700 volt connection and it was the fault of the way the inverter was designed. This started a long process for which I hired the attorney, David Medvedov, my previous employer for testimony at trial. To make a long story short, I had the wrong kind of insurance and had to settle the claim for about the cost of a low-end Mercedes Benz. I was quite beside the point that all the engineers at the test site could not believe I was being sued by an experienced technician who had intentionally failed to wear his gloves

ARCO Solar paid to have the inverters rebuilt so that a plastic shield covered all electrical connections with the door open. The inverters were reinstalled and performed very well. Subsequent tests elicited the comment from the site engineers that the inverters were "bulletproof" This was a curious comment as the site was about 200 yards north of the Davis Police Department firing range. One of the young engineers had a 9 mm round go through a solar array next to where he stood. Once I heard two .256 rounds go overhead in a northerly direction.

* * *

PG&E let a contract to Bluepoint Associates Ltd. (my consulting company) to do a paper design of an 80 Megawatt utility scale solar power scheme. I would work with Luz Inc. an Israeli company located in Tel Aviv. This turned out to be interesting, but had some peculiar aspects. The Israelis would talk about the job and then say, just before they went out to lunch, "Let's talk with Art." They phoned and of course this would be about 4 am in California. I learned to wake up quickly.

The design was completed and the Israelis got quotes from European suppliers for the switchgear and from US suppliers for the solar arrays. The costs looked pretty good, but PG&E as well as other US utilities were simply not in a mood to build solar. This put an end to the market for my inverters as they were only economic in large sizes. However, the experience of doing a complete design for a utility-scale system was exciting, even though the subsequent bankruptcy of Luz left my bill of $1024.unpaid. It struck me that 1024 was the $10^{th}$ power of 2, a number well known as "kilo" in digital circles. I was owed a kilobuck.

In succeeding years the progress in new semiconductor switching devices in both high current and high ratings obsoleted the circuitry of my inverter. Thus the whole four year exercise was educational, but not profitable. The cost for the right kind of insurance was found to be $40,000. per year. My company went out of the high voltage equipment business.

The cost of solar power systems continued to decrease by half each five years. By the early 2000's the economy was such that solar become the vogue first in Europe and then in the U.S. which was the source of that decrease in cost and increase in technology.

* * *

Collie continued to paint 8 hours a day, mainly flowers and a few still lives. She did original investigation of citrus solvents for acrylic paint, but usually returned to her favorite, watercolor. Shari continued her work as an insurance adjuster and developed a reputation for creativeness in settlement solutions. She also taught insurance at night. Chris continued her work as a teller and her son Travis started training as a fire-fighter and paramedic. Grandchildren were developing their own courses.

# Yugoslav War, Problems In Iraq, Rodney King Riots,

In the year 1992 the Socialist Federal Republic of Yugoslavia quite literally unwound with secession and fighting among Serbs, Bosnians, Herzegovians, Slovakians and Croatians. The UN authorized a peace keeping force which landed, but was forced to evacuate when the city of Sarajevo was besieged. Sniping of civilians by militia was horribly portrayed on personal cameras.

In the Near East, a U.S. F-16 shot down an Iraqi MIG-25 which was violating the UN no-fly zone. multiple scraps occurred between UN inspectors and Iraqi soldiers when the inspectors were refused entry to possible manufacturing sites for excluded weapons. Clearly Iraq did not consider itself defeated in the Gulf War.

In an early signal of future concerns the space shuttle Atlantis was dispatched with instruments to study earth warming.

Earth warming of a different kind occurred in Los Angeles when the four police officers indicted for the Rodney king beating were acquitted at trial. The resulting riots lasted 6 days and 53 deaths occurred. Damage was estimated at over $1 billion dollars.

Expanding technology was evident when sales of CDs exceeded sales of audio cassettes for the first time.

* * *

I received a Social Security Number at the age of 16 in 1942 while repairing radios on Saturdays as a regular job. Fifty years later, for the first time since then, I was unemployed except for my own consulting engineering company. Regular pay disappeared and was replaced with intermittent pay for whatever jobs I could land.. One of these was with Kilovac in Carpenteria, CA. They were a progressive company making vacuum interrupters for switching medium voltage AC circuits (up to 5 kilovolts) at moderate current (up to 100 Amperes). There was a need for DC interrupters on the International Space Station (ISS) to handle the new 270 volt DC power system. NASA had asked for proposals as no such product was then on the market. The attractive possibility was that the defense department might adapt the 270 volt DC system as standard replacing the 24 volt DC systems in use since the late 1939's. Interrupting AC is relatively simple with vacuum switches as the voltage on a 60 cycle system goes through zero 120 times each second, but the DC voltage stays fixed. However, in a vacuum as a switch opens, there are opportunities for the arc to simply stop, owing to the statistical nature of the ionization that maintains the arc (up to 5000 amperes). Kilovac had tried their switches and found that they did indeed interrupt 270 volts at the required current of 100 amperes.

The problem of their entry was that the regular test equipment to prove this in production came at a cost of $65,000. One of my former students was on their staff and told the engineering manager that Professor Dickerson had developed DC switches up to 100,000 volts and 2000 amperes -- maybe he would have an idea.

I received a call from the chief engineer and volunteered to come down and discuss their test problem. This was a marriage made in heaven, as I had developed a very low cost test scheme some years before and had government approval for it. The cost would be $2,000. instead of $65,000. The Kilovac staff gave me a thorough questioning and the next day called NASA who checked the Department of Energy and found that indeed the low-cost scheme was approved and had done a good job. As a result I had intermittent consulting work for about 6 months during their product development. They did get the contract for the ISS interrupters and found that there were other applications for this product. We were both happy and further intermittent work occurred over the next two years.

A second job occurred with the Bruce Anderson Company (BACO).. Although Bruce Anderson lived in San Luis Obispo, his company worked out of an office in Montana. They wanted to do a job for Montana Power and Light in estimating ways to reduce power consumption at a former SAC base which the Air Force had donated to the township of Glasgow. The Boeing Company wanted to lease the base for testing of the developmental 777 aircraft. The base was ideal for Boeing as it had a 15,500 foot runway and was located well away from other airport traffic patterns. Thus, they could fly about at moderate altitudes without clearance and do such things as create a 1 inch water layer on the runway to test the effect of landing in rain. Montana Power and light did not want to build a new generation site as the loads on their system grew, but at a rate too slow to pay for the new generators.. Thus, they wanted to eliminate existing unused load as a way to postpone a large capital expense. Boeing wanted their electrical bill to be minimized on a huge base of which they used only a small part. There was a common goal and that's why BACO was hired to survey the ways to minimize the overall load at the base.

BACO asked Cal Poly for the names of two professors that might help in the work with Montana Power and Light. My name came up as well as the head of the Electrical Engineering department. BACO interviewed both of us. Because the department head was primarily skilled in digital techniques and my advanced degree was in electrical power, I got the job.

The head of BACO and I flew to Glasgow and met with his Engineering manager as well as representatives of Montana Power and Light (MP&L) for a tour of the airfield. This was a trial for me as I was new to BACO and the whole idea of hiring an outside company to survey their system was new to MP&L.

I began by asking MP&L to show me their substation that supplied the base. This was partly to recognize the utilities importance and partly because I wanted to understand the local system. They were proud to show off and we all drove to the station. When we parked, I commented, "It's good that you have a 100 kilovolt substation, we will have no problems of supply." They responded that it was a 69 kilovolt substation, eyebrows questioning my 100 kilovolt statement. I had used the trick of counting the insulators on the line and multiplying by fifteen to estimate the line voltage. No designer would put as much as 20 kilovolts per insulator onto a line for safety reasons or less than 10 kilovolts for economic reasons. .I responded that the line looked to me like 100 kilovolts. The BACO people were uneasy that I questioned the customer. Then the older of the MP&L men scratched his head and said, "You know you're right. I forgot, but when that line was built we designed it for 100 kilovolts, but the substation was designed as 69 kilovolts.

I guess you know what you're looking at." I was now "in" with MP&L and BACO was relieved. .

Everything seemed in order at the station, so we went to the base. As we drove along a rode adjacent to the residential area, I noticed that the drawout fuses were still in place on one large 69 kV transformer and asked the MP&L people what load was on it. The reply was, "Nothing, that's all vacant." I avoided telling, but tactfully asked if it would be worthwhile to pull out the fuses and thus shut off the excitation load of the transformer. The answer was, "Yeah, we ought to do that, I'll check all the transformers on the base that have no load." Now I was "in" with BACO too.

We met with Boeing's site people and MP&L explained their desire to minimize load and how that would reduce Boeings' bill. It would all be done at the expense of MP&L and would be done only with Boeings' approval of the changes. Boeing had nothing to lose, so the site manager was immediately on board, but the older Boeing site engineer thought he smelled a rat and was evidently cautious.

His caution was tested when we inspected the base pumping station. He was sure this academic guy would tell him to install new higher efficiency pumps and motors. That equipment was almost as old as he was and he had put in a lot of loving care and maintenence. When he asked, "What should we do about this stuff?" I replied in all sincerity, "The new equipment might improve efficiency by 1 %, but these older systems often have a better match between pump and motor than the newer stuff. Can you get a motor rewound if it fails?" He quickly replied, "Sure, there's a good outfit in Billings that does that kind of work." I shrugged and said, "Well, you can do whatever you think is best, but if it were me I'd keep the old stuff on line." He tried to hide the smile that came across his face, now I was "in" with Boeing's engineer too. However, my next statement nearly ended that. "I see that you have the air-conditioning turned on for the whole pump-house, turning it off would save a lot of energy and there's no one working here now to know the difference." That went into the log of changes and was one of the larger savings in MP&L's load.

A lot of time went into the loads in the hangars and flight-line. The Air Force had installed hangar lighting to allow precision maintenance tasks at floor level. Boeing would not be doing precision maintenance at this base. Reducing the lighting by 50% added greatly to the swelling load reduction log. Similarly, shutting down the pumps and controls on all but one flight-line fuel tank added more saving.

I had several personal experiences working alone on a base of that size where the Air Force had simply walked away and the tightly sealed buildings kept out the dust leaving the impression that the people were gone for only an hour, not the year since they left. In the flight-line fire station, the names of the men on watch were still chalked on the blackboard and pencil notes lay by the microphone of the radio. Yet all was incredibly quiet. I had the feeling that at any moment an MP might put his hand on my shoulder and say, "What are you doin' here Mac?"

I drove out to check the runway lighting in the rental car BACO had provided. I parked at the numbers at one end of the runway and looked down the concrete at the other end. Surprisingly, the ILS antennas at the other end could not be seen, they are about five feet tall and can hardly be missed. I drove to the other end to investigate. The rental car I had was sweetly tuned and adjusted by a BACO acquaintance in Glasgow. On that marvelously flat and level runway, I was surprised to see the speedometer reach 120 mph without a vibration in the car. I slowed own and at the end, there were the

ILS antennas. I did the mental math and sure enough, it was the earth's curvature that caused the antennas to be invisible from the other end. Visible confirmation that the earth is not flat.

\* \* \*

Collie went to a week-long watercolor training in Arizona and enjoyed it immensely. She continued her plant and landscape photography and painting, acted as a docent at the SLO Art Center and displayed her work also at the Morro Bay Art Center. Shari continued her work as an insurance adjuster and taught insurance at night. Chris continued as a bank teller and her son Travis completed his training and became a firefighter. The family pursued their individual courses

# Some Brightness In A
# World Gone Insane

The year 1993 was filled with fore-runners of future world events. Iraq refused to allow UNSCOM inspectors to fly into the country and started military operations in the area closest to Kuwait. The U.S. fired 40 Tomahawk missiles at Iraqi factories linked to Iraq's nuclear weapons program. The inspectors were allowed in. A bomb in a van parked underneath the North Tower of the World Trade Center exploded killing 6 and wounding over 1000 workers in the complex. North Korea withdrew from the Nuclear Non-Proliferation Treaty and refused UN inspectors. China performed a nuclear weapons test, ending a world de-facto moratorium. The world seemed mad or at the least off track.

On a more positive note, South Africa officially abandoned its'nuclear weapons program. Its'weapons had been dismantled in 1990. The North Atlantic Free Trade Agreement (NAFTA) was approved in the U.S., Canada and Mexico. Yasser Araffat and Itzac Rabin shook hands after an agreement at Camp David to promote peace between Israel and Lebanon. This looked very good. In retrospect, one out of two in world events isn't too bad.

Clearly on a bad track, a plot in Iraq to assassinate former president George Bush caused President Bill Clinton to order a cruise missile attack on Iraq. Two U.S. Blackhawk helicopters were shot down in Mogadishu, Somalia. Over 1000 Somalians died and 19 U.S. servicemen were killed in the surrounding events. Clearly American power was great and unforgiving.

\* \* \*

In my personal career, 1993 was not a year of real accomplishment although my company Bluepoint Associates received enough business to stay profitable. A brief job was done for my prior employer, Hughes Aircraft when they considered a business venture installing solar power systems on residential roofs. I produced an accounting of material, labor and miscellaneous costs for this endeavor. It was not a business for a large company such as Hughes and although the market would in time grow, the ones to succeed would be small fast movers such as San Luis Obispo's REC. Hughes saw that and decided against entry. That was correct, but ended my work for them.

Another customer was Higher Logic in San Luis Obispo . They made lighting controls for the movie industry. A need arose for direct current (DC) controls to eliminate the flicker produced in the film image when the camera shutter was not synchronized with the AC power supply. This required conversion from AC to DC and then a dimmer to control for the DC output. The design was straight-forward and did a good job for lighting up to 1500 watts.

The next job was to produce a control for 2500 watts to go on a Michael Jackson European tour. There was a short deadline for that one and I'm sorry to say that I was unable to meet it. The control worked, but was unstable in some conditions and there was not enough time to cure the problem. Jackson went to Europe with old style controls.

A European customer was Alpha Real in Switzerland that wanted a solar-power battery charger. This was a straight-forward design which was close to the one that had been produced for Sandia National Labs. I executed the changes on computer simulator and then did the mechanical design, It was constructed and worked well with no new changes. That was good news, but no real thrill. Alpha Real was pleased. I was discovering that simple straight-forward engineering was profitable, but not real fun like invention and new fields of endeavor.

* * *

Collie discovered a new painting procedure which she used on landscapes. Some time back I had bought an overhead projector for her and more recently at a Col Poly surplus sale a 200 ft roll of clear plastic about 10 inches wide. She projected a 35 millimeter slide onto an 8x10 sheet of the plastic taped to a foam-core board. Using a black marker pen she traced the outline of the objects in the slide. Then, taking the slide to her drawing table she added imaginary items to balance the composition. Then to the overhead projector shining on a full sheet of watercolor paper where the drawing was made in pencil. Then back to the painting table and while looking at the projected 35 mm slide, the colors were put in to match nature's display. This proved to produce lovely improvements on matures subjects while preserving their beauty of color.

In Los Angeles Shari was holding down 5 jobs, manager of her apartment house, book-keeper at her husbands place of employment, teaching two classes on insurance adjusting and her full-time job at MDM Associates as an adjuster.. It got to be tiring.

Chris with Jessie was living in San Luis Obispo and working as a bank teller.

The family was fully loaded with work and health concerns.

* * *

# MIXED NEWS ON THE WORLD SCENE, HEALTH PROBLEMS ARISE

The year 1994 opened with several positive events in international relations. BillClinton and Boris Yeltsin signed the Kremlin Accord in which it was agreed to end the practice of preprogrammed missiles aimed at each others country. Later in the year Russia and China also agreed to de-target their missiles. South Africa held its' first multi-racial election, ending apartheid. Nelson Mandela became it's first democratic president. China allowed its' first connection to the internet. After 7 years of labor by 15,000 workers the Channel Tunnel between England and France opened to traffic, minimizing conflicts going back 1000 years interspersed with brief co-operative periods. Clintons first State Of The Union Address endorsed reform in health care and welfare plus a ban on assault weapons. It seemed that the world was coming to its' senses.

However, conflict still flourished. Four U.S. F-16s shot down 4 Serbian J-21aircraft that violated the no-fly zone in Bosnia-Herzegovina. Iraq stopped UNSCOM inspectors and moved troops to the border with Kuwait. The U.S. moved troops to Kuwait in a protective stance. The presidents of Rwanda and Burundi were both killed when a missile struck their aircraft.

This initiated the Rwandan Genocide. The Red Cross estimated that in the first two weeks over 100,000 Tutsis were killed. This estimate was raised to 1 million by year end. The world sat by and simply watched.

\* \* \*

Early in the year I developed symptoms which were finally diagnosed as Lyme disease. This apparently came from small tick bytes that occurred while working outdoors in the Solar array field at PVUSA in Davis, California. Only once did I remember seeing small red spots in a line just above the top of my socks. I showered and thought nothing of it at the time. I was referred to the care of a specialist who prescribed what I later found was 2.5 times the maximum allowed dosage of steroids. This caused me to have stomach ulcers, which I had never before experienced. The ulcers broke while I was at French Hospital and precipitated a "Code Blue" in which the emergency surgery team reported to the operating room. There I was coughing up blood. They started a transfusion and then decided on inspection that they would have to go in and sew the ruptures closed. At that point I was under anesthesia and did not know what was happening. The surgery was excellently performed and I was taken to recovery. Here a peculiar thing happened with an out-of-body experience. From my perspective I fell out of the sky and through the stick and paper roof of a Japanese house where my body lay on the floor. The noise was a great crash to me even though the hospital was quiet. However, the problem I saw was that I had not re-entered my body and needed help to get back in. So I yelled. This mustered three nurses asking where I was and who was president. By the time I passed that exam, I was back in my body and happy with the world, apologizing to the nurses for my behavior. This was my second out-of-body experience in a medical situation and was brief compared to the several minute experience when my fingers were amputated at the age of 13.

* * *

At mid year I was acting as a technical expert at Federal Court in a case of fire on board a boat in a San Francisco marina. I had been hired by David Medvedov who had been my attorney in the earlier suit of the electrocuted technician buddy at PVUSA.

The fee for appearing in Federal Court is charged in my scheme at twice the rate of a continuing technical consulting job. This is certainly earned as the job of the attorney on the other side is to take the witness apart and thus discredit his testimony. In this case I had been offered as an expert on small boat operation and maintenance as well as on electric arcs since there had been a short circuit aboard before or during the fire. The question was whether the short circuit caused the fire or something else did it. My statement for certification stated that I had owned three small boats including one exactly the type and size of the subject boat. The statement for certification on arcs claimed that I was a full professor at Cal Poly and had managed a research operation on high voltage switches. The attorney had consulted his own technical expert who must have said something like, "Look at his age. When he studied physics they didn't know about plasma temperatures in an arc. Here's a question that will trap him. State that you understand that the temperature of an arc increases as the current increases, then ask, is that so? When he says "yes", you have him trapped. Actually strange as it seems the temperature is constant for increasing current until you get to very high values. Here's a recent book that states it." The attorney must have listened carefully as in his questioning he repeated the statement ending with, "... the temperature increases with current, is that right?" When I answered "No". He said, "Well how can that be?" Unknown to him and his expert I had a thorough re-education in arc temperatures while managing the high voltage research at Hughes. I replied, "The arc temperature is set by the plasma that you see as the bright light of the arc. This plasma is a property of the gas in which the arc occurs and is independent of current up to about 5000 amperes. I've done the calculation of current for the short circuit in this case, it could not be over 2000 Amperes. So in this case the temperature would be the same regardless of the current level." This stopped him dead and he went to another topic. Finally, I was stipulated to be an expert in both small boats and arcs.

We did not win on this one as a yard worker testified that he might have dropped a lit cigarette on the boat and this seemed more likely than a short circuit with no known cause.

* * *

Another type of work which began in 1994 was the evaluation of research proposals for the Department of Energy at the National Renewable Energy Lab (ENREL) in Boulder, Colorado. This was sweet work as it put me in touch with the most advanced thinking in my field and required a great deal of imagination on my part. There were three parts to the evaluation work. First to see the proposers technical dream and envision the pitfalls: Second, to envision the management problems that ensue from that work in that field at that time; third to envision the economic and technical effect of a successful program. The evaluator then must write up his views in each of the three areas and rate the proposal based on the extent to which the proposer addressed the problems and the questions of success in advancing the goal of economic renewable energy.

Only a small number of the proposals were in the "hopeless" class. These typically proceeded from the idea that the government gives away money freely to anyone with an idea. These still required effort to enumerate the questions that appear to obstruct a successful program and for which the proposal presents no cure.

The better class of proposals range from long shots to straight-forward, well thought-through efforts to make progress in a limited, but economically effective manner. The long shots deserve careful review as they may produce huge changes for the better, but face severe odds of success. The field of electronics has experienced several of these technical earthquakes that rearrange the landscape and provide new, lower-cost routes to the basic required functions. I once worked for a very intelligent and effective boss who said, "If your success rate is over 80% your not taking enough chances." That first review job would in time lead to several more over a period of two decades. Perhaps the most enchanting work I've done.

* * *

Collie and the girls were very concerned over my health problems and supportive in my recovery. Collie continued painting in both watercolor and acrylic. She sold paintings through both the San Luis Obispo and Morro Bay Art associations. Shari continued her insurance work in Los Angeles, but left MDM Associates to go with A.G.Gallagher, a change she would come to regret. Chris continued her work as a teller. Health was not the family keynote that year.

# A Year Of Terrorism, The Opening Of Personal Electronic Communication And A Bad Year For Family Health

The year 1995 saw the start of personal communication electronically. The first web browser, Yahoo, was put on the market and the DVD digital communication disk became available. Against todays' background of everyone under 40 tied to a cell-phone or I-pad, it seems impossible that a world with no e-mail, texting, personal photo transmission or DVDs existed as recently as 20 years ago.

Terrorism assumed many forms in several countries. In Japan Sarin gas was released in the Tokyo subway by the organization Aum Shinoikyo, killing 15 and injuring 5510. In Oklahoma City the bombing of the Alfred P. Murray building killed 168 persons, many children in a day-care center. President Clinton closed a portion of the street passing the White House as a protection against a repeat of a truck bombing as was done in Oklahoma City. Many personal vendetas occured in the Bosnia-Serbian war as talks with terrorist organizations failed and NATO began bombing raids as a sanction.

One hundred seventy countries signed the Nuclear Non-Proliferation agreement. Jacques Chirac announced that France would perform nuclear weapon tests in Polynesia. The world's most horrific weapon to be tested in the world's most placid region? What had we become?

* * *

At the end of 1994 I testified as an expert witness at the Federal Court in San Francisco. When I awoke the following day I had completely lost the sight of my left eye. I immediately drove to San Luis Obispo to avoid hospitalization in San Francisco and obtained an emergency examination at Pacific Eye. They immediately diagnosed this as the result of Grave's Disease, an auto-immune disorder that caused swelling of the material behind the eye and cut off the function of the optic nerve. Fortunately they knew of a recently developed operation to relieve this condition and were able to get a surgery scheduled at USC Medical Center in Los Angeles the next day. I was driven to LA by Shari with Collie accompanying. I went straight into surgical preparation where the inventor of the new operation described it as a sectioning of the floor of the orbit, or eye socket, so that the eyeball could drop a few millimeters and relieve the pressure. The novelty was that the operation was performed from inside the lip and up into the orbit from below, without an external cut. He said they normally did both eyes at the same time. I was doubtful of this as a failure might cause the loss of sight in both eyes, but was tactful and simply requested one eye at a time. In deference to the fact that I had taught at USC, he agreed.

The operation went well and I went to sleep in the hospital early that night. At 0500 the next morning the assistant surgeon wakened me to see if sight had returned. It had, although the image was a little blurry. He said this was normal and I would be released that morning. He removed an incredibly bloody bandage from my face and wished me a pleasant day. Indeed, I was released and driven back to San Luis with no ill effects.

As the surgery healed, we faced with the question of what to do about the Graves Disease. The opthalmologist felt there was no qualified physician in SLO and suggested I be analysed and treated at Cottage Hospital in Santa Barbara. That was an excellent suggestion and I was checked in to the hospital the night before my thyroidectomy. I cannot say too much about the care and consideration I was given at Cottage Hospital. I had a good night's sleep after a long talk with the anesthesiologist and early in the morning was wheeled across a parking lot roadway to surgery. Before noon I was out of recovery and back in my room. Shari and Collie drove me home and I was a happy camper to be through this double ordeal of optical and then thyroidal surgery. Recovery was quick and soon I was back at my computer, simulating circuits of new inverters in solar power systems. The work would come later that year.

* * *

Collies' painting was interrupted by my surgeries and her severe case of influenza. However, she recovered and by year end was back to regular daily painting.

# AN UNUSUAL YEAR OF AIRCRAFT CRASHES AND NUCLEAR TESTING

The year 1996 saw two major commercial aircraft crashes in the U.S. with an extraordinary number world wide. Flight 800 exploded and crashed off Long Island New York shortly after takeoff. All aboard were killed. A second commercial aircraft crashed in the Florida Everglades after a fire occurred in the cargo hold. Again all aboard were killed. While America's attention was on its own crashes, it was a heavy year for airline accidents worldwide. In total, 1866 lives were claimed in 12 crashes. Five of these were into oceans, with the loss of 755 passengers. One hoped that this brought on improvement in airline safety when the causes were determined and safety measures implemented.

In a remarkable reverse preview of 2014, Russia received from the International Monetary Fund a loan of 10.2 billion dollars to improve economic reform. The O.J. Simpson trial began in Santa Monica and Americans were caused to wonder on the nature of their justice system. In the U.K., Dolly the sheep became the first animal to be cloned from a cell. At the other end of the scale, the IBM computer "Deep Blue" defeated chess champion Gary Kasparov in their first match. He responded with a victory in their second match, but humans wondered what have we come to when a human designed machine defeats a top human in a game of creative strategy.

On the world scene, 44 nations signed the Comprehensive Nuclear Test Ban Treaty after France exploded what it announced as "the last atomic weapon". Unfortunately that proved to be optimistic, but at the time it was greeted as a worldwide milestone.

* * *

My health was improving slowly and I did go through a cardiac conversion at French Hospital to correct the spasms of weakness that came occasionally. This worked well and things began to look up.

I did more research evaluation work for National Renewable Energy Laboratory in Golden, Colorado. This comprised both review of printed material at home and meetings in Golden. The meetings were a delight as the team members had no private agendas and were all dedicated to improving the art of solar cell power systems. One member of the team was an Austrian who had been captured by the U.S. Army during the Battle of the Bulge in World War II. Although a member of the Austrian army, he was wearing a U.S. fatigue jacket and in the heat of the moment was about to shot under the assumption he had killed an American prisoner for his jacket. He explained in good English that he had taken it from a frozen American soldier to keep from freezing himself. An understanding 2nd Lieutenant stopped the execution and sent him off with the other prisoners, but minus the jacket.

Let me explain the type of research proposals we were evaluating by citing the case of the two-material solar cell conceived to produce more electric energy from sunlight than the conventional single material type. The single material type accepted sunlight on one face of a metal panel about the thickness of a sheet of paper. There were layers of conducting material on the front and back of the sheet. The sunlight excited the material and electrons were released. They were picked up by one of the conductors and sent out to do useful work. When they returned through the other conductor the process was repeated and thus sunlight was converted to useful work.

The amount of voltage generated by a single such cell was a function of the internal energy levels of the material. The current was a function of the amount of sunlight. The energy produced was the product of voltage times current. The internal energy levels and hence the voltage produced were a fundamental property of the type of material. Silicon, for example had relatively high internal voltage from absorbing high energy light near the ultra violet range. Indium at the other end of the scale responded to light near the red range and produced a lower voltage. In the single material cell, after a thin strip of material absorbed its color of light, the remaining light passed right through and out the backside.

The idea arose that one could get more energy out of a solar cell if it had two layers of material, one behind the other, with the top absorbing the light near ultra violet and the bottom layer absorbing that near the red end. That was true and easily demonstrated. The voltage of the compound cell was higher than the single layer cell just as the physics demanded. However. the current through the two layers had to be the same as they were electrically in series. This presented problems in design as the current was a function of how much of its color of light each layer absorbed. That was a matter of the thickness of the layer. Thus a precise matching of thickness of the two different materials was essential. The thickness of each layer was much less than a sheet of paper and the two materials were laid down by two different processes. Thus, tight manufacturing control would be required. The question then in evaluating the research proposal was whether the manufacturing process could be controlled to the required degree at a level of cost that would be competitive with the dollars per watt of single layer cells. There is no way to answer that question definitely except to try it. The basic question of whether it was close enough to the realm of possibility could only be determined by spending the money to find out.

My view was that the required complexity of control made success unlikely. However, success promised a real technical and economic improvement. Thus, I was in favor of a high risk venture. After all, that's what research is about, testing the economics at the limits of existing technology.

The team did approve the research and initial results were promising. However, costs for single layer cells dropped steadily and even today they produce more watts per dollar than compound cells. The compound cell research did work well, just not well enough. It did produce some good new physics. Was it worth doing? I think so, although it did not end up where it was supposedly headed.

* * *

Collie's painting continued steadily at eight hours per day. She sold through the SLO art museum and enjoying her artwork and gardens. Shari divorced her husband Jerry, however they remained friends. He moved to Washington State. The family was experiencing their individual problems, but hanging together.

# Scientific Progress And Only Minor Wars

The year 1997 revealed significant scientific accomplishments. In Scotland the Sheep Dolly, cloned in 1996, was announced to the world. President Clinton banned any government funding to organizations working on human cloning. He was right on with the majority of US citizens. This might be useful for animal husbandry, but tailor-made human copies were just not right. I agreed completely.

The Toyota Prius, the worlds first hybrid vehicle went into production. A good technical contribution toward fighting the earth-warming crisis. On the side of putting down humans, IBM's Big Blue computer defeated world chess champion Gary Kasparov in a final match. I was less worried by this. As a one-time chess player I was aware that the game had a fixed board and rigid rules with no chance occurrences. It was ideal for a fast computer, but introduce chance and I felt that humanity would triumph. There was however, no way to test this

In the political arena, there were no major wars. However, there were repeated massacres in Algeria at the rate of about one a month. In Iraq, the United Nations inspection force, UNSCOM, was repeatedly attacked by "citizens" in its attempt to disarm the Iraq nuclear program. Finally the government announced that it would shoot down UNSCOM aircraft flying over Iraq. This did not happen.

The United States finally admitted that it had aided in a secret war in Laos during the recognized Viet Nam war. This was not news to the family as Chris's husband, was loaded onto a ship for secret transport to Laos three times during the war. Each time the ship set sail and was called back before reaching its destination. This tore Chris up terribly.

The UK parliament transferred Hong Kong to China. Later Hong Kong killed all of its chickens when it was found that they were the source of a severe flu epidemic. The world took serious note that international air transport could move a infectious epidemic from one country to another in hours.

Diana, Princess of Wales died in Paris following an automobile crash. The world loved that lady who seemed to be a welcome bit of humanity in the UK nobility.

* * *

My work during 1997 was virtually all for the National Renewable Energy Labs, or NREL. That was for evaluating proposals for research which they had received. The work was both in San Luis Obispo and on site at NREL in Boulder, Colorado. I came to have a very high regard for the quality of people at NREL. Their meetings occurred with no private agendas and although there was always some difference of opinion on the merit of a specific proposal, it was possible to reach an evaluation acceptable to the six or seven people around the table. This was a delightful and rare experience.

We did not evaluate the money which went to the PV panel manufacturer that went bankrupt. It was my view that had we seen their proposal we would have killed it as we did in many cases where the proposer simply felt that there was money to be had just for a novel idea without consideration of the chance of success or the progress that success would bring.

The evaluations not only involved the technical idea, but the proposer's plan for managing the research and subsequent engineering. All of the reviewers had both personal research experience as well as research management experience. Unifying a group of wild egotistic researchers to a team eagerly cooperating toward a single goal is not a simple task. Finally there is the matter of the skills required for the program and assurance that all of these skills exist in the proposing group, which may be multiple companies joining ad hoc for a single task. It was indeed fun.

* * *

Collie continued to paint 8 hours a day. However, she had developed a breast cancer which would require surgery early in 1998. I tried to help where I could, often cooking dinner so that she could concentrate on her painting. The family was having new experiences, not always good.

# International Space Station Launched, Trouble In Africa

The first two sections of the International Space Station, ISS, were launched from Russia and America and successfully docked in space. This was a great pleasure to me as I had participated with Kilovac in Carpinteria, California in the development of a new circuit breaker which met the unusual voltage needs of the ISS.

The Second Congo War began if Africa. Before it would end in 2003 over 3,900,000 people were killed. US embassies in Kenya and Tanzania were bombed. Those fatalities were 224 and the injured over 4,500. The bombings were linked to Osama Bin Laden. I was saddened by the Africa tragedies and puzzled as to what the rest of the world might do to prevent them and whether America could help in a remote civil war.

Both Pakistan and India conducted nuclear weapons tests as threats to each other across the territory of Kasmir and the Indus River. Their efforts would accelerate until today the nuclear weapons total of the two countries is over 650 warheads. I was horrified at the lengths to which a dispute over the uses of the Indus River and the Kashmir territory could escalate.

On the positive side, 120 countries created the International Criminal Court to try crimes against humanity, war-crimes and aggression. Google was founded in Menlo Park by two Stanford Phd candidates. The US Clementine probe found enough water in the moon's polar regions to support a human colony in a rocket re-fueling station.

\* \* \*

I apologize to my readers for the section on my activities over the next 4 years until 2001. I must write only about non-technical matters as during this time I was working mainly for the National Renewable Energy Laboratories, NREL. My new contract with them specified that I must destroy all notes, burn any discs that I had made and not talk in detail about the evaluations that I made on their research proposals or evaluations of ongoing research. As a result, I have only my invoices for that period. I can tell you how many times and when I went to meetings with six-person evaluation teams in Golden, Colorado or how many hours I worked at home. However, I cannot tell you the detals of what I worked on except that it was the evaluation of research on alternative energy sources. The work was not classified, but was fascinating and the people I worked with were excellent, intelligent and free of personal agendas. It was a happy work time.

During this period I joined SCORE, the Service Corps of Retired Executives. That organization counsels and assists small businesses and start-ups. It also sponsors workshops and originates printed materials on starting and running a small business. In this organization I worked with John Wolcott on originating workshops, Dick Ponemon on evaluation of customer satisfaction. Rich Loomis supervised my initial training, which was thorough as SCORE maintains an exceptional code of performance and conduct. I took to SCORE like meeting an old friend. It was a way to give back something to the community and the work ethic from which I had so much benefitted.

Dick Ponemon and I undertook to write and institute a means for clients to evaluate SCORES' counseling. This produced ratings on 10 different efforts and counselor techniques. It proved to be very effective in reinforcing good effort and in spotting poor performance. Over the next 10 years it applauded and reinforced the efforts of over 60 counselors and caused the resignation of 3 whose efforts were offending to clients and who refused to alter their performance when the problems were explained to them.

I discovered in the one-hour counseling sessions, which always included two SCORE members, that that two heads were far better than one. This permitted much improved listening to what the client was saying and thinking about it while the other counselor was speaking. In addition, two heads often produced extra ideas that would not have occurred to one. Most SCORE chapters use only a single counselor in their sessions, but The San Luis Obispo chapter holds rigorously to the two-counselor principle.

* * *

Shari resigned from her job in Los Angeles and moved to San Luis Obispo where she readily obtained a job as an insurance claims adjuster. She felt much happier away from the pressure of the Los Angeles management where she had worked. Jessie married and started work as a photographers' model. Chris moved in with Shari in a rented apartment. Collie continued painting 8 hours per day. Her paintings began to sell at the local Art Museum and in Morro's Art Museum. These sales appeared in the income tax returns of Bluepoint Associates Ltd. along with my receipts from NREL.

# Less War, Varied World Events, Computers Face 2000

In comparison the year 1999 was relatively peaceful with only the Kosovo War and the two-month conflict between India and Afghanistan. The Kosovo War was notable as the first time that NATO attacked a sovereign nation. However, NATO intelligence was poor resulting in their planes attacking Albanian refugees for two hours under the assumption they were Serbian military trucks. When a NATO B-2 later mistakenly bombed the Chinese embassy in Belgrade their intelligence appeared ridiculous.

A 7.6 magnitude earthquake in northwestern Turkey killed over 17,000 and wounded 44,000. This ushered in a series of severe earthquakes in 1999 and 2000. It seemed strange to me, but studies found they were not linked to a common cause.

The EURO was established as a common currency for the European Union. I saw this as an excellent economic advance which would bring a common European market to the world stage.

On the sad and hard to understand list was the Columbine High School shooting in which two teenage gunmen killed 12 students, 1 teacher and themselves. This would be seen again and again in subsequent years, no more understandable to me then than it was the first time. What terrible waste.

Much more understandable and through that knowledge correctable was the common computer problem of not recognizing the first two digits of date change from 1999 to 2000. Some software writers saved storage space by neglecting the first two digits of the year entries and then later simply putting "19" in their place. Thus the year 2000 would become 1900. This could have been a catastrophe, but early recognition and a lot of effort kept it to reasonable levels. Some things did go right.

* * *

My work for NREL continued and was both challenging and exciting, but I will stick to the activities of SCORE.

One SCORE counseling was related to the problem of the year 2000, which came to be known popularly as "Year 2K, or Y2K". A young man in his 20's came in with the idea to sell food packages over the internet for people to stock so that shipping to stores, which would be ruined by Y2K would not be a worry.. His father accompanied him. I assumed this was because Dad had been asked to finance the endeavor.

The young man did a good job of describing what might happen on1/1/2000 when computers could not give correct shipping instructions and thus ruin the whole food distribution system. He knew what he was talking about, but none of us knew how much effort was being put into correcting the computer programs, and thus whether a market would exist for his emergency food supply.

I listened carefully, was worried too and had actually scouted out places where I could buy bulk supplies of food. The question that I then posed was the dietary balance of his proposed food package. If he was going to take over the customer's complete food supply, he should be furnishing a balanced diet. He had not given this any thought. I glanced at his father and saw a poorly hidden smile on his face. I interpreted that he felt his son would not do the work and so he would be cleared of the need to finance the project.

SCORE insists that it's counselors listen carefully and observe human reactions to achieve the closest relationship to the client. I was trying hard.

* * *

John Wolcott and I discussedvarious types and subjects for SCORE workshops. We tried groups for 3 hours also groups that met together for one hour and then separately with a counselor for 2 hours. We also tried a small fee of $10. or $5. versus no fee at all. We settled on no fee at all and have held to that over the years. That seems to convince the clients that we really want to help them. Further, the small money collected would not significantly help. for the rental space.

* * *

Shari and Chris found living separately preferable to shared space. Shari had fallen from the bed in their shared space and seriously injured her back. That was an injury which still requires care.

Collie continued to paint and sell her paintings. Jesse invited Collie and I over to dinner at her apartment with her husband. It was her first family dinner and went very well. I never though to be invited to my granddaughters dinner party. That's something new.

# A Calm World Year
# Relatively Speaking

The year 2000 did not experience the earlier forecast of computer chaos called Y2K or year 2000, when many computer programs would not correctly recognize the date change from 1999. Fortunately nearly all companies spent the money to fix the software and only a few government programs went berserk. So Y2K became a non-event, thank God.

It was also the last year in which there were no humans in space. The International Space Station, ISS has been continuously occupied ever since. This would have seemed unthinkable as little As 20 years before. I was again proud to have been involved in the design of the electrical circuit breakers to protect the power system on the ISS. They were a new voltage class 100% above that available before and have been very reliable.

It was not a good year for naval ships. The Russian submarine Kurtz sank in the Baltic during fleet maneuvers, killing all 118 men aboard. Russia refused help offered by the U.S. and Britain. The report said that damage came from a torpedo explosion in a bow firing tube. I could not help but wonder why an armed and fused torpedo was in use during fleet maneuvers close to Sweden. I knew from my visit to the

Swedish Navy in the 60's that they did not trust Russia and were specifically trained and armed to fight the Russian Navy. What a waste of time for the good men on both sides.

In Aden, Yemen, a U.S. destroyer *Cole* was approached by a small boat that detonated a charge killing 37 and wounding 80. The opponent was Al Qaida of Yemen. It was the first terrorist attack on the U.S. I could not see how the deck officer allowed this to happen, but we were more trusting then before 9/11 in the next year.

*

I was still under restriction on the details of my work for NREL and so this account will concentrate on the volunteer effort for SCORE, the Service Corps of Retired Executives. John Wolcott and I were trying to produce a workshop that would be both effective and popular. We tried one titled "Finding the Problem in Your Business". It was based on our observations that many SCORE clients had trouble finding and fixing the true problem in their business. They were overwhelmed by the immediate symptom and thought of it as the problem that needed fixing. In fact the symptom was only the surface manifestation of a deeper problem.

The workshop outlined several symptoms and introducing the technique of questioning why that condition existed. The answer to this first question was then subjected to the same process, "why does this exist"? When the process reaches the point where there is no further answer, the true problem has been found and the process of fixing it can begin. An example would be "My problem is that I need money!" This should lead to the question "Why do you need money? Low pricing, or poor inventory turnover, or excessive overhead costs"? Which in turn might lead to further questions until the true problem is located and the plan to fix it laid out.

The workshop seemed straightforward to John and I, so we put together the necessary slides to carry it out and presented it to a group that signed on to review their business problems. We found out from the responses that it was a failure. The idea was "you don't know my business and I do. I know what my problem is, you don't have to tell me."

We put that workshop into the file and started work on another.

\* \* \*

Collie continued to paint 8 hours a day, but developed a breast cancer and opted for a complete mastectomy to limit the spread of the malady. She recovered physically very well, but the loss of a breast was a partial loss of self-esteem. I continued to cook dinner 3 or 4 nights a week to ease the load and allow her more time for painting.

Shari continued her work as an insurance adjuster in San Luis Obispo. Chris found work as a cashier at a bank. The family had individual problems.

# A Poor Year For Everyone

With the catastrophe of 9/11 the year 2001 became a turning point for America and a sad year for nearly everyone in the western world. Shari called on the phone to say, "Turn on the TV, I can't believe it!" She spoke for all Americans. With this alert Collie and I watched the fire in the World Trade Center building and later the crash of a third aircraft into the Pentagon in Washington. My first reaction was to remember the crash of a B-25 into The Empire State Building in 1942. That was only a small fire, but when it was announced that this 9/11 crash was from two planes that took off from east-coast airports with fuel loaded to fly to California this was clearly a different situation. I imagined the fire in the center elevator structure like a steel chimney as the fuel burned through to the lower floors. I did not anticipate that it would soften and melt the steel to the point of collapse of the entire building. It was evident from the two aircraft involved that this was a carefully planned and coordinated terrorist event

The TV coverage was exceptional. All watchers saw the cloud of smoke and dust chasing New Yorkers down to the riverfront. We did not learn until much later that about 500,000 people were taken off the Hudson River docks and transported to New Jersey by prompt action of barges and ferries under the impression that New York was being bombed. A third plane crashed into tghe Pentagon.

Brave passengers overpowered the high-jackers in a fourth plane that crashed in Pennsylvania. A total of 2,977 people were killed in these acts. I could not help but wonder where our intelligence services had been that this had not been picked up in the money transfers, visas and planning for such a large job. It also raised the question of how many additional terrorist actions were in the works. Oddly enough, Donald Rumsfeld had only the day before given a speech concerning the Pentagon's difficulty in accounting for $2.3 trillion in spending. The next month President George W. Bush announced the formation of the Department of Home Security. I sadly wondered who had been looking after home security before.

Anthrax attacks occurred later in the month through letters mailed to 5 broadcast and newspaper offices on the east coast. Five people died of the 22 exposed. Fast action by Health Services and the Postal Service prevented it from being higher.

On October 7,2001 The U.S. invaded Afghanistan with help from other nations. The rational was that the 9/11 terrorists had been trained there. Later in October President Bush signed the Patriot Act, which opened the door to all manner of spying on Americans and their communications. In December he announced the U.S. would withdraw from the 1972 Anti-Nuclear Weapons Treaty.

* * *

In a much calmer vein, John Wolcott and I developed a new SCORE workshop to replace the unpopular one "Finding and Fixing a Problem in Your Business". The new workshop would be "Starting a New Business In San Luis Obispo". At least the title would not be a problem and it would aim at the larger segment of our clients who were starting, not running a business.

The workshop comprised three sections of approximately one hour each. These were; 1) The procedure of starting a new business, 2) The financial data necessary to start and run the business, and 3) What this means to you personally.

Part 1) was a revelation to the folks with "a new idea". It covered the details of a business plan describing the business, the legal structure and the procedure to implement it. There were also the mundane matters of insurance, banking records for taxes and local licensing. I undertook to present part 1). Part 2) introduced the clients to the balance sheet, profit & loss, and cash flow. It stressed the necessity of all three separate records for management and tax purposes. It also introduced more details of the business plan and the procedure of applying for a loan. A local accounting firm supplied a CPA to present this part. She was exceptional in handling a detailed technical subject without inducing sleep. Part 3) undertook the personnel activities and stress of starting and managing a small business. This was psychology in contrast to the math of part 2) and the procedures of part 1). SCORE member Jim Murphy presented this part.

The workshop was a success from the first presentation. The general client reaction was, "Whew! I had no idea. I'm glad to discover this and the SCORE counseling that is available afterward at no charge." Many signed up for counseling after the workshop. In all the workshop has been presented every month for 14 years to over 1500 attendees in generally the same basic format. I presented part 1) about 150 times with Lorna Whiteaker taking over as age limited my ability to walk and talk for an hour. She has done a magnificent job.

*

In the family it was a difficult year for all. Collie's sight in one eye went bad limiting her depth perception and interfering somewhat with her painting. In addition her back developed pain that added injury to the insult of vision problems. During the course of the year a chiropractor helped greatly on the back problem and Doctor bloom referred her for laser treatment with Dr. Higginbotham. This procedure was very helpful and by year end she was back in good shape. During the year Shari, Chris and I all cooked dinners to relieve her of that load, permitting more time for painting. Her paintings sold well at the SLO Art Museum. She came to the understanding that all she wanted was to paint and not to be a marketer or leader. This was a great and useful revelation.

During the year I bought a computer for her and she bravely learned to use it and explore the internet for libraries and art supply houses. At Christmas I gave her a color printer that could reduce/enlarge images. This became a primary tool in her studio.

Shari gained much weight and decided to have stomach bypass surgery. This would not occur until 2002, but the decision was a landmark for her. Chris and Shari were stopped at a traffic light on CA1 in Cayucas when they were run into by a truck. Both were injured and taken to the hospital and Chris's car was totaled. There was much delay by the insurance company in making a settlement, but help came to the scene. The accident occurred in front of a fire station at a time when all of the firemen were outdoors, There were many witnesses and help getting them to the hospital. When the the insurance company delayed, there were several firemen who signed on as witnesses and finally the issue was settled. Chris got a replacement car. I got a replacement car when mine was run into while I was stopped at the crossing of a country road and a highway. The insurance settlement this time was straight-forward and I got a nice used car which I still drive.

Jesse divorced her husband. She received no support. I fell in the house and sprained my ankle in both directions, invert and evert. This put me in bed for 2 weeks, but has healed well and gives no problems. At Christmas Collie gave me an electric rotisserie which I found delightful for cooking roasts. The family had individual problems, but ended on a happy note.

# A Year Of Violence In The Middle East With U.S. Attack

In March 2002 George W. Bush ordered the invasion of Afghanistan as an outcome of the 9/11 attack. I was confused as it was clear that the terrorists needed to be found and killed or punished, but to invade a nation to accomplish this seemed a bit heavy. I felt this was going to be expensive in lives and treasure and the cause might better be served by actions of special services such as the Navy Seals. That would require local intelligence which once again we seemed to be lacking. This was maddening as we seemed to get deeper and deeper into foreign commitments because we lacked understanding of the situation on the ground.

Bush and Putin signed the Strategic Offensive Weapons Reduction treaty to replace the 1972 Anti Ballistic Missile Treaty. This was a positive note in U.S. and Russian relations. The countries of western Europe, except England, adopted the Euro as a common currency. This was viewed as threatening by Russia, which was a sour note in what was otherwise a very sensible move to unify trade and migration in Europe.

The United States declared seven nations as supporters of terrorism. These included Iran, Iraq, Cuba, Libya, North Korea, Sudan and Syria. The action seemed sensible. We should not be attacking countries that were sources of terrorism, but we had to stop the terrorists before they strike. I wondered again if we were getting the local intelligence to make it work effectively. In Iraq, UN weapons inspectors were finally allowed to make their inspections. It was a positive move as they had been repeatedly stopped in their tours. I was pleased, but still anxious over Iraq's bellicosity and our seeming inability to get local intelligence.

* * *

In the work area matters changed markedly. I continued my work with NREL which could not be discussed, but in addition obtained a sub-contract to do the design, supervise construction and test of a 36 kilowatt solar power system for a new hospital in Visalia, CA. This would be working for the prime contractor, a gentleman in Morro Bay. After we signed the subcontract, but before the design work could begin, the gentlemen

The contract passed in his estate to his daughter who worked at a hospital in San Luis Obispo. I contacted the daughter and made her a generous offer for the contract if I could gain the agreement of the Visalia hospital. The doctors felt out on a limb and as they had already accepted me for the actual work and were happy to pass on the complete contract. So I began the design work, which was anything but straightforward. The air-conditioning units had already been installed. These projected upward about five feet above the roof. They thus cast a significant series of shadows across the roof where the solar panels were supposed to be mounted. An analysis of the pattern through the day-light hours showed there was no hope of getting all 36 kilowatts of solar panels on roof.

I suggested that some be mounted on top of the sunscreen of the parking area. I was not the one who signed on for 36 kW so when I explained that the cost would likely be about the same as if it were possible to mount all 36 kW on the roof, the doctors agreed. I did not tell them that this would be the first time that two physically displaced solar arrays would be used to feed the same inverter. I had done the calculations and felt confident. The details were not something they needed or wanted to know.

I completed the design of the electrical portion of the array, including all the safety provisions required by the National Electrical Code, which said nothing about separate arrays feeding a common inverter. Now it was necessary to do the mechanical design. The contract specified that no part of the array should be higher than the parapet that surrounded the roof. This involved considerable effort in design of the beams to join the roof to the array. This had to consider wind speed and direction, necessary tilt to optimize sunlight and the need for a watertight joint. Patients would not appreciate a constant drip. There was also the safety consideration of wiring together the two arrays from the roof and parking structure. Finally the design was complete.

The next consideration was bids for the material. The total job was $220,000.

Thus the material was a significant item. I found that the cost for steel pipe to make the array supports was significantly less from China than USA. I was also able to get the pipe threaded, a significant item. I got an excellent quote on the solar panels from Japan. However, the metering and protective equipment was all bought from U.S manufacturers. The inverter came from Canada. Thus, I an American in doing what I was hired to do, sent most of the purchases offshore. None of the goods were second rate. I just could not get a good price in the U.S. In the final analysis the job cost came in well below the going average rate of $/kW for solar. I had mixed feelings. Proud that I could bring the job in below average cost and angered that the country that developed all this solar technology could not make the parts at a competitive cost.

Supervision of the construction was enjoyable. The electrical contractor had never built a solar system and was a little anxious. We talked daily at the job with little tips from me like, "When you mount the aluminum panels to the steel support, insert a thin cardboard piece between the panels to offset the difference in thermal expansion.

That way they won't crumple in the summer." He appreciated the field experience and practicality so much that he did a few extras for me such as wrapping all structures that a person might run into with black and yellow tape. We got along well.

When the electrical inspector came to inspect and approve the job, he confessed that he had never inspected a solar system. I handed him a list of all the citations in the National Electrical Code that applied to solar with one column for the requirement and another for the design level on this job. He looked astounded and then said, "This thing is worth its weight in gold." I gave him a copy. The inspection was approved.

Then, came the day for turn on. I checked the carport array against the rooftop array and found they were virtually identical. The Japanese had done a first-rate job on these solar panels. Then we turned on and waited for local noon. When the power topped out it was 0.5% above the projected noon value for that date. The doctors were pleased. I was astounded. In matters of hourly solar power 5% is considered agreement.

The final pleasure came when the California State Safety Inspector came to see how the joining of two arrays was handled. This required that the wiring from the external array must enter the building with the roof array. He and I were both concerned about that safety item as a direct current short circuit and arc is nearly impossible to extinguish. Whereas an AC arc has a chance to extinguish itself 120 times a second when the voltage goes through zero, the DC arc is continous. Further, this was a hospital which would be hard to evacuate in a fire. When he saw that the Visalia design brought the carport wiring in through steel pipe that never entered the building, only penetrated through the parapet, he said, "That is exactly the way it should be done." I was delighted.

* * *

Collie learned quickly on her new computer and was absolutely delighted with the color printer and the digital camera. She continued to paint and to sell via the SLO Art Museum. In the fall she caught the flu, despite having a preventive shot and was in bed two weeks. Her eyesight was improved greatly after a second action with Dr. Higginbotham. Shari cooked for her while I was away on the Visalia job. By year end she was cycling back to normal. It was a varied year for the family.

# Iraq War Begins, Columbia Disintegrates Over Texas, Big Blackout In The East, European Union Grows

U.S. declared war on Iraq to eliminate weapons of mass destruction. Over ten million people worldwide protested the war, but the invasion began March 19 with "shock & awe" visible on TV coverage. One month later saw Baghdad captured and Saddam Hussein overthrown. Later, Hussein is captured in Tikrit. I was appalled at the lack of have presented". Events showed that we didn't. There were no weapons of mass destruction. Even worse we didn't understand the internal politics of Iraq and that Hussein was using dictatorial power as the only way to obtain peace among a set of warring tribal powers. Where again was our intelligence? Space shuttle Columbia disintegrated on re-entry over Texas, killing all seven astronauts aboard. Chris's son Travis was a qualified EMT and fireman. He was sent to Texas to search for bodies and clues. He was successful on both. I felt deeply sad for him.

Khalid Sheik Mohammad, mastermind of the 9/11 catastrophe was arrested in Pakistan by CIA and local forces. It felt good that for once we had enough intelligence to operate internationally and bring to justice the leader to 2300 deaths in America.

The European Union grew as former parts of the USSR joined up. These included Poland, Estonia, Latvia and the Czech Republic. A constitution for the European Union was written. I welcomed the freedom of these peoples to join in creating a new trading block with the ability to travel free of interference.

Massachusetts was the first U. S. state to legalize same-sex marriage. I welcomed This. All the homosexuals I knew were intelligent, well behaved citizens and did not deserve to be excluded from forming families.

* * *

I continued to work for NREL, about which I am not allowed to write. In addition I found a new customer headquartered in New Jersey who needed design work on low power inverters for solar systems that would be mounted on light poles. This was very Interesting as small size was a key requirement. The company was using its own engineers in New Jersey and a group at the University of Florida. We held conferences by telephone with simultaneous display via internet-computer after we had exchanged drawings of our work. This was a new form of communication and it was far more effective than I had expected. We got to the point of exchanging ideas readily and knew each other by first name. The discussions were lively with a good sense of humor among the three sites in New Jersey, Florida and California. Only once did I see a command given. In discussion, I made a suggestion of the circuit for the inverter input, saying It might increase efficiency and even be cheaper. Florida said they had looked at it and didn't think it was a good idea. A new voice immediately came on. The president of the company said "That's the second consultant that has made that suggestion. Take another look." The hospital solar job in Visalia was finished with the lengthy set of documents required by the state to qualify for their rebate. It went well if slowly. Finally I was paid and happy with a well done job.

* * *

Collies health during the year was a multifaceted problem. Her eyes produced a very bright image that induced soreness and fatigue. Sunglasses helped, but reduced the colors visible in a scene. For an artist this was unbearable. Late in the year, she fell and broke her upper leg. This led to a complete replacement of her hip. She went through car for over a month and began to worry that she might never drive again. This was therapy at the hospital and a recovery center, then at home on a walker. She didn't drive a car for a month. Her concerns were exacerbated by renewal of her DMV license. After two tries she passed and looked forward to the freedom and independence of her own car.

Shari took up with Allen in New Mexico. She went out to visit him and he came to visit with her in San Luis. It did not develop and he went back to Albuquerque. Chris went back to Cal Poly to study Anthropology.

The house needed much attention with painting and in the fall a complete wrap up and termite extinction performed by Jim Batchelor, our next door neighbor. We spent the 3 days of the house treatment at a top notch motel and ate out daily. We had a view of the ocean and a grand time together. When it was completed, the world looked much better.

In the events of the year, Chris, Shari and I cooked dinners to relieve Collie. In the end, it went well and Collie began to paint again

# A Generally Quiet Year Except For Indian Ocean Tsunami

The Iraq war continued with a major conflict at the city of Fallujah. U.S. forces finally prevailed and the formal conflict in Iraq cooled down. George W. Bush was re-elected in a close race with Kerry. I could not help but wonder how the man who got us into this Iraq conflict could not be defeated. What were Americans thinking? Were they thinking? Kerry was not the strongest candidate, but Bush had established a terrible record in my view.

The dissolution of the USSR continued as seven former members joined NATO.

these were Bulgaria, Estonia, Latvia, Lithuania, Romania, Slovakia and Slovenia. I was in favor of these moves, but could not help but wonder how this looks from inside Russia. Surely this must be a wound to the self-esteem of the once world power to see their former western states joining their former military foe.

Libya dismantled its' nuclear weapons voluntarily. British Prime Minister Tony Blair visited Libyan dictator Muhamar Gaddafi to express the pleasure of the worlds' nations. I was delighted. Libya, of all nations had no basis or need for nuclear weapons. It was good that they now recognized this. Blair's move was good, but I would have and preferred something from the United Nations.

A massive earthquake measuring 9.3 on the Richter Scale occurred in the Indian Ocean. Tsunamis struck all bordering islands and nations with massive destruction. All told the dead exceeded 200,000, with injured uncounted. Whole communities on the ocean islands were completely destroyed. It was thoroughly covered on TV, leaving me with a great sadness and sympathy for the far-away populations. I stood in awe at the power of the earth and the destruction it could release. It was impossible not to think of earth warming and the ruin it will create. The debate as to whether it results from human activity is foolish. Regardless of cause, only humans can do anything about it. It is past time to start.

\* \* \*

I continued to work for NREL, about which I cannot write although the people I worked with were a fine, skilled lot without personal agendas. It was a pleasure. Work with SCORE was also a pleasure. I bought an excellent software that permitted accurate simulation of the circuits used in a complete solar power inverter. This prompted several new ideas which were tried out on the simulator. From these came a design for a compact inverter to mount under the rail of a single solar panel. I discussed this with the engineers in Sandia National Labs in Albuquerque New Mexico. They were interested and as a result I was invited to an inverter conference in Baltimore, Maryland. I showed a mechanical model of the inverter and was pleased to find that several people in the audience remembered me from past associations. They came over to comment favorably on the compact inverter idea. This was a true heart warmer to see old friends and be recognized for past and present work.

This resulted in a small contract to produce a feasibility model of the inverter. It would not completely cover costs, but would be a boost on the road to a producible design. Counseling with SCORE proved to be a great pleasure along with that of presenting workshops on starting a new business.

\* \* \*

Collies health was variable during the year. She received therapy following her hip replacement.. On top of this she had four teeth break. By mid-summer these were either crowned or received implants. In October she gave up driving the car and depended on the girls or I to drive her. Strangely, with this severe health came a new interest in gardening with pot plants and a return to photographing flowers. By year end she had adjusted and returned to watercolor painting and gave up smoking.

Shari bought a module home and set about decorating and repainting it. Chris graduated from Cal Poly with a BS in Anthropology. . The family was on a set of varied courses.

# Hurricane Katrina -- North Korea Goes Nuclear

Hurricane Katrina with a storm surge up to 14 feet struck the Gulf coast just east of New Orleans. There were 1836 deaths resulting from the flooding when 53 breaks occurred in the New Orleans levee system. About 80% of the city was flooded. There were delays and confusion in the governmental systems at federal, state and city level. The only heroes in the catastrophe were the Coast Guard and one U.S Army unit which on its' own moved relief supplies into a nearby area to be ready when the waters receded. The head of the Federal Emergency management Agency, FEMA, Michael Brown resigned within a week when the mismanagement of his operation was disclosed. It was only days after President George W. Bush praised him. Subsequent professional examination showed flaws in the Army Corps of Engineers design of the levee system which did not even meet its' own internal standards. I was overcome with empathy for the terrible fear and pain evident in the trapped survivors faces. This was almost matched by my anger as the errors and delays emerged at seemingly all levels of government. At the lowest level, school busses were supposed to be used to evacuate survivors from un-inhabitable areas. Buses were available but the authorities would not authorize anyone but school bus drivers to use them. There were not enough drivers available. One brave soul simply stole a bus and drove 74 survivors to Houston. The mayor of New Orleans delayed and told higher authority this was her territory and she had the evacuation in hand.

What is government for? If it cannot overlook its' politics in the face of major disaster. We appeared to have a broken political system.

* * *

On the world scene, North Korea announced that it had nuclear weapons which it developed to protect itself from the United States. What a ridiculous claim. What evidence of a self-centered view of the world. Later in the year they proposed giving up nukes in exchange for supplies from the U.S. We can see today, with North Korea armed with numerous nukes and submarine launched missiles to carry them, where these promises lead.

* * *

Work continued with NREL and action started on the compact inverter contract from Sandia National Labs. This proved to be very fascinating. Using the new simulator software I was able to prove out a new circuit for the inverter. This was done before the contract with Sandia was signed, so the rights to the invention were mine. To fund a patent would cost about $10,000. at that time, but a Provisional Patent Application could be obtained for about $1,500. I decided this was the way to go and wrote the provisional application myself. This is only good for 12 months and then it must be changed to a regular patent or abandoned. It is unusual to sell rights to a provisional application, but in this case it was done. I made the mistake of asking a very low initial payment and depended instead on the annual percent of sales of products using the patent.

To make a long story short, the buyer in writing the final patent made a gross mistake which virtually destroyed its' value. I did not see this until the patent issued. He made no product and so I got no percent of sales. The curious end to this story was that two years later I was asked if I could design around my own patent. That caused me a day's worth of thinking on ethics -- I decided YES, I could and did on a new consulting contract which turned out to be a happy payment in this fiasco.

In the Sandia contract, I finished the design and construction to the small dimensions and started the tests. Here I had a problem. For some reason my hands were shaky and my handwriting was hardly legible. Fortunately, Chris stepped in to make the entries in my lab notebook as the tests proceeded and changes were made. This was a great help as I could dictate my lab notebook entries and keep my mind on the physical work. Chris had a problem and a question. I had dictated a change in a capacitor as 10 pico-farads, a Farad is a measure of a capacitors size. It is impracticably large and hence the usual values are in micro-farads (a millionth of a farad) or pico-farads (a billionth of a farad). Chris had heard farad as ferret, the small furry animal. She knew that pico was one billionth and so was puzzled as to what a billionth of a ferret would be -- maybe a millionth of a hair. We got a good laugh out of that one.

The tests went very well with high conversion efficiency, 96%. Even the temperature tests were OK at an ambient air value of 140 degrees F.

* * *

Collies health during the year was poor. She had more teeth repaired or replaced. Late in the year she fell and hurt her knee. This temporarily limited her walking, but she had given up driving a year before. She bought a digital camera and liked it very much, then bought a better one that would hold still more readily. Her interest increased on the garden and taking pictures of her flowers. She also began to paint in Chinese style. This was a variation of watercolor.

Chris bought a mobile home in the same park as Shari and almost across the street. Shari developed a kidney cancer. It was removed successfully, but left her with only one kidney. She took this with good psychological strength, but I'm sure there were a lot of tearful nights. My health was not the best, with back problems and high blood pressure. It was a problem year for the family's health.

# Iraq Religious Conflict, Mexican Drug War, Israel Into Lebanon

The only pleasant indicator of the future was the forming of Twitter in 2006. Otherwise it was wall-to-wall conflict. In Mexico President Felipe Calderon sent federal troops into the state of Michoacan to stop drug movement. This initiated the Mexican Drug War. I was saddened because the family had enjoyed many trips into Mexico in our camper. Now such trips would not be wise. In effect, outdoor Mexico was closed to us. This brought to an end enjoyment of a rural, neighboring country of unusual charm. All of us spoke enough Spanish to be readily understood by the populous. It had been a pleasure.

In Iraq religious conflict raged between Shiites and Sunnis. The Sadr City uprising was indicative, but the actions occurred through the year. In this Shiite slum of Baghdad 215 people were killed in one night by Sunnis. The following day 6 Sunnis were caught, doused with kerosene and burned alive by Shiite militiamen. who also attacked 4 mosques. How can religious beliefs inspire such actions? I was puzzled, greatly saddened and angry at what we had done in Iraq. To think that all this came because we just had to unseat Saddam Hussein and his non-existent weapons of mass destruction. And we did all this without understanding that he was a dictator holding together a complex political/religious melange. Where indeed was our foreign intelligence and understanding? The United States had 16 intelligence agencies. Were they all just spying on each other and neglecting the rest of the world? In 2006 Saddam Hussein was tried and sentenced to death by hanging. I had mixed feelings about that.

North Korea announced that it had conducted its' first nuclear weapons test. It was judged small, but still nuclear.

\* \* \*

I published a technical paper on the compact solar inverter and its' test results. This created some interest and a request for a proposal from a New England company for a quote to complete the product design to compliance with the National Electric Code, NEC, standards. I submitted this proposal with a lengthy writeup on the inverter principle. However, I heard nothing back from the New England company. Then I discovered they had lifted the technical part of my proposal to them and included it verbatim in their proposal to the Department of Energy without my permission. Further, there was no money for me in their proposal and they said, "That will not be necessary." I learned that day to include the phrase "This document contains confidential information that is the property of Bluepoint Associates, Ltd."

I also did some research evaluation for the Department of Advanced Research Projects, DARPA of the Department of Energy. This was technically satisfying, but was all at home and provided no meeting with other technologists on the same topic. I missed the human interactions that were satisfying in the NREL meetings. However, my contract allowed me to talk about the work. One evaluation was for development of a solar power inverter with associated battery energy storage. I particularly liked this proposal and rated it highly. Others must have rated it highly also as it did receive a development award. A few years later I checked the company and found the research had gone well and they had a product which they thought they were ready to sell.

A few years later the news was not so good. The management had failed to put money behind marketing the product and although it had won several technical awards, it was not selling. The finances were in poor, but not hazardous shape. Two years later the management was replaced, but the finances looked to be on the last road. Ah well, not all good technology becomes a winner in a business sense.

* * *

The house and grounds got a good work over. The huge pine tree in the front yard was cut down and hauled away. The house got a new roof. It looked great! My left knee gave a lot of pain until the OTC drug Glucosamine/Chondroitin was found. For reasons not clear only 20% of patients respond to this for a lacerated meniscus in the knee. Fortunately I was one of the 20%. The case went from assured surgery to a cure in a short period of time.

The whole family switched to a no-sugar, reduced salt, no-fat diet and all began to lose weight. Shari recovered slowly, but well from her kidney removal. Chris was delighted with her new house in the mobile home park. Collie got a new computer and was delighted with it. She also began to see painting sales at the SLO Art Museum. A great ego boost! In general it was a good year for the family except that Jessie and boyfriend broke up. Well, you can't win 'em all.

# Putin Cuts Europe's Winter Oil Supply, U.S. Infrastsructure Ages

On January 8, 2007, Russian Premier Vladimir Putin cut off the oil supply to Poland, Germany and Ukraine. This in the middle of a cold European winter. I felt that this was inhumane and done simply to show his power. What a cruel politician he must be. There was never an accounting of the resulting deaths, but it took little imagination to see shivering small children held by parents in an unheated apartment. Isn't the function of government to serve and protect humanity, even if it's in the neighbors jurisdiction?

North Korea agreed to shut down its' nuclear facilities in exchange for 50,000 tons of fuel oil. Strange how winter heating works differently at the two ends of Euro-Asia.

In the United States, the unsupported maintenance of our infrastructure was demonstrated terribly when the 35W bridge in Minneapolis, Minnesota collapsed totally, killing 13 citizens. Once again government seemed to be ignorant of it's function in serving its' citizens. Where indeed do politicians get their education? Or should the question be where do they get their corruption?

On the campus of Virginia State University, a South Korean ex-patriot with a rifle killed 32 students before he committed suicide. What a loss, what a waste. The families will never understand and forgive. I was hit with sadness for the families and for the students who would not live the years they envisioned. To a lesser extent I was sad for the nation's loss of educated adults whom we definitely need.

There was at least one bright note. Steve Jobs, founder and CEO of Apple announced the availability of the first I-phone. I saw this as a broadening of intercommunication and availability of information. I did not foresee some of the negative factors that would develop.

* * *

As a result of the technical paper on the compact inverter, I received a call from Petra Solar's president to ask if I would design a compact inverter for them to use on a solar panel mounted on a utility pole for data collection and communication. I was delighted, but we had some discussions over the terms of the contract. I had no problem with Petra owning the rights to any design or invention, that's what they were buying. I did have minor objections to the terms of indemnity. However, discussion produced agreement and I think a mutual respect.

I started the design with a new microprocessor that could handle the data collection and communication. They also wanted a different mechanical layout, flat and rectangular rather than long and thin. These were accomplished and simulations run on the computer software. The electrical operation looked good. The thermal properties were calculated and the operational losses put into these to discover the temperature rise at the outside of the case during a summertime air temperature. It all looked fine and the drawings were shipped to Petra. They were pleased and readily paid the agreed fees. However, I heard nothing from then for several months. Then a letter came explaining the situation, this was appreciated but not really necessary. They had used my design as "The Gold Standard" and given a charge to their engineers to reduce cost and size. The engineers had made a slightly smaller unit which tested OK. They had put it out for sale and were having a good success. The letter thanked me for the original design. It would have been nice to have the design constructed, but at least it was a "Gold Star Design" model. I continued to work for NREL.

\* \* \*

The house got a considerable make-over to match the new roof. Shari repaired many inside wall cracks and repainted them. We contracted to have the outside painted in a new light yellow color to compliment the tan roof.

Chris took a trip to China with her Tai Chi instructor and class. She enjoyed it immensely and returned eating with chop sticks and carrying a load of presents for each one in the family. A great experience!

Collie got a new camera, a Canon Power Shot which she learned to use rapidly and started taking landscape photos for reference in painting. Chris often drove her to the key photo areas. Collie began painting in acrylic as well as watercolor. Her printer failed utterly and she got a new one which operated fine with the new camera prints.

Art went in for a second cataract operation which came off very well. It was a good year for the family and for the house.

# THE SECOND GREAT RECESSION, OIL HITS $140. PER BARREL

Banks began to put together packages of loans which were then sold to other banks as "derivatives". Many of the loans in these packages were made without careful assessment of the borrower. In fact, loan procedures became simply automatic approval in some banks. These risky loans became part of the derivatives. I applied for a refinance on my house. It was approved and granted before I even signed the agreement. I pulled out of that bank in a hurry.

The visible result on a national scale came with the filing for bankruptcy by Lehman Brothers, the 4th largest bank in the U.S. Bankruptcy was also filed by Bear Sterns and many other banks. These actions sparked a crisis that came to be known as "The Second Great Depression". The Dow Jones average dropped 1000+ points in one day. In all stock market prices dropped 57% as measured by the S&P 500 index. George W. Bush signed off on a $700 Billion bill to buy the assets of failing banks. Barack Obama, of the opposite party won in the fall election. No great surprise.

I had noticed the unusually high ratio of loans to assets as high as 35 to 1 at Citibank among others. I asked people who should know how this could be safe as a 3% loss on loans could wipe out the bank. I was assured that the bank examiners were on the job. I wondered later what job that was.

Like many retired persons, I had stock investments which paid dividends that made the budget a little more pleasant. The value of these equities dropped over 40%. It was much later before they recovered. Fortunately many of the dividends continued. I felt very sorry for those who lost their savings and sometimes their homes as well. Where were the bank examiners? In fact where was the government oversight that we expected would be there?

Bernie Madoff was arrested for running the worlds' largest Ponzi scheme. People sympathized with those who lost their money. I couldn't see it. Anyone who expected to continue getting 30% on an investment had to know it was a Ponzi scheme where the 30% for the older investors would come from the investment funds of the newer investors. I simply could not feel sympathy for participants in an illegal game.

On a happy example, Bill Gates, founder and CEO of Microsoft, stepped out of industry and devoted himself to philanthropy. I didn't like Microsoft, but Gates did a grand human thing.

\* \* \*

My professional work took on a fascinating task. A former student of mine at Cal Poly, who had worked for me on research contracts I brought into the school, called to ask if I was interested on a speculative bid for an installation in Nigeria. This would not involve going to Nigeria, but would involve the complete design of an off-grid solar power system for rural communities of about 10,000 people. It would be capable of operation independently or tied to the unreliable Nigerian electric grid. The design would be a package which the Nigerian Government would fund for various locations to upgrade the living standards of the rural populations. This sounded great. Technically interesting and challenging plus a humanitarian boost to the farmers. I immediately volunteered.

My first chore was to learn about Nigeria. Like most Americans I knew only that it was somewhere in Africa. I discovered that it was the largest country in Africa with a population of 170 million, equal to that of the U.S. in the 1940s. It was a community of 240 tribes speaking 500 languages and dialects. Two religions were predominant, Christians in the south and Muslims in the North and Northwest. Its primary export was crude oil, which was refined abroad and shipped back to be sold at high prices in the country. The primary source of oil was in the Niger delta in the southwest of the country.

Directly affecting the power system design, it had the heaviest rainfall in Africa and the highest rate of lightning strikes. However, the rain mainly came at night so that the annual sunlight availability was moderately high. I found several well-written technical papers from Nigerian university faculty on the experiences with prior solar power installations. A curious thing was that the rural population greatly valued the street lights that came with the solar power. They were tribal oriented and in the fields working all day. The street lights gave an opportunity to walk around, meet, talk and generally tribalize. One negative item was the near total absence of skilled mechanics to maintain diesel-electric generators. As a result many diesel units were simply rusting away out of service. The government and organizations outside the tribe were viewed as thieves of Nigerian resources, thus stealing from the utilities and pipelines was frequent.

\* \* \*

A simple calculation showed that the 5 Megawatt solar field required would be struck by lightning about once every two years. This meant that it had to segmented such that after a strike it could return to service with the damaged portion easily isolated. This is not difficult to do if the array was designed that way, but impossible if it was not a built-in feature. The thievery plus lightning meant that the lines from the solar field to the village should be underground in concrete trenches or pipe. Obviously, good street lights were an essential.

One aspect of the design about which I was not happy about was the need for a strong power source to bring the system back up after it crashed, for example from a lightning strike. Solar alone is not a sufficiently powerful source to overcome the extra power needed for a cold start. Battery backup to the solar wiould accomplish this, but is very expensive. The only option was diesel-electric generators. I designed in two units so that one could be out of service for delayed repair. Battery backup was designed for the medical service, street lights and police unit.

\* \* \*

With the price of oil up to $140. per barrel, income to Nigeria was great and it appeared that the job would be financed for a location in the center of the country. Then religious conflict showed up between Muslims and Christians and killings occurred right in the center of Nigeria, where the installation was to be. Then Boko Haran rose in the northeast and the government had more than it could handle. So the program was abandoned before it could even start. I was struck with sadness. Religions are supposed to lead mankind to humanity and improved living conditions. Here we had exactly the reverse, technology was available to improve living conditions, but zealous religious people were killing others and preventing the improvement in living conditions. What had religion become?

* * *

Collie had trouble with her feet and could only wear SAS sandals. She cleaned out a closet of shoes. Her greatly loved cat, Star died. Of the dozens of cats we had, I think she loved Star the most. Our next door neighbors, the Batchelors, tore down their old house for completion of the new one. They gave us the old front door, a real beauty. It was installed on our house and looked great with a glass window in the center. Shari lost weight and felt great about herself. She also lost a kitty of long standing. Not a good year for cats.

Chris knitted finger-free gloves and an arm warmer for Collie. She thinks they are great and kept her hands in shape for painting. I went to Boulder, Colorado to work with NREL. I walked too rapidly inside the building and collapsed. NREL insisted I be taken to the ER. It turned out to be lack of oxygen at the 6000 foot altitude of Boulder. I was sent home immediately. It was the end of work for NREL.

* * *

This is a good point to close my memoirs. It is the last year my technical work had any depth. It marks the passage of 67 years from that day, December 7, 1941, which changed the future of 4 young men and initiated an explosion of technology that has changed our lives. That technical evolution was accompanied by a change in industrial, political and religious orientation which often inhibited the use of that technology in the service of mankind. This is in contrast to the professed goals of religion and politics. The world has changed.

# Epilogue

Collie died in 2010 from a widespread internal cancer. Fortunately there was little pain until the last two weeks. I controlled her pain medication until the last four days which she spent in hospital on a morphine drip. I had come to the end of my ability to avoid overdosing her in response to her cries. Our doctor admitted her and she died quietly in the hospital. That closed sixty four years of married life. Shari, Chris and I still live in San Luis Obispo, California, a beautiful spot on the central coast.

After Collie's death I felt terribly alone in a large house with attached studio and an acre of land. In 2011, I sold it and bought a small house on a tiny lot with views of a lake and three ranges of mountains. The lake has many swans, seagulls, ducks and migrating Canadian Geese. Shari and Chris call the view from my back window "The bird channel." Granddaughter and great granddaughter enjoy visiting and feeding the "duckies" stale bread.

I have started writing. This is my third book. The second, "A Mature Single Man's Cookbook" contains 41 recipes and advice to a man who finds himself single after many years of married life. It uses culinary arts as a means to re-enter society. The cover features a photo of a delightful lady friend and I serving dinner to guests. We are content.

Printed in the United States
By Bookmasters